George Liele's Life and Legacy

MERCER
UNIVERSITY PRESS

Endowed by
TOM WATSON BROWN
and
THE WATSON-BROWN FOUNDATION, INC.

George Liele's Life and Legacy

An Unsung Hero

Thank You!
To the Tifre Family
Enjoy your history.

DAVID T. SHANNON, SR., SENIOR EDITOR

JULIA FRAZIER WHITE AND
Julia F. White
DEBORAH VAN BROEKHOVEN, EDITORS

MERCER UNIVERSITY PRESS
MACON, GEORGIA

The James N. Griffith Series in Baptist Studies

This series on Baptist life and thought explores and investigates Baptist history, offers analyses of Baptist theologies, provides studies in hymnody, and examines the role of Baptists in societies and cultures around the world. The series also includes classics of Baptist literature, letters, diaries, and other writings.
—Walter B. Shurden, Series Editor

MUP/ H853

© 2012 Mercer University Press
1400 Coleman Avenue
Macon, Georgia 31207

First Edition

Published with assistance from the Porter Fleming Foundation, Augusta, GA

Books published by Mercer University Press are printed on acid-free paper that meets the requirements of the American National Standard for Information Sciences—Permanence of Paper for Printed Library Materials.

Cover painting by Averett P. Shannon

Mercer University Press is a member of Green Press Initiative (greenpressinitiative.org), a nonprofit organization working to help publishers and printers increase their use of recycled paper and decrease their use of fiber derived from endangered forests. This book is printed on recycled paper.

ISBN 978-0-88146-389-7
Cataloging-in-Publication Data is available from the Library of Congress

Contents

This book is dedicated to the memory of

Dr. David T. Shannon, Sr.
September 26, 1933–March 22, 2008

A Tribute

Dr. David T. Shannon, Sr., was committed to excellence in education, historical integrity, and walking in love. He cared about the human family and did his best to share his knowledge, love, and understanding about what he called "The Predicate of God" with humanity and in particular the African-American community. He worked tirelessly to empower underserved children with knowledge that would allow them to one day stand toe to toe with giants like he did. He was giving and selfless to levels that I didn't understand as a child and that marvel me as an adult. He was made from the fabric of agape love.

As an academic, he was a king among kings.

As a free thinker, he was a giant among giants.

As a father, he was what I can only aspire to live toward.

The world had a unique and powerful gem of a man, a fountain of pure knowledge, in the great Dr. David T. Shannon, Sr. I was privileged to see his greatness, his commitment to leadership, and his unconditional love as a father daily. As a black male, I have yet to see another who can hold a flame to him...and don't think I ever will.

—David T. Shannon, Jr.

Foreword

HELEN K. THREATT

A complete history of the African and African-American contributions to the history of religion remains to be written. George Liele, an African-American evangelist, began his ministry in the 1770s. He was certainly one of those people who understood the promise of freedom embedded in the Christian doctrine. He is credited with establishing the first Baptist churches for African Americans in the United States and Jamaica and mentoring other early African-American Baptist evangelists.

George Liele's life and legacy have been given new momentum thanks to the interest and work of Dr. David T. Shannon, Sr. (recently deceased). A noted African-American theologian and visionary, Shannon was well aware of the gap in historical information concerning early black evangelicals and their contributions to theology. He was determined to help remedy this academic vacuum during his lifetime. Shannon's education seemed to have prepared him for the task.

Earning degrees from Virginia Union, Oberlin, and the University of Pittsburg, where he received a PhD in Higher Education, David Shannon became a leader and administrator in academics. Named a remarkable graduate of Oberlin Graduate School of Theology by former students and ministers, Shannon's career in higher education was extraordinary. In addition to professorial accomplishments at Virginia Union and Bucknell universities, he served as dean of the Pittsburg Theological Center, dean of faculty at the Interdenominational Theological Center, Atlanta, and as president of three universities, including Andover Newton Theological School, Newton Centre, Massachusetts; Virginia Union University, Richmond; and Allen University, in Columbia, South Carolina.

As a scholar, Shannon became interested in theology from a black perspective. In addition to many other publications, Shannon is known for his articles and books about African-American preaching. "An Antebellum Sermon: A Resource for an African American Hermeneutics" in

Stony the Road We Trod: An African American Biblical Interpretation (1991) and *Black Witness to the Apostolic Faith* edited by David Shannon and G. S. Wilmore (1988), are examples of his published works in African-American theology.

A Baptist minister, who pastored churches in Liele's birthplace of Virginia, Shannon became passionate about research on this Baptist pioneer. His interest evolved into the George Liele Research Project, a group composed of scholars and theologians recruited by Shannon. The group's objective was to chronicle the history of George Liele's evangelism in America and Jamaica and produce an anthology containing biographical and critical essays for educational purposes in college and university seminars. By producing a comprehensive anthology, Shannon, as senior editor, believed that he would be making a significant contribution to theological studies. Although articles in journals and books exist about Liele, there are no anthologies devoted solely to his story except this work.

This anthology, consisting of never-before published articles by scholars of religion and other disciplines, provides a unique approach to studying Liele. It is further enhanced by essays reflecting Shannon's own research on Liele, contributed by his widow, Averett, and daughter Vernitia Shannon. Indeed, *The Life and Legacy of George Liele: An Unsung Hero* is a remarkable testament to David Shannon's vision and an important addition to the Liele canon and world religions.

RESOURCES

Felder, Cain Hope, ed. "An Ante-bellum Sermon: A Resource for an African American Hermeneutics." In *Stony the Road We Trod: An African American Biblical Interpretation*. Minneapolis MN: Fortress Press 1991, Eerdman's Pub. Co. for Commission on Faith and Order, National Council of the Churches of Christ in the U.S.A.

Shannon, David, and G. S. Wilmore, eds., *Black Witness to the Apostolic Faith*. Grand Rapids MI: W. B. Eerdmans, 1988.

Acknowledgments

Dr. David T. Shannon was the genius and guiding spirit who drew together the many persons involved in the research and writing of this book. It would be impossible to mention all of them by name, since the indebtedness is great. There were several people, though, who deserve special mention and gratitude because of their dedication.

The research team for the George Liele Research Project included the staff at the Woodruff Library at Atlanta University Center, especially research librarian Mrs. Helen Threatt, who devoted countless hours researching critical information; and the Auburn Avenue Research Library on African American Culture and History, with its committed and accommodating staff, particularly research librarian Ms. Akilah Nosakhere, who did much to facilitate the use of the library in research. Thanks to the Fulton County Library research staff and the Library of Congress library staff, especially archivist Conway Clark.

Thanks to Dr. Earle D. Clowney, professor emeritus of Clark Atlanta University and the Rev. Dr. Charles Washington, former Dean of Arts and Sciences of Clarke Atlanta University, both of whom read, edited and made critical and helpful suggestions. Thanks, also, to Mr. William Glass, who offered his insights and accompanied the group on trips to do primary research.

Thanks to Mr. Milledge Galphin Murray and Pastor Linda Birchall of St. James United Methodist Church. They facilitated a meeting that took us to several sites significant in the life of George Liele: Silver Bluff; Dead River; the Kimberly-Clark Beach Island Mill, where there are well-maintained slave graves; Springfield Baptist Church; the site of the Galphin Plantation, which was owned by the ancestors of Milledge Galphin Murray; and the Augusta-Aiken Audubon Society, Jacksonville, South Carolina, and to Daniel Connelly, Audubon staff, for enriching our research in the gathering of slave information, identifying how their graves were marked, and relating some of their predicaments during that time in history.

Sincere appreciation goes also to the Kimberly-Clark Corporation and staff at the Beach Island, South Carolina plant for allowing the group to tour the slave gravesites on their property. We are very grateful that Kimberly-Clark protects and maintains the slave gravesites in good condition.

We are grateful for the late pastor of Springfield Baptist Church of Augusta, Georgia, Rev. E. T. Martin. Reverend Martin has since passed away and is buried in front of Springfield Baptist Church. Reverend Martin and the staff and members of Springfield Baptist Church provided an informative and memorable tour of their church while telling and depicting rich historical facts about George Liele (who was one of their former pastors), the environment, and memorabilia from that period.

Thanks to Rev. Dr. William V. Guy, pastor emeritus of Friendship Baptist Church, who provided helpful insights, and to the Friendship family for making us welcome at the church facility as a meeting site.

We are thankful for Rev. Dr. Winston A. Lawson, who welcomed us to Hillside Presbyterian Church for several meetings of the George Liele Research Group. Dr. Lawson provided a Jamaican meal to the group and explained each item on the menu. This helped us to understand more about the Jamaican heritage Liele adopted after he left America.

A sincere debt of thanks goes to Dr. Deborah Bingham Van Broekhoven, director of the American Baptist Historical Society, the staff of the American Baptist Historical Society, and to the staff of Mercer University for hosting the George Liele Research Group several times. Dr. Deborah VanBroekhoven's contribution has been a valuable asset to the group.

We are grateful to Mr. Don Perkins of Augusta, Georgia, a longtime resident of the area and a walking historian on that part of the state. Mr. Perkins provided a tour of the exact location south of Waynesboro where George Liele was converted in 1773, at the age of 23, at Buckhead Creek Baptist Church. Of this inspiring tour, Dr. Driggers said, "Milledge [Murray] and I both felt that we were walking on the very land where George Liele lived and worked and became an ordained Baptist minister. We just want you and Dr. Shannon to know of our visit and of how very pleased we are with the information we received, which will be of help to us as we fulfill our writing assignments for the book."

We give special appreciation to Dr. Julia Frazier White for her persistent commitment, dedication, and inspiration to the George Liele Research Project. As project manager, Dr. White worked very closely with Dr. Shannon to guide the George Liele Research Group, facilitate the meetings, and provide written records of the meetings and of conversations with Dr. Shannon. Dr. White tirelessly wrote, edited, and assisted in successfully completing this project.

Dr. Shannon often expressed special thanks to his wife, Averett P. Shannon, whose understanding, patience, and helpful insights added immeasurably to the preparation of the manuscript and for sharing his dream of completing this notable project. Dr. Shannon always thanked his three children, Vernitia, Davine, and David, Jr., for their participation in bringing the George Liele story to the world. To his six grandchildren (Jylyan, Myriah, Nicole, David III, Malachi, and Isaiah), Dr. Shannon stated, "I pass on to them the love and thirst of learning and the deep respect of those who have dared to improve the fate of others as they sought to live better lives through their Christian faith."

The George Liele Research Group gives a special note of appreciation to the Porter Fleming Foundation. Because of the beliefs of the Porter Fleming Foundation in the educational and intellectual merits of this project, they helped us to realize our goal: to research and tell the story of the life and legacy of George Liele, an unsung hero.

George Liele's Life and Legacy
An Unsung Hero

DAVID T. SHANNON, SR.,

Introduction

About the title: George Liele's life and legacy have long been underappreciated. He launched a mission movement that reached from Georgia to Jamaica and from Jamaica to Sierra Leone and Nova Scotia—all before William Carey, Adoniram Judson, Richard Allen, or Lott Cary. Yet writers of church and mission history have devoted very few pages to Liele's pioneer ministry, and most mentions ignore the global nature of his work and influence. Beginning as a slave preacher, Liele learned the Baptist story and theology—a message he preached in South Carolina, Georgia, and Jamaica. Through the preachers he taught, the same message reached Nova Scotia and Sierra Leone. In providing a comprehensive introduction to Liele's life and work, this book draws readers into identifying with Liele and those who lived through a difficult historic period and who in the process developed a theology that guided them through the challenges of being a Christian leader in an enslaved society. Now the time has come for one to recognize that George Liele's life was one that helped to unbolt the enslaved and free people out of their darkness. Whatever insights have come from this research are perhaps most useful to others if the book is approached with an open mind. It is hoped that persons interested in history will find new truths based on the research from this book.

This body of work is written as a tribute to the life and legacy of George Liele, an enslaved man who became the first ordained African-American Baptist preacher. George Liele's life and theology bring into focus the indisputable reality of God's action in the life and history of humankind, especially among those of lowly status. Liele was enslaved when baptized. He was enslaved when he was ordained. Enslaved persons were thought of as illiterate and often punished for displaying or sharing thoughts and actions that bespoke of freedom of any kind.

Liele lived and preached during the First Great Awakening of the eighteenth century, one of the greatest Christian movements of all times. His life and influence came earlier than the nineteenth century, the period in which scholars have argued that Africans in England and the United States created a literature that bore witness to their strong desire to be free and literate.

The Christian movement has always been greater than any individual or local church community has imagined it to be. It was so strong that a slave was able to allow his faith to direct his life in spite of the perils of slavery. Liele was an organizer, mentor, church and school founder, an abolitionist, and a master negotiator. Many people, however, have never acknowledged George Liele's rightful role in history and some have never heard of him. This book is the product of a collaboration of scholars and historians who share the belief that George Liele is truly an unsung hero who needs to be recognized at this particular time in history. It is hoped that those reading these perspectives on Liele will find new truths about Christian ministry and missions.

Writing the history of George Liele from a global point of view requires the insights of more than one individual or community. With this realization in mind, the fourteen authors set out to shape this book from its inception in close collaboration with a wider body of consulting scholars and researchers. These scholars, chosen for their leadership in the field, represent a wide array of methodological approaches to the study of theology, history, and literature. Our initial theme was George Liele, unsung hero, and this theme shaped our thinking, research, and writing.

For several months, small groups met in Shannon's home to discuss, share, and marvel at the life of such a dynamic, unheralded servant. The George Liele Research Project was initiated. In 2004, the members of the George Liele Research Project team met to shape the outline and suggest revisions for the next stage. Several members of the team provided critical resources and specific insights from their own areas of expertise and research. The George Liele Research Project members also visited several of the sites where George Liele lived, was baptized, was ordained, and preached in the area of Augusta, Georgia, and South Carolina. We visited sites in Burke County, Georgia; the site of Silver Bluff Baptist Church (South Carolina); and the Galphin Plantation (South Carolina), where Liele preached. Also we visited several slave gravesites, which gave us a sense of early slave culture. One of the slave gravesites is now owned and preserved by the Kimberly-Clark Company, and the other is preserved through the National Audubon Society in Augusta, Georgia.

One of our members, Milledge Galphin Murray (the great-grandson of the owner of the Galphin Plantation on which the first African-American Baptist church was founded in 1773), provided a very informative tour of the Springfield Baptist Church, where Liele was a cofounder and preacher. The tour was hosted by congregation members and Pastor E. T. Martin, who identified important historical papers, artifacts, and newspaper clippings used during the George Liele period.

A significant visit to Big Buckhead Church, where Liele was ordained, was hosted by Donald Perkins in Jenkins County (Perkins, Georgia). We were also warmly hosted by one of our members, Milledge Galphin Murray, vice president of Sun Trust Bank. The meeting was held in the board room of the bank. The George Liele Research group also met at the St. James United Methodist Church in Augusta, where Milledge G. Murray, members, and Pastor Linda Birchall welcomed the research group.

American Baptist Historical Society director Deborah Van Broekhoven and staff from Mercer University have been extremely accommodating, hosting and providing space for many of the meetings in the Atlanta area at the American Baptist Historical Society's new headquarters on the Mercer University campus. Pastor William V. Guy of Friendship Baptist Church (Atlanta) welcomed the George Liele Research Group during one of its research meetings. Rev. Dr. Guy noted the special interest of Friendship Baptist in the George Liele legacy, in part because of close ties between Friendship Baptist and the Springfield Baptist Church in Augusta, the first two homes of Morehouse College.

George Liele preached before the first members of Springfield Baptist Church, a number of whom were former slaves from the Galphin Plantation. Three of our contributing authors were born, reared, and educated in Jamaica. Two of them (Noel Erskine and Winston Lawson) were members of the East Queen Street Baptist Church that George Liele organized in Jamaica in 1816. One of our members, Horace Russell, served as pastor of that same church for many years.

George Liele's life in America as well as in Jamaica illustrates his commitment to the preaching of the gospel. He also exercised great influence on the life of David George, a colleague who immigrated first to Halifax, Nova Scotia, and then sailed on to Sierra Leone, Africa. As a way of continuing the mission, one of the members of the George Liele Project (Jeneen Roscoe) is currently a missionary to the very church that David George founded in Sierra Leon, Regent Road Baptist Church, in 1782.

Each session's engaging participation presented some newly uncovered resources that had been overlooked or forgotten through the years but related to our theme of George Liele as an unsung hero. Our team expanded to include dedicated and enthusiastic research librarians from America and London, England.

As a result of these significant efforts, the consultation over the last five years has taken on a life of its own. We have reached remarkable consensus on many issues. The members have been faithfully committed to the research project, working together as well as individually, and have expanded on one another's areas of interest and concern. Several individuals who were unable to attend various meetings nevertheless read portions of the text and provided critical comments that proved to be very helpful. To each of you we extend our thanks. Many readers will benefit from your having made this a much better book than we could ever have accomplished without you.

The members of the George Liele Research Project are the following: Dr. Deborah Van Broekhoven; Dr. Earle D. Clowney; Dr. B. Carlisle Driggers; Dr. Noel Erskine; Dr. Ernestine Pickens Glass; Dr. Winston Lawson; Mr. Milledge Galphin Murray; Dr. Linda Reed; Ms. Jeneen Roscoe; Dr. Horace Russell; Mrs. Averett P. Shannon; Dr. David T. Shannon, Sr.; Mr. David T. Shannon, Jr.; Vernitia A. Shannon, Esq.; Dr. Thomas Scott; Dr. Davine S. Spark; Dr. Charles Washington; Dr. Love H. Whelchel; Dr. Julia Frazier White; and the Reverend Victor Williams.

During the last five years, the goal of the George Liele Research Project team has been to come to a mutual understanding of the true story about George Liele's life and legacy in the United States and Jamaica, as well as his significant influence upon his associates, based upon the research. Other goals included maintaining channels of communication for mutual as well as self-understanding, identifying new sources and avenues for common witness and agreement, and addressing those prejudices that exist between races and confessional families.

Three Keys:
Experience, Understanding, and Crossing Points

The following three key points will serve as a guide to begin our examination of the life of George Liele: experience, understanding, and crossing point.

1. What were the experiences of George Liele that formed the bases of his ministry?

2. What was Liele's understanding of these experiences?

3. What are the crossing (significant) points from George Liele's experiences and understanding to our lives today?

This method presents the religious history and experiences of George Liele's liberating faith.

1. Experiences in Scriptures, particularly Liele's interpretation of John 13:13 ("Ye call me Master and Lord: and ye say well; for so I am") and Hebrews 12:1–2 ("Wherefore seeing we also are compassed about with so great a cloud of witnesses, let us lay aside every weight, and the sin which doth so easily beset us, and let us run with patience the race that is set before us. Looking unto Jesus the author and finisher of our faith; who for the joy that was set before him endured the cross, despising the shame, and is set down at the right hand of the throne of God.") KJV.

2. Experiences in circumstances as an enslaved and as a free man (comparison chart of Paul and Liele).

3. Experiences of the community (George Liele's influence on others).

The point of focus of this work reflects the biblical writer's belief of how the experience of God had (and still would) come in dire circumstances. The essay,

"George Liele: Apostle of Liberation and Faith," concludes with a discussion of the linage of the hermeneutical elements in Liele's life with his ministry in the United States of America, Jamaica, and London. Further, this work contains an additional ten chapters, a prologue and an epilogue. The chapters include information on George Liele's life previously unknown to many scholars and the general public. Chapters about Liele's economic environment, his last will, his literacy, his evangelical environment, and his legacy in Sierra Leone, Africa, provide unfamiliar material about the evangelist Liele. The chapters focusing on comparative studies of Liele with the Apostle Paul, the poet Phillis Wheatley, and the Native Baptists with the Revival church in Jamaica are expected to broaden perspectives on the teaching of Liele. The prologue and the essay on Liele in British Jamaica reveal the extent of renewed interest in Liele today in academia as compared to his negative, early reception in Jamaica. Conclusively, this work is a monumental effort to raise Liele from a relatively obscure person to one of immediate recognition and appreciation by scholars and lay people alike.

Prologue

HORACE O. RUSSELL

So is the Kingdom of God as if a man should cast seed into the ground; and he should sleep and rise night and day, and the seed should spring and grow up, he knows not how. For the earth brings forth fruit of herself; first the blade then the ear then the full corn in the ear.

—Mark 4: 26–28

George Liele (1750–1828?), a Baptist of African descent, may have remained in relative obscurity had he not been the central figure in the bicentennial celebrations of the Jamaican Baptist churches in 1983. These celebrations brought together the leadership of the four churches which claim Liele as their founder: two in Savannah, Georgia, and two in Kingston, Jamaica. They are the First African and the First Bryan in Savannah and the East Queen Street and Hanover Street Baptist churches in Kingston. Liele's move to Kingston placed him in the sphere of dominant British influence, and so in time he reached out to British Baptists while remaining in contact with his friends in Georgia. Thus began a tripartite relationship, which led to formal ties between Jamaican and British Baptists for more than two centuries with looser associations with the Baptists of the United States over the same period.

Prior to Clement Gayle's book, entitled *George Liele: Pioneer Missionary to Jamaica* (published in 1982), Liele had been relegated to a few sentences in books on the history of Baptist life in Savannah and Jamaica. Dr. Gayle's book was published to celebrate particular events in the church calendar.[1] It was also included in the invitations to the pastors of First African and First Bryan to preach at the East Queen Street Baptist and Hanover Street Baptist churches[2]. Although Liele received greater exposure during this celebration, Gayle's book did not stimulate any concerted scholarly attempt to evaluate his work or to set Liele within the global framework of either Christian missions or ecclesiastical history.

---

[1] Clement Gayle, *George Liele: Pioneer Missionary to Jamaica Kingston* (Kingston, Jamaica: Jamaica Baptist Union, 1982).

[2] Ibid.

Since then, progress has been made. George Liele is currently the subject of several unfinished missions and Baptist history studies, and his biblical interpretation and insights were the subject of a scholarly discussion at the American Academy of Religion devoted to the Study of Biblical Literature at Philadelphia in 1994. He was included in the final communiqué which Baptist leaders, under the auspices of the Baptist World Alliance, produced from the Summit on Baptist Mission in the 21st Century, which charted the course toward a new understanding of missions among Baptists, held at Swanwick, England, in May 2003. There is every indication that at last Liele is coming into his own, and this publication will aid the move forward.

Liele was a product of the evangelical movement. His early life and conversion was in Savannah, Georgia. Georgia was a colony founded by General Sir James Oglethorpe (1696–1785), whose plan for a free colony for all people was corrupted by greed and the exigencies of the time. The precipitate events in the aftermath of the independence movement of 1776 and the rout of the British garrison from the colony set in motion significant political and social changes, which led to a mass exodus to the Maritimes in Canada and the islands of the West Indies. However, these migrations were to redound to the glory of God in the spread of Baptist witness to Canada, the Bahamas, Trinidad and Tobago, and Jamaica, and eventually to Sierra Leone and Cameroon.

The evangelical movement, with the imprint of Jonathan Edwards, the Clapham Sect, and the Methodist Movement in English-speaking church life, the Pietist movement of the German and Danish churches, and the endeavors of Count Zinzendorf and Unitas Fratrum, had spread the ideals of the Reformation beyond the borders of Europe and North America. A variety of missionary endeavors with social, and later political, implications emerged from this movement. Among the sociopolitical institutions affected were colonialism and the institution of slavery, which the movement challenged and confronted to reverse current negative stereotypes of Native peoples and Africans. While the most radical impact of evangelicalism on politics took some time to evolve, in time it did lead to the American Revolution and its aftermath, and in Britain to succession of governments in Westminster. However, its social impact was more immediate. The Quakers had already led the way with their universal antislavery stance and prison and child-labor reforms. Kindred movements began to blossom in other churches, and these causes found their way into print. In worship, evangelicalism produced an enthusiasm in religious affairs that had been lacking in the previous century, and this provided grist for the mill, with social consequences. This was the environment in which Liele heard the gospel and responded by establishing a nascent witness, at first in Silver Bluff, South Carolina, and eventually in Savannah, through which David George and Andrew Bryan were involved. The political events of 1776 and their aftermath forced David George to migrate to Canada and later to Sierra Leone, where he was the pioneer of Baptist witness in Africa. Andrew Bryan remained in Savannah and his work, it could be argued, strengthened the foundations of the black Baptist church in the United States. To escape re-enslavement, Liele and his family went to Jamaica.

George Liele arrived in Jamaica in January 1783 with his young family in fortuitous but constrained circumstances. It appears that he was in debt to Colonel Moses Kirkland (1730–1787), the commanding officer for the evacuation of Savannah, who had served under General Sir Archibald Campbell (1739–1791) while both were in the service of the British East India Company and also when he was the provincial governor of Georgia in 1779. Campbell had subsequently been appointed acting governor of Jamaica in 1781 and confirmed in the post the following year. Kirkland gave Liele a letter of introduction, and Liele worked as an indentured servant for some time to pay his debt to Kirkland, who had also evacuated to Kingston soon after. Liele's job was to carry shot from the naval base in Port Royal into Kingston and to collect abandoned pieces about the town. It appears to have been a large enterprise, and according to his account in the *Jamaica Gazette* (an official government publication) and from his will and that of his wife, Hannah, it appears Liele bought enslaved persons to carry out his business. It was not an unusual practice in Caribbean urban centers for former enslaved persons to own slaves. There is evidence that there were enslaved persons who did business on behalf of their owners and shared the profits with them. There was even a woman in Kingston who allowed her enslaved person, a Baptist, to be an evangelist for the Moravians. Liele was a creature of his social times, and his action was a compromise.

In spite of this lapse he did lay the foundation for Baptist witness in Savannah and Kingston and in that sense is a pioneer of the Baptist missionary enterprise and Baptist global relationships. Liele arrived in Jamaica ten years before William Carey preached his famous sermon which created the Baptist Missionary Society (BMS). He was in touch with other British and American Baptist leaders, and his recommendations were accepted and respected. Over the years, Liele recommended several of his members to churches in London, including the Carter's Lane Church. This congregation and John Rippon (1751–1836) had been active in the British and Foreign Anti-slavery Society led by Joseph Sturge (1793–1859) and the rehabilitation of freed peoples through the Committee for Poor Blacks (1786) and in 1807 arranged celebrations for the Abolition of the Slave Trade. When the numbers of freed Africans increased over time, John Rippon invited Liele to come to London to help him, which he did for six years (1822–1828). Liele's work in England remains an area of fruitful research. It would be helpful to know not only what were his tasks and the reception he received, but also to understand what the enduring legacies of his work are. Of some interest would be an answer to whether the black membership was eventually absorbed into the larger congregation, thereby all but disappearing, or whether some or all sailed with David George under the auspices of the African Association (1788) and the Sierra Leone Company (1791) to establish Baptist witness in Sierra Leone. Regardless, it can be said that Liele's visit to England at the request of the BMS through Rippon set a precedent which was to be followed in international church relationships and mission strategy for years to come.

There are two other areas in which Liele was a pioneer. The first is in the understanding of himself and his Christian faith in relation to Africa, and the second concerns the positive stance of the Baptist churches to all aspects of the life of the community in which they are set. There are no extant writings in which Liele addresses the identity question per se. However, in his descriptions of himself and the churches he supervised to Rippon, he calls himself and the members "Ethiopians." It is a description drawn from Psalm 68:31, and its abiding significance lies in its usage over the decades. It became the rallying cry of Jamaican Baptists in the post-Emancipation era, around which they organized the Jamaica Baptist Missionary Society in 1842, to send missionaries to Africa and the Calabar Theological College in 1843 to train men as ministers and teachers for the Caribbean churches. While it cannot be argued that Liele and the Baptists were solely responsible for the decision to identify persons of African heritage in Jamaican society with Ethiopia, still it is among the Baptists that the earliest references occur. In the late nineteenth and early twentieth centuries the designation "Ethiopia" continued to find acceptance among social and political groups seeking to identify with Africa and can also be found in the writings and sayings of Marcus Mosiah Garvey in the 1920s and other leaders of Pan-Africanism in the '40s, '50s and '60s. "Ethiopia" has also been given a global reference through the Rastafarian movement and its music.

Liele's understanding of the Baptist church and her place in society can be inferred from the Church Covenant he drew up for the church he established in Kingston which was to inform Baptist witness island-wide. The theology and structure of the covenant appears to have been drawn from the Georgia Association and was forwarded to London in 1792. A second covenant quite similar to the first (probably belonging to Moses Baker, an early convert of Liele's) was dispatched in 1796. The covenants show that Liele had charted for himself a middle ground between Calvinism and Arminianism. In his letter of introduction to Rippon, Liele wrote that he accepted "election, redemption, the Fall of Adam, regeneration and perseverance, knowing the promise of all that endure in Grace, Faith and Good Works to the end will be saved."[3] Ernest Payne,

---

[3] George Liele to John Rippon, 18 December 1791, letter published in Rippon's *Baptist Annual Register for 1790, 1791, 1792, and part of 1793*, vol. 1 (London: 1792) 332–37.

the celebrated Baptist church historian, observed that "the simplicity and sincerity revealed" in Liele's letter, alongside perceived "dangers of lapses into fanaticism and heresy" and "the difficulties and opportunities" among those newly "covenanted in this fashion," meant that these West Indian Baptists were seen as the responsibility of Englishmen. So it is not surprising that Dr. Ryland and his friends "did not rest" until they were able to send missionaries to Jamaica.[4]

These covenants are important because together with several letters of recommendation from William Wilberforce, they were the fundamental reason why the BMS decided to respond to the invitation to work with and coordinate the scattered and persecuted Baptists of Jamaica after Thomas Coke, the Methodist, on principle refused help, due to his theological differences on baptism. It was on receipt of the covenants that plans were put into place that eventually led to the arrival of John Rowe, the first BMS missionary, in Montego Bay in 1814.

The covenant might be read from two points of view, depending on whether it was being read by the enslaved or the slaveholder. This was not because it was a deceptive document. There was no duplicity here. But in any polarized society, each person reads documents with their own self-interest in mind. The covenant appealed to the slaveholder because of its defense of "law and order." For instance, it noted that there was to be no "shedding of blood." While this appears to rule out insurrections for the slaveholder, for the enslaved it meant humane treatment. No enslaved persons were allowed to join the church without the slaveholder's permission, with 1 Peter 2:13–16 and 1 Thessalonians 3:13 cited as justification. While on the surface this section of the covenant appears to be an enquiry into the moral standing of the enslaved, the very fact that the slaveholder is consulted ensures support and lessens suspicion. The fact that Liele had been enslaved and was now a slaveholder gave him a perspective from both sides.

There was another important aspect of the covenant. It contained regulations for settling disputes out of civil courts in accordance with Matthew 18:15–18 and 1 Corinthians 6:1–8 as well as providing for marriage and burial. Here we have in embryo an alternative community that in time would challenge successfully the prevailing culture of slavery and slave society, specifically in the uprisings of 1832, called the Baptist War, led by Samuel Sharp, a Baptist leader from Montego Bay, and the Morant Bay Rebellion of 1865, which was led by another Baptist deacon, Paul Bogle. In the first instance the confrontation led to the abolition of slavery in the British colonies in 1833, and in the second it led to new

---

[4] Ernest A. Payne, *Freedom in Jamaica: Some Chapters in the Story of the Baptist Missionary Society* (London: Carey Press, 1933) 19.

educational, social, and fiscal policies under Sir John Peter Grant, tailored to the many and not just the privileged few. Liele's covenantal Christianity laid the foundations upon which participatory government in Jamaica was built; for after all, it is recorded in holy Scripture that any true covenant with God involves true covenant with one's fellow citizens (Rom 12:1–8.).

A third contribution of Liele was his emphasis on education and land ownership. While it is true that education was Bible-based, it did provide the enslaved with the ability to read other material. We know that there were local newspapers, and the London newspapers were readily available in Jamaica. Some urban slaveholders were not averse to their enslaved people having basic reading and calculating skills. There is evidence that in some cases it was the enslaved person who ran the slaveholder's business, especially in shipping and fishing. It would appear that Liele's school had two important consequences. Firstly, it provided instruction in the Christian faith within the Baptist tradition, and secondly, it gave the educational tools to the learners to negotiate for themselves alternatives within their society.

Liele established a school with a schoolmaster who also doubled as his assistant in the church while he was traveling to the other stations he had established. Indeed, by 1816, when the BMS missionary Lee Compere (1789–1871) arrived to assume the pastorate of East Queen Street in Kingston, Baptist witness was well established in several centers across the island. Baptist witness in the east looked to Liele for leadership, and several of his members appear in the founding lists of the churches in the eastern portion of Jamaica.

In order to establish the witness, land had to be procured. While there are not many land titles extant in the names of Baptists before the incorporation of 1847, there are worshipping congregations in the east and central areas of Jamaica that trace their origins to original Liele witness. In the 1830s Baptists were to expand this custom to include not only church property but also personal property, with dimensions which would enfranchise them.

Liele provided for Baptists not only a sense of identity, partially drawn from Psalm 69 and rooted in the memory of Africa, but set within a global framework of Baptist witness. It was a logical progression for Jamaican Baptists to be among the founding members of the Baptist World Alliance in 1905. Liele also gave to Jamaican society covenantal Christianity, which was to be the basis of the participatory democracy for which Baptists strove and died in the ensuing centuries.

That Jamaica is today a democracy is in no small measure due to the theological underpinnings of Baptist witness, individual freedom, and communal responsibility before God. Still, we must never forget that Liele's wife, Hannah, was illiterate, although he built a school; that his deacon and school master, Nicolas Sweigle, took him to court, which landed him in prison for almost four years and led to a split in the church; or that on his return from

11

England the church split again, this time on the issue of speaking in tongues and the fact that he was a slaveholder. It might therefore be said that God can find great use for imperfect people in order to carry out his ultimate purposes, and in this is hope.

Resources

Brooks, Walter H. *The Silver Bluff Church: History of the Negro Baptist Churches in America.* Washington DC: Press of R. L. Pendleton, 1910.

Clarke, John. *Memorials of Baptist Missionaries in Jamaica 1869.* London: Yates & Alexander, 1869.

Gayle, Clement. *George Liele: Pioneer Missionary to Jamaica Kingston.* Kingston, Jamaica: Jamaican Baptist Union, 1982.

Martin, Sandy. *Black Baptists and African Missions.* Macon GA: Mercer University Press, 1989.

Rippon, John. *The Baptist Register 1791–1802.* Volume 1. No publisher. No date.

Russell, Horace O. *Foundations and Anticipations: The Jamaica Baptist Story 1783–1892.* Columbus GA: Brentwood Christian Press, 1993.

Russell, Horace O. *The Missionary Outreach of the West Indian Church: Jamaican Baptist Missions to West Africa in the Nineteenth Century.* New York/London: Peter Lang, 2000.

Russell, Horace O. *Understandings and Interpretations of Scripture in Eighteenth and Nineteenth Century Jamaica: The Baptists as Case Study: Religion and Tradition in the Caribbean.* Edited by Henchand Gossai and Nathaniel Samuel Murrell. New York: St. Martin's Press, 2000.

Geographic and Socio Economic Environment at Silver Bluff: George Galphin, Indian Trader and Plantation Owner

MILLEDGE GALPHIN MURRAY

The Savannah River, which forms a natural boundary between Georgia and South Carolina, is a winding river that became a very valuable resource for commerce and trade. The early inhabitants of Georgia and South Carolina were Indian tribes which resided in this region for centuries. Many names are associated with the tribes. For geographical purposes the English adopted the names Upper Creeks, Middle Creeks, and Lower Creeks primarily to describe where they lived. British General James Oglethorpe, founder of Georgia, reported on 12 March 1733 that the three most powerful nations dwelling between the coast and the mountains were the Upper Creeks, the Lower Creeks, and the Uchees. The Indians lived near waterways, including the Savannah River, due to the convenience of travel by canoe and water resources.

The earliest European expedition into the state of Georgia, and the Augusta area in particular, appears to have been at the Indian settlement called Cutifachique by the Spanish explorer Hernando de Soto in 1539. According to Georgia historian C. C. Jones, the location of Cutifachique is identical with that of Silver Bluff, on the north side of the Savannah River, about fifteen miles by water below the city of Augusta. The river here stands against a bold bluff rising some thirty-five feet above the level of the river tributary and extending along the line of the stream, with an unbroken front, for the distance of nearly a mile. It was at this place that George Galphin, an Indian trader originally from Ireland, established his trading post and named this place Silver Bluff.

Augusta, Georgia, is located on the Savannah River some 130 miles upstream from Savannah, which borders the Atlantic Ocean. The colony of Georgia was founded on 2 February 1733 at Yamacraw Bluff, later named Savannah. General Oglethorpe and the original founders gathered together and held religious services to thank God and ask blessings upon the plantation settlement. At the conclusion of the religious services, General Oglethorpe stressed the importance that the seed now sown would yield a harvest either for good or bad in the coming generations. He urged the people to establish good relations with the native Indians. In the specific words of James Oglethorpe, "It is my hope," said he, "that through your good example the settlement of Georgia may prove a blessing and not a curse to the native inhabitants."[1] The colony of the Carolinas had been founded earlier in 1707. The principal trading establishment with the Indians was at Savanno Town, better known as Fort Moore, located at the base of the Savannah River near present-day Augusta. The main population of Indians from the Carolinas was the Cherokees. In Savanno Town, the Carolina Indian traders kept their warehouses and formed caravans to transport goods to the Cherokees at the headwaters of the Savannah River, to the Lower Creeks along the Chattahoochee, to the Upper Creeks of the Coosa and Tallapoosa waterways, and to the Chickasaw Indians beyond.

Oglethorpe understood the importance of trade with the Indians and the importance of establishing a trading establishment and township inland. The natural place for this establishment would be Augusta. Fort Moore already had been established there in 1716, and this location was at the base of profitable trade with the Creeks and the Cherokees. A delegation of Indians visited Oglethorpe in early 1735 and asked him to establish a town on the Georgia side of the upper Savannah River. Oglethorpe had already decided to establish the township. He instructed Noble Jones, the surveyor, to lay out a town with the same forty-lot pattern that had been done at Savannah several years before. Augusta was established in May 1735 and was named for Princess Augusta of Great Britain, mother of King George III of England. Augusta was developed to help with defense of the colony and to promote trade, principally with the Indians. It was easier for the Indians to travel to warehouses at an inland trading post rather than having to travel to coastal seaports such as Charleston, Savannah, or St. Augustine.

During this early period, the Carolinas permitted Negro slavery, but Georgia (primarily due to Oglethorpe's influence) prohibited it. Negro slaves were used by Southern white plantation owners to help run their plantation business operations. There were reasons for prohibiting slavery in Georgia. It was thought that the white man, in possessing a Negro slave, would himself be less inclined to labor and that much of his time would be spent keeping the Negro at work and guarding against any dangers he and his family might apprehend from the Negro. Georgia's Trustees felt that the state's products would not require the labor of Negro slaves, and their plan for the colonization of Georgia was for farmers to own and operate their own farms without the use of Negro laborers. The Trustees also did not want to create the possibility of poor Georgia farmers mortgaging their properties to Negro merchants and creating the possibility of being indebted to and losing their lands to these merchants. It was also thought that the introduction of slaves into Georgia would create the opportunity for

[1] Charles C. Jones, Jr., *History of Georgia*, vol. 1 (Boston: Houghton, Mifflin, and Co., 1883) 121.

desertion of the Carolina Negroes through Georgia into Florida, thus defeating one of the prime intentions of the founders of the colony: to make it a secure barrier and sure defense to Carolina against the negative influences and malevolent designs of the Spaniards at St. Augustine, Florida.

The early years of the colony of Georgia proved very difficult for the colonists trying to establish themselves in the new land. There were many pressures associated with the operation of farms and businesses as well as violation of slavery prohibition. Over time there was pressure to repeal Negro slavery prohibition in Georgia. On the 10 January 1749, the president of Georgia, James Habersham, his assistants, and a number of Georgia inhabitants forwarded to the Trustees a petition suggesting certain restrictions and regulations, under which they prayed that Negro slaves might be admitted to the colony. The Reverend George Whitefield actually felt that Negroes would be better off and treated more humanely in a Christian land rather than the barbarian land from which they came. On 7 July 1749, a formal act of petition enacted by the Trustees of Georgia allowed the introduction of Negro slaves into the colony. There was a desire within this petition that all slaves be treated in a humane manner and that they be given ample provisions for their labor. In addition, there was a restriction on the number of Negro slaves to white servants that could be owned. It was also unlawful for Negro slaves to work on the Lord's day. If a slave owner did not provide some time on Sunday for instruction in the Christian religion, they would be deemed guilty of a misdemeanor and would be fined.

Thus we have the environment of the Augusta area that borders South Carolina at the Savannah River around 1750. This area was very vibrant with the Indian trade, and many tribes brought animal hides (primarily deerskin) for exchange with the Indian traders for British goods. A very prominent Indian trading company operating in the Augusta area was Brown, Rae and Company, which included traders who were acquiring property in the Augusta area. This included Patrick Brown, who owned and operated an indigo plantation below Augusta, and John Rae, who owned 500 acres along a creek named Rae's Creek. Another trader associated with Brown, Rae and Company was George Galphin, who settled on Silver Bluff plantation, fifteen miles below Augusta on the Carolina side of the Savannah River. Galphin also was interested in acquiring lands in Georgia in addition to building an extensive Indian trade.

Galphin was an enterprising and adventuresome young man who was originally raised in Ireland and who, at the young age of twenty-seven in 1737, sailed from Ireland to Charlestown in the Carolina colony of America. When he arrived in Charlestown, Galphin noticed the bustling activity associated with the warehouses stocked with British merchandise for trade with the Indians. He became fascinated with this business and made an early decision to enter the Indian trading business. Galphin learned that success in this business would require an understanding of Indian customs, characteristics, and an effective means of communicating with them. He sought to learn their language, becoming an interpreter, and he tried to cultivate relationships with them, particularly the chiefs and other Indians in charge.

Galphin liked people and had a personality that drew people to him. He was known to be fair, kind, and honest, which was beneficial in establishing relationships with Indian tribal leaders. He developed early friendships with other Indian traders, such as Lachlan McGillivray and John Rae already explained. Brown, Rae and Company had control of the majority of trade with the Creeks of Georgia and Alabama. The base of this operation took place at the inland port of Augusta. When George Galphin decided to move to Augusta, he was looking for the right spot to establish his own trading operation. It was natural for him to select a spot along the Savannah River, due to its convenience as a means of transportation. British goods would have to be transported by water from the coasts, and Indians would bring deerskin hides by river to the trading posts by canoe.

Galphin knew about Fort Moore, which was located on the river and had been established in 1716 as a defense against the Indians. A settlement of Swiss immigrants known as New Windsor was located on the Carolina side of the river near Fort Moore. About ten miles below Fort Moore, Galphin discovered a place along the river with a high shiny bluff. It immediately attracted him as the best place to settle due to its proximity to the river and its closeness to Augusta. Galphin decided that this is where he would live and establish his trading post. He named this place Silver Bluff because of the way the sun made this spot shine like silver. He began to acquire real estate holdings, and since he intended to become a very active trader in British goods and merchandise, he learned the art of acquiring land grants through the British Crown.

Galphin always had an affinity for the ladies, and early on he acquired an Indian wife named Nitechucky from a Creek tribe, who gave him a daughter named Rose. Galphin was very astute about Indian culture and customs, and he had learned the Indian custom that required a trader operating a store in one of their towns to marry one of their women. His reputation among the Creek Indians grew, and when it was apparent that he would be very involved with them, he acquired another Indian wife named Metawney, daughter of a powerful Creek Indian chief. His marriage to Metawney gave him two sons, George II and John, and a daughter, Judith. This was the beginning of George Galphin's large multicultural and multiracial family which grew to include Indian wives and children, a wife and child from a mulatto slave named Sapho, and two white children from a wife named Rachell Dupree, who originally was from France. It can be assumed that these three multicultural families lived together and developed a common bond of community.

As Galphin's Silver Bluff trading empire grew, he acquired many slaves to help operate his growing business enterprise. Galphin's Silver Bluff Trading Post was located on the Carolina side of the river, and Carolina always had been a colony that allowed slaves. Galphin probably obtained his slaves in Charlestown, where slaves were bought and sold and where slave ships actively traded in the marketing of Negro slaves. There is evidence that Galphin was probably the largest slaveholder in the area. Besides being widely known as an Indian trader, he also was very prolific in the acquisition of land holdings, having much property in Georgia as well as Carolina. He conducted much of his business in Georgia and is credited with founding present-day Louisville, where he had a remote trading post on the Ogeechee River. This trading post was named Galphinton, and the community was known as Queensborough. Louisville would become Georgia's first planned capital. The secret to Galphin's success was his fairness with the Indians and the relationships he developed with the chiefs and leaders of the various Indian tribes. Naturalist William Bartram visited George Galphin in 1774 and described him as a "gentleman of very distinguished talents and great liberality who possessed the most extensive trade connections among the South and the Southwest Indian tribes."[2] Bartram was able to witness a very vibrant settlement bustling with activity in which Indians, blacks, and whites lived together and enjoyed freedoms not generally associated with a normal slave-holding environment. From 1740 to the time of the American Revolution, Galphin was developing a reputation among the Indians that drew Indians to his plantation from Georgia, Carolina, Alabama, Tennessee, and beyond to trade deerskins and small animal hides.

The Silver Bluff Trading Post has been the subject of archaeological investigations with evidence of a number of buildings, including a large two-story brick house said to be the first brick house built in the area. The archaeological findings have revealed many slave quarters, the site of Galphin's original house, trade warehouses, the guards' quarters, and a large staging area where many activities took place. There were several landing areas at the Savannah River where river barges and canoes came to conduct business. Since this was an active living establishment for slaves, Indians, and whites, there was much hospitality associated with the environment. At times Indians conducting trade at Silver Bluff were invited to eat and stay overnight at the plantation, another type of diplomacy that helped build relationships and establish a reputation among Indians far and wide.

Galphin also had a sawmill and a gristmill. In addition to trading English goods, he had an agricultural operation that grew tobacco, corn, and indigo, and he relied on slave labor for his farming. The archaeological investigations conducted by the Archaeological Society of South Carolina have identified more

---

[2] Charles C. Jones, Jr., and S. Dutcher, *Memorial History of Augusta, Georgia* (Syracuse NY: D. Mason & Co., 1890) 55.

than 14,000 artifacts at Silver Bluff, with the majority of them being eighteenth-century ceramics, including Delft, Westerwald, white salt-glazed, British brown, scratch blue, Staffordshire, combed yellow lead-glazed, Jackfield, creamware, colonoware, and porcelain. Other items recovered include brass buttons, buckles, cuff links, musket balls, tobacco pipe fragments, wine bottle shards, lead bale seals, brass furniture tacks, wrought nails, and many brick and limestone mortar fragments. The Indians were very happy to trade animal skins in exchange for British goods for cooking, eating, tools, beads, blankets, and other items, including rum and tobacco. The British needed the animal skins from Indian trading activities. The Savannah River was busy with river barges carrying goods and merchandise to and from the traders and merchants, and there was constant activity from the Indians in their canoes visiting the traders and Galphin at Silver Bluff and at his remote trading post on the Ogeechee River near Louisville.

At the time of Galphin's death in 1780, he had amassed more than 7,000 acres in Carolina and another 7,000 acres in Georgia. Although he had a relationship with the British Crown and also the English merchants with whom he did business, he sided with the American colonists during the American Revolution and was very much an American Patriot. Galphin had tremendous influence with the Indians and this proved very valuable to the American cause of independence from Britain. From 1775 until 1780, Galphin served as Commissioner of Indian Affairs in the southern district of the Continental Congress, effectively encouraging and influencing the Indians from fighting on the side of the British. This diplomacy included meeting with more than 200 chiefs near Augusta and telling them that the conflict between the American colonists and the British was not their fight. Galphin is listed in the papers of George Washington, where he reported the number of arms Indians were to bring if brought into the fight. Governor George Walton (a signer of the Declaration of Independence), Major Joseph Habersham, the Honorable William Stephens, and Major Peter Deveaux all signed affidavits to the patriotism of George Galphin. General Howe, Revolutionary leader, in writing to his commander-in-chief, General George Washington, spoke in the highest terms of the unwearied efforts of Galphin to conciliate the Creek Indians.

The American Revolution almost caused the dissolution of Galphin's plantation. The British captured the Silver Bluff Trading Post and nicknamed it Fort Galphin and also Fort Dreadnaught. They were intrigued by all of the warehouses of goods. Most of the slaves retreated to Savannah or nearby Augusta. It is believed that George Galphin died in 1780 at Silver Bluff Plantation. The plantation was later recaptured by the American Patriots led by Colonel "Light-Horse" Henry Lee, father of Confederate General Robert E. Lee.

In John Rippon's *Baptist Register* (1793) one of the Galphin's slaves, David George, gives an account of life on the Galphin Plantation. George, who became the first black minister in South Carolina, was an escapee slave from Virginia taken in by one of Galphin's Indian traders. Galphin purchased David George, who became Galphin's personal servant. Throughout his service at Silver Bluff, George described Galphin as kind. David George wrote that in 1770, a black evangelist named George Liele visited Silver Bluff and preached a sermon to some of the slaves, during which David George himself was converted. George learned about repentance from a sinful life, forgiveness of sins through Jesus Christ's sacrifice on the cross, and a new relationship in Jesus Christ as personal Savior.

Other preachers periodically came to Galphin's plantation to preach the gospel to large congregations of mostly slaves but also to whites. They would congregate under a brush arbor and hold baptisms in a place known as Dead River. This was a tributary of the Savannah River where the river was stationary and water did not flow. One white pastor who preached at Silver Bluff was Wait Palmer, who formed the slaves into a black congregation church, while Liele, the black evangelist from nearby Burke County, Georgia, continued to preach to the slaves at Silver Bluff. David George became one of the elders in the church who wanted to learn more about the Bible. Galphin allowed George to attend classes, taught by his white schoolmaster, in reading and writing along with Galphin's white children, Thomas and Martha. In 1773 George helped establish the first Negro Baptist church in America at Silver Bluff where Liele preached to this congregation. Another member of this church was Jesse Peter Galphin, who also became a Negro preacher. After the American Revolution, David George went to Nova Scotia, where he established churches. Jesse Peter Galphin and other Silver Bluff slaves likewise did the same in Augusta, where they formed Springfield Baptist Church with Galphin as the first pastor.

By 1790 Springfield Baptist had 180 members and continues to this day at its original location on Reynolds and Twelfth Street in downtown Augusta. This church also is the birthplace of Morehouse College, now in Atlanta, and has a State of Georgia historical marker located beside the church telling of this very important landmark in Negro Baptist Church history. In the celebration of Augusta's bicentennial in 1935, a Pageant Book commemorating the important events of Augusta's first 200 years recounts the founding of Springfield Baptist. The Pageant Book states:

> This church was organized on Sunday, August 12, 1793, by the Rev. Jesse Peters and George Liele, men who belonged to Silver Bluff Baptist Church, better known as Dead River Church which was organized in 1750 near Silver Bluff landing on the Carolina side of the Savannah River, originally built for the whites but turned over to the Negroes in 1773. The Reverend Jesse Peters Galphin was pastor of this church until 1814. There is not an exact record of the 1750 date but one can conclude a possibility of religious instruction in the Christian religion on the plantation as far back as 1750. There is evidence in the

Rippon Baptist Journals of the Church Formation at Silver Bluff in 1773.

A central premise in the Bible and the Christian religion is that God created man in his own image. Black individuals had to suffer through long periods of slavery in which they were considered as property rather than as persons. The author of this chapter believes an important conclusion should be the will of George Galphin, a very remarkable pre-Revolutionary War document that includes the names of many Galphin slaves. These slaves were presented as persons and not property in this document and recognized as persons with names rather than mere property owned by Galphin. Obviously the pastors who preached at Silver Bluff, including George Liele, had a profound effect on Galphin and his personal faith. Most of Galphin's estate was left to his son Thomas, whose mother was white Rachel Dupree. Galphin referred to her as "Rachel Dupree" not as "my wife" or "Rachel Galphin." In addition to Thomas, Rachel gave George a daughter, Martha, who received a generous 1,050 acres and one-third of the assets of the estate. Three of Galphin's heirs with a Creek woman, Metawney, were George, John, and Judith, and each was endowed at Galphin's death. Barbara, Galphin's "mulatto girl," the daughter of Rose, who died before Galphin, received her freedom and 300 acres and twenty slaves. Unlike the wills of most of his peers, Galphin's carefully disposed of his 128 slaves, each by name.[3]

---

[3] The author is grateful to Isabel Vandervelde, *History of Aiken County* (Spartenburg SC: Art Studio Press, 1999) for permission to include the complete text of her excellent transcription of Galphin's will in appendix D of this book.

Resources

Augusta Bicentennial Scrapbook. Augusta GA: Bicentennial Commission, 1935.

Cashin, Edward J. *Lachlin McGillivray, Indian Trader.* Athens: University of Georgia Press, 1992.

———. *Old Springfield: Race & Religion* in Augusta, Georgia. Augusta: Springfield Village Parks Foundation, 1995.

———. *The Story of Augusta.* Augusta GA: Richmond County Board of Education, 1980.

Cros, D. C., B. R. Penner, T. Forehand, J. Huffman, L. Potter, and L. Potter. *Excavations at New Windsor Township, South Carolina.* Columbia: South Carolina Institute of Archaeology, 1997.

Cruickshank, Helen G. *John and William Bartram's America.* Greenwich CT: Devin-Adair, 1957, 1990.

Galphin, G. Billings. Scrapbook. University of South Carolina Library. Special Collections.

Jones, Charles C., Jr. *History of Georgia: Volume I: Aboriginal and Colonial Epochs.* Boston: Houghton Mifflin, 1883.

Jones, Charles C., Jr., and Salem Dutcher. *Memorial History of Augusta, Georgia.* Reprint of 1890 edition, Spartanburg SC: Reprint Company, 1966.

Lawrence, K. *Heroes, Horses, and High Society.* Columbia SC: R. L. Bryan Co., 1971.

Rippon, J. *Baptist National Register.* Volume 1. No publisher. 1790–1793.

Vandervelde, I. *George Galphin: Indian Trading Patriot.* Aiken SC: Art Studio Press, 2004.

Vandervelde, I. *History of Aiken County.* Spartanburg SC: Art Studio Press, 1999.

Christianity in the World of George Liele

DEBORAH BINGHAM VAN BROEKHOVEN

There is a large body of writings about American religion in the colonial and Early National Period, as well as numerous books about slave religion in the Americas and about the Baptist denomination in which George Liele was a leader and preacher. Some of these works even provide a sentence or paragraph about Liele. But to understand George Liele's Christianity, influences, and impact on his world, he must be understood in a broad, transatlantic perspective. That global perspective requires a look at the Christianity in colonial Virginia, South Carolina, and Georgia, along with the Baptist movement in England and her colonies, including Jamaica, Nova Scotia, and Sierra Leone, as well as the mainland colonies.

Much discussion of religion today is framed globally, with recent atlases of religion using color coding to map concentrations of Christians, Muslims, and Buddhists. The assumption behind these studies of world Christianity or Islam is that the global nature of religion is a new phenomenon, the product of inexpensive and ubiquitous internet, cell phones, and transcontinental air flights. What is less frequently noted is the global movement of Christianity in the late eighteenth century as it continued into the nineteenth century, a period most often depicted as the great century of Protestant Christian missions and expansion. Often these narratives begin with the Eurocentric stories of the English missionary William Carey and the American missionaries Adoniram and Ann Judson, whose journeys to British India in 1793 and 1813 provided the dramatic stories needed for large-scale organizing and fundraising in support of international missions. Reframing our understanding of Christianity and mission efforts by focusing on the life and times of an earlier pioneer, George Liele (c. 1750–1830), suggests that a more nuanced, global, and multicultural view of this expansion of Christianity is possible and desirable.

Beginning with George Liele, one sees that the great century of Protestant mission and the accompanying diaspora of Christians began earlier than Carey and Judson's work, and this movement was fueled by both voluntary and involuntary movements of people and included preachers such as George Liele. As someone born into servitude, this preacher traveled almost as broadly as George Whitefield, from the mainland colonies and the new republic in the United States to Jamaica, and from Jamaica to England. Yet no organization or congregation commissioned him as a missionary, and reports of his itinerant preaching around South Carolina, Georgia, and Jamaica that appeared in his time are much more fragmentary than those documenting the travels of Whitefield and Wesley in the Americas.

Examining Christianity through the life and times of George Liele allows us to better understand both Liele and his transatlantic world. Looking at the factors which influenced his conversion and ministry allows for a more integrated and holistic view of Christianity than is commonly emphasized in the scholarly literature, which is traditionally divided into "black" church and "white" church studies and within a national, not a global, framework. The Christianity practiced by Liele was not limited to one nation, colony, or ethnic group but was a faith formed and spread through interaction with colonists and national leaders in the Americas and England. In turn, this broad vision of Christianity shaped and spread a variety of Christian experience that became widespread and influential in black, white, and integrated congregations in Georgia, South Carolina, Jamaica, Nova Scotia, Sierra Leone, and beyond.

Historians cite the Great Awakening, a series of preaching journeys and revivals associated with Englishman George Whitefield and New Englander Jonathan Edwards, in explaining the spread of revival-oriented Christianity in this period. Writers focusing on the southern colonies of Great Britain also emphasize the importance of Shubal Stearns and Daniel Marshall, who migrated from Connecticut, down the Shenandoah Valley, and eventually into the Carolinas and Georgia—a route that parallels the involuntary journey of many slaves, including Virginia-born George Liele.

Both migrations suggest that alongside the political and economic upheavals in Europe and its New World colonies (most often labeled revolutionary wars or wars for independence), equally important was the forced migration of peoples. Those exiles included German Anabaptists of several varieties, along with Methodists and Baptists, the groups that experienced the most dramatic growth in the Revolutionary and post-Revolutionary period. Among the background factors that contributed to the spread of revival-oriented Christianity in this period, the most important were the political and economic upheavals in Europe and its colonies, both of which encouraged the voluntary and forced migration of peoples. Anabaptists of several varieties, along with Methodists and Baptists, were the groups that experienced the most dramatic growth, for the message inviting listeners to come to liberty in Christ was a powerful attraction to those desiring to escape, even temporarily, the shackles of political and economic servitude.[1]

---

[1] This article builds on Alfred L. Pugh, "The Great Awakening and Baptist Beginnings in Colonial Georgia, the Bahama Islands, and Jamaica (1739–1833)," *American Baptist Quarterly* 26 (Winter 2007): 357–73; also Mechal Sobel, *Trabelin' On: The Slave Journey to an Afro-Baptist Faith* (Princeton NJ: Princeton University Press, 1979); Sandy D. Martin, "National

Looking at Christian movements during Liele's life and times also suggests a legitimate path through which we today can understand better the complexity of religion and religious peoples moving across political and geographic boundaries. The diaspora of Christians and Christianity was a transatlantic phenomenon that involved travel and people moving between Europe and the Americas, between the Americas and Africa, and between Africa and Europe. These movements of people and ideas shaped George Liele, and he in turn became one of the more influential preachers converted during the series of transatlantic revivals that began with the first Great Awakening and extended through the nineteenth century. This expansion and cross-fertilization happened more slowly between 1750 and 1830, Liele's lifetime, than did the spread of Pentecostalism or the Muslim religion in the twentieth century, because this earlier movement and its leaders were bound by the rhythms of transatlantic shipping. Letters, pamphlets, and itinerant preachers traveling on sailing ships served as the engine of this movement. The pamphlets and serial publications circulated in this fashion included formal minutes printed by the Society of Friends and regional Baptist associations, most often carried to other regions and countries by traveling preachers or very slow mail service. The letters and association minutes circulated by Baptists around the edges of the Atlantic world provide details about this movement in which Liele served as a leader.

That he lived in a world in which most people of African descent were enslaved complicated and shaped Liele's ministry and theology. During the span of his life, conviction that modern slavery was not Christian and should be abolished grew to become a frequent part of Christian conversation, preaching, and pamphleteering. The twin subjects of slavery and freedom were in the air, stirred up by the political upheaval of the American, French, and Haitian revolutions and by the religious conviction that began with Quakers and Baptists that slavery was evil and slaveholding problematic, particularly in a world where Christians were holding other Christians in slavery.

Baptists," in W. Glenn Jonas, Jr., ed., *The Baptist River: Essays on Many Tributaries of a Diverse Tradition* (Macon GA: 2006): 68–92; Sylvia R. Frey, *Water from the Rock: Black Resistance in a Revolutionary Age* (Princeton NJ: Princeton University Press, 1991); Timothy James Lockley, *Lines in the Sand: Race and Class in Lowcountry Georgia, 1750–1860* (Athens: University of Georgia Press, 2001); Philip Morgan, "Lowcountry Georgia and the Modern Atlantic World, 1733–ca. 1820," and Erskine Clarke, "'They Shun the Scrutiny of White Men': Reports on Religion from the Georgia Lowcountry and West Africa," in Philip Morgan, ed., *African American Life in the Georgia Lowcountry: The Atlantic World and the Gullah Geechee* (Athens: University of Georgia Press, 2010): 131–50 and 13–47. For details of the mission outreach from Liele's Jamaica to West Africa, see Horace Russell, *The Missionary Outreach of the West Indian Church: Jamaican Baptist Mission to West Africa in the Nineteenth Century* (New York: Peter Lang, 2000).

One can easily overstate the extent to which American Christians believed that slavery was wrong, especially if looking only at the earliest declarations against slavery in the Americas. These include a formal declaration against slavery issued by a Germantown (Pennsylvania) meeting of Quakers and Baptists in 1698 and an antislavery tract issued by a Kentucky Baptist preacher, David Barrow, in 1802. Most churches refrained from antislavery comments as they knew slavery was a sensitive subject among slave-holding Christians. As a slave and then former slave, George Liele was as careful as St. Paul when dealing with the issue of legal bondage, perhaps understanding that his liberty to preach was conditional upon the approval of the slaveholders he encountered and not just the approval of his own master or patron.[2]

Liele and others in the evangelical world were aware that prior to and after the American Revolution, some meetings of Quakers and Baptists had issued statements condemning slavery. But who was on the side of liberty was not always easy to discern, especially for African Americans, who understood that fighting against the rebel revolutionaries and for the British would more likely lead to their own emancipation. "Coming into liberty," a phrase used in this period to describe a conversion experience, might within the church or religious meeting mean finding personal release from the bondage of sin. But outside the church and a revival setting, "coming into liberty" connoted political freedom, change, and possibly revolution. With this type of religious experience so closely associated with Baptists, many of whom were also slaves, rulers in the slaveholding portions of the Americas grew nervous. This nervousness increased as Baptist and Methodist congregations grew and multiplied, with Baptists often typed as the church for "lower sorts." The earliest Baptist congregations in the Southern colonies included both white and black members, with black membership most often the majority. These demographics meant that the growing number of Baptist congregations, along with the increasing size of their preaching assemblies, was by itself threatening, even without talk of freedom from legal slavery. So however careful Liele was to refrain from direct criticism of slavery, British authorities in Jamaica still found cause for jailing him as an incendiary preacher.

With little known about the content of Liele's sermons, much less the preaching for which he was arrested (conducted at a racecourse in Kingston, Jamaica), we cannot know whether he emphasized that converts would find "liberty in Christ." Arguably he would not have been that bold. But as Baptist congregations multiplied in Jamaica, Georgia, and elsewhere, established leaders

---

[2] See Whittington B. Johnson, *Black Savannah, 1788–1864* (Fayetteville: University of Arkansas Press, 1996) for a discussion about the difficulties Liele and other black preachers faced in Savannah (8–12).

often did view Baptist preaching as threatening their authority. From their seventeenth-century beginnings, Baptists and other evangelical preachers had evoked similar fears. This was because so many of the early Baptist ministers were itinerants, traveling from place to place, constantly in and out of different legal jurisdictions. Because of their movement, these Baptist leaders were not as accountable to or concerned with temporal authorities. In a real sense they did undermine the status quo in churches and communities.

Historians of Jamaican politics and religion distinguish between itinerant "native Baptists" and more settled pastors like Liele, who became the "settled" pastor to a congregation in Kingston. Liele also gained a level of respectability because of his literacy and the opportunity this skill provided for him to correspond with leading Baptists in Great Britain. His alliance with British Baptists, in part for funding and moral support, might suggest he supported the status quo, in contrast to the wilder "native" Baptists, whose backcountry locations and free-form theology seemed unorthodox and directly threatening to authorities. But one can make too much of these distinctions. When the Baptist Wars, as they were called, erupted in Jamaica in 1831, it was Baptists of all types who were viewed as the heart of the rebellion. And to this day, George Liele is considered one of the fathers of Jamaican independence.

It would be wrong and an oversimplification to argue that all or most Baptists taught rebellion against one's owners or rulers as divinely sanctioned. Yet Baptists did challenge authority, and their opponents decried this evangelical religion as disruptive and leading Baptists into immoral practices. By stressing the individual's responsibility to convert and follow Christ, both in baptism and holy living, Baptists did, for example, authorize some women to act independently of their husbands who were not converts. Likewise, Baptists encouraged slaves to convert—sometimes without regard to a master's wishes or religion. So while church leaders stressed that converting African Americans to Christianity would make them better and more obedient slaves, not all slaveholders or community leaders agreed.[3]

The Baptist Network

George Liele did not stand alone as a preacher or church leader. Like their Quaker contemporaries, Baptists developed an organizational structure that supported, disciplined, and empowered itinerant and local preachers. Regular association meetings, as Baptists called them, paralleled the quarterly and annual meetings of "Friends," as Quakers called their organizational structure. And just as traveling ministers among the Friends carried news, advice, and questions

---

[3] John Parmer Gates, "George Liele: A Pioneer Negro Preacher," *The Chronicle* 6/3 (July 1943): 118–29.

from meeting to meeting, so Baptist associations appointed "messengers" to travel to distant meetings, where they brought greetings, encouragement, and advice. Unlike the Friends, Baptists published these records of annual meetings, including details about preachers and elders present, though not always with care to include "Negro" ministers such as George Liele.

Perhaps because they began as the least literate of the evangelical denominations, Baptists worked hard to establish their structure as legitimate, with ties and support from near and far. Beginning in 1707, Baptists in Philadelphia began publishing the annual minutes of the regular association meetings, a practice that grew after the first Great Awakening, when Baptist congregations and associations multiplied. In the ministry and travels of George Liele, several Baptists associations provided support and encouragement. Most important were the Philadelphia and the London associations, which provided the only denominational structure for linking Baptists in joint enterprises, including mission efforts.

Perhaps the reason Liele's earliest activities are not recorded in association minutes is because his conversion and early preaching occurred in the low country of Georgia and South Carolina, far from the center of Baptist work, and ahead of the establishment of Baptist congregations of white colonists. Under those circumstances, Liele's itinerant preaching was neither recorded by a literate companion nor forwarded for publication in the minutes of the Philadelphia, Pennsylvania, or Charleston, South Carolina, associations, which were the earliest Baptist associations in the Americas. During the 1770s and 1780s, the period in which Liele preached in South Carolina and Georgia, and also when Morgan Edwards preached and collected histories of early Baptists, Morgan records very little about black Baptists, occasionally noting unnamed "negro servants" joining an early congregation, alongside their owners who are named. In Morgan's records nothing is recorded about African-American preachers, though from other sources we know of largely black congregations of Baptists in several parts of Virginia, including its capital at the time, Williamsburg.

The single best source for information about Liele, interestingly, comes from the other side of the Atlantic and was published about the same time that Morgan Edwards published his *Materials Towards a History of the Baptists*. In London the Rev. John Rippon (1751–1836), created *The Baptist Annual Register for 1790, 1791, 1792, and part of 1793, including Sketches of the State of Religion Among Different Denominations of Good Men at Home and Abroad* as a tool to connect Baptists on both sides of the Atlantic. So while Liele's manuscript letters do not survive, nor is there much mention of him in association minutes, detailed reports about him and copies of his letters do survive in the registers published by John Rippon in the 1790s.[4] It is within Rippon's *Register* that the letters and voice of George Liele survive, including the classic account of his religious background and conversion.

That Dr. Rippon was Liele's biographer is significant, given that Rippon held the most prominent Baptist pulpit of his day,[5] one that allowed for his leading role in strengthening the transatlantic network of Baptist leaders. And it was the British leaders in this network who provided the crucial support Liele and the Jamaican Baptists received. This aid came because Rippon was not just a pastor and publisher, but also a leading member of the Baptist Missionary Society. Based in London, this group was the only national or transnational organization for Baptists until the Triennial Convention was formed in the United States in 1814. But that convention movement largely ignored the needs of the Jamaican Baptists in favor of a focus on missions in India and Burma. Understanding the special relationship between Liele and Rippon allows us to envision the Baptist world of Liele's time in ways sometimes excluded by an exclusively theological description of the Baptist world. The more traditional approach to Baptist history divides Baptists into two theological types, regular or Calvinist Baptists and general or Armenian Baptists.

Such theological distinctions are difficult to pin on either Rippon or Liele, who are generally ignored by those tracing the historical theology of Baptists. A more helpful categorization for Liele may be the label he suggested in his writings about an Anabaptist covenant. Regardless of how one interprets the covenant, Liele's choice of the term "Anabaptist" sets him apart from theological quarrels of the most doctrinaire Baptists (whether general or particular) and instead suggests Liele was more comfortable in the broader world of Anabaptist faith, one that included the Moravian contemporaries of Liele in Georgia. The Moravians offered another distinction in their emphasis on devotional and congregational music—a worship practice not commonly accepted by Baptists

---

[4] Morgan Edwards published his compilations between 1770 and 1792, with a modern two-volume edition annotated and indexed by Eve B. Weeks and Mary B. Warren (Heritage Papers, Danielsville GA, 1984). For students of Liele, most helpful is the first volume published by Rippon in *The Baptist Annual Register, for 1790, 1791, 1792, and Part of 1793, including sketches of the state of religion among different denominations of Good Men At Home and Abroad* (London: Vestry, 1793); see especially pages 332–37 and 541ff.

[5] Rippon's pastorate in London followed that of the Rev. Dr. John Gill and preceded the pastorate of the best-known preacher of his century, Charles H. Spurgeon, though he did not share the extreme Calvinist theology of Gill or Spurgeon.

this early, and which Baptists and Methodists first heard in the worship of the Moravians sailing to or newly arrived in the American colonies.[6]

Scholars have long acknowledged the importance of singing and hymnody in the black church and to some extent in American church life in general. Less well known is the extent to which singing as worship brought Christians together across racial, geographic, and denominational barriers. Yet hymnody was central to the ministry of both Liele and Rippon. Liele began his ministry by teaching hymns, and as one observer wrote to Rippon, Liele "began to discover his love of other negroes, on the same plantation with himself, by reading hymns among them, encouraging them to sing, and sometimes by explaining the most striking parts of them."[7] Rippon too was convinced that singing could instill in believers the meaning of Scripture, so he devoted much more time to collecting, publishing, and distributing hymnals than he did to sermons or theological treatises, in sharp contrast with his predecessor in London, the Rev. Dr. John Gill, and his successor, the Rev. Dr. Charles Spurgeon. Rippon led Baptists to accept more and more congregational singing as part of worship through his *Selection of Hymns* (1790). That hymnal was such a steady seller that by 1830 the volume had run through more than thirty editions.[8]

A letter from Rippon written in 1786 to the Rev. Thomas Ustick, a leading minister of the Philadelphia Baptist Association, emphasized the ties of religious affiliation and affection that bound the men, regardless of their inability to travel across the Atlantic for a face-to-face meeting. Fully half of an eight-page letter is taken up with hymnody, as Rippon concludes his letter with a request for Ustick to send him some American hymns for his forthcoming *Selection*, and then writes out all the stanzas for three hymns that he suggests "for singing in an Association or meeting of ministers."[9] In the rest of his letter, Rippon stressed the importance of Baptists developing close ties through the exchange of association

---

[6] David W. Stowe, *How Sweet the Sound: Music in the Spiritual Lives of Americans* (Cambridge MA: Harvard University Press, 2004). Here I am following and elaborating on the analysis and narrative Stowe offers in his first chapter, "O for a Thousand Tongues to Sing," 17–40.

[7] Rippon, *Baptist Register* (1793): 333.

[8] *Selection of Hymns from the Best Authors, intended to be an appendix to Watts's Psalms and Hymns* is advertised as early as 1790, with the "first American edition" advertised in 1792. That American edition seems to be the earliest imprint surviving. See Edward C. Starr, *A Baptist Bibliography, Being a Register of Printed Materials By and About Baptists; Including Works Written Against the Baptists*, Vol. 19 (Rochester NY: American Baptist Historical Society, 1973): 252–55.

[9] John Rippon to Thomas Ustick, 18 August 1786, Record Group 1285, American Baptist Historical Society, Atlanta. Rippon's emphases and spelling are uncorrected from the original.

minutes and letters, noting he would happily receive more than fifty association letters from America, distributing them at the various association meetings he attended in England.

Rippon did not expect he would travel to meet Ustick and other brother Baptists in Philadelphia, but he envisioned a time when they would all assemble "on Mount Zion." And then his imagination soars: "Yes we shall all meet, not as you will at Philadelphia, but we shall meet & never never Never part—O what an Association will that be, an Association of Universal Harmony & of everlasting Happiness—don't you long for it, Mr. Ustick, I feel a pleasure this moment in the Anticipation of it, not to be described by a pen even if it were dipped in ye Ocean of celestial happiness which flows from the throne of God & ye Lamb." And since mere words failed to match his imagination of this heavenly scene, Rippon envisioned a "celestial" choir singing with "joy,...shout,... [and] Harmony," that "Christ is the Alpha & Omega of the Song," and "Worthy is the Lamb that dy'd." He imagined "the noble army of martyrs" gathered in triumph singing "Worthy the Lamb," and "our lips reply, for he was slain FOR US. But I must come down from the Mount of Songs above to describe the songs which I have lately been preparing for the Church below."[10] With Rippon expressing such ties of Christian affection to brothers he had never met face-to-face, one can better imagine why George Liele, also the recipient of letters (and material aid) from Rippon, would travel to England near the end of his ministry, perhaps hoping for a foretaste of that heavenly reunion imagined so well by Dr. Rippon.

Conclusion

In part, Jamaica's Baptist War of 1831 to 1832 was a response to the half-measures taken toward emancipation there as the truth came home that the West Indian emancipation bill languishing in parliament (finally passing in 1833) might not bring immediate and unconditional liberty to Jamaican slaves. But this Baptist War and the fever for liberty was also the consequence of the deep faith found in the Baptist congregations spreading throughout Jamaica. Sadly, only Rippon, not Liele, lived to see the emancipation bill pass. Any portrayal of Wilberforce's long fight in parliament against slavery misses the grassroots Baptist dimension of the antislavery campaign. It was the reality (one might even argue the threat) evoked by Jamaica's Baptist Wars against slavery and for independence that strengthened support for Wilberforce's moral position. Without the so-called Baptist uprising in the New World, British Parliament would have been even slower to move from a gradual emancipation law to

---

[10] Ibid.

unconditional abolition of slavery. Though Liele did not live to see his world transformed by an end to slavery, his legacy of freedom is well known in Jamaica and many other parts of the world, including Sierra Leone, Liberia, and Nova Scotia. To these far-flung places, those converted and ordained by Liele traveled to bring the gospel and to find a more secure living than Liele had found in the plantation countries of Georgia and Jamaica.

This legacy of global mission outreach and Baptist liberty is often unknown among American Baptists and Christians today. Arguably this hole in our understanding of the Christian movement globally is because Liele took what many historians judge to be the "wrong side" in the American Revolution. Deciding temporary servitude with a friendly British officer would allow him a brighter future for his family and ministry, Liele left Georgia and the pages of most American history books, preferring the broader work of evangelism and church-planting allowed in British Jamaica to the continued trials of life in low country Georgia. If he had sided with the American revolutionaries rather than the British, Liele's ministry would have remained in Georgia, limited by the legal codes governing the daily life of slave and free. His loss to the American Republic was Jamaica's gain, and one that translated into a Jamaican missionary movement reaching into Canada, England, and West Africa.

The Early Baptist Roots and Religious Environment of George Liele

B. CARLISLE DRIGGERS

Tracing the life and ministry of the Reverend George Liele is a fascinating journey. He was by all accounts the first ordained black Baptist preacher in the new world called America. There have been bits and pieces written about him through the years, but never before now has there been an exhaustive attempt to know all we can about him and his legacy. It is a story that begs to be told.

In order to see where the importance of George Liele fits into the total picture of Baptist history, it is necessary to trace that history from the earliest days of the Baptist movement. Even though many details have been lost over time, much data has been preserved and is most interesting to recall. As is well documented, the journey of Baptists worldwide can be traced back to the Anabaptists in Switzerland in the sixteenth century. The origin of Anabaptists is obscure, but it is widely accepted that the designation of Anabaptist came from the belief that one's baptism as an infant was without Scriptural justification and that the only baptism that was biblical was by immersion based on personal regeneration. Consequently, severe persecution was inflicted on the Anabaptists, or rebaptizers as they were called, by government officials and the Roman Catholic tradition.[1]

Anabaptists also surfaced in Germany, England, and Holland in the sixteenth century, similarly suffering rejection and persecution. There was no firm, institutional relationship between the Anabaptists and emerging Baptists, but there was nevertheless a spiritual connection of several mutual beliefs, such as believer's baptism, regenerate church membership, the absolute authority of Scripture, and civil and religious liberties.[2]

Early Beginnings of Baptists

Even though there is much uncertainty about the actual beginnings of the Baptists, there are certain facts that are well known. It must be recognized that sincere and well-meaning Baptists for decades have believed that their forebears can be traced to the first-century followers of Jesus Christ as outlined in the Book

---

[1] Henry C. Vedder, *Short History of the Baptists* (Philadelphia: American Baptist Publication Society, 1907) 129–66.

[2] Robert G. Torbet, *A History of the Baptists* (Philadelphia: Judson Press, 1950) 35–55.

of Acts and even linked to John the Baptist.[3] Such convictions remain by some fundamentalist Baptists to this day, but those assertions are largely refuted by numerous other Baptist groups and church historians.[4]

What can be determined is that the acknowledged history of Baptists began with John Smyth in 1608 and 1609. He was a religious refugee who has been named by some as the founder of the modern Baptist churches because he adopted believer's baptism and ascertained to a marked degree the Baptist principles in his historic Confession. Smyth led about eighty nonconformist church members from England to Holland to escape persecution because of their practice of believer's baptism. He was joined by Thomas Helwys in leading the group to separate from the Congregational Church at the town of Gainsborough on Trent and relocate in Amsterdam. Soon Smyth baptized himself by affusion; then he baptized Helwys and some forty other believers. He was at first the pastor of the group but in a short time became an Anabaptist and then a Mennonite after settling in Holland.[5]

Sometime around 1611 or 1612, Thomas Helwys and eight to ten members returned to England and started the first recognized Baptist church that was located at Spitalfield, just outside London. In time, the little church grew and helped give rise to other Baptist congregations. Helwys and his members opposed the teaching of John Calvin and Calvinist adherents because of their strict predestination views, and so became known as Arminians or General Baptists while the Calvinists, sometime around 1638, became known as Particular Baptists.[6]

Thomas Helwys stood up for religious freedom. He spoke against the Church of England and the Roman Catholic Church for supposedly taking away man's freedom in Christ. In his book *A Short Declaration of the Mystery of Iniquity*, which was the first claim for freedom of worship to be published in the English language, Helwys wrote:

> Let the king judge, is it not most equal that men should choose their Religion themselves, seeing they only must stand themselves before the judgment seat of God to answer for themselves.... We profess and teach that in all earthly things the king's power is to be submitted

---

[3] G. H. Orchard, "Introductory Essay" by J. R. Graves in *A Concise History of Baptists from the Time of Christ Their Founder to the 18th Century* (First published in London in 1838, republished in 1855 in America by J. R. Graves, and republished later in 1956 in Lexington, Kentucky, by the Ashland Avenue Baptist Church) iii–xxiv.

[4] Robert Ashcraft, *Landmarkism Revisited* (Mabelvale AR: Ashcraft Publications, 2003) 5–29.

[5] Torbet, *History of the Baptists*, 62–64.

[6] Ibid., 66, 69–72.

unto; and in heavenly or spiritual things, if the king or any in authority under him shall exercise their power against any, they are not to resist by any way or means, although it were in their power, but rather to submit their lives as Christ and his disciples did, and yet keep their consciences to God…. The king is a mortal man and not God, therefore hath no power over the immortal souls of his subjects to make laws and ordinances for them and to set spiritual Lords over them.[7]

In response, an irate King James I placed Helwys in Newgate Prison where he later died in 1616.[8]

Throughout the seventeenth century in England, the two Baptist bodies, Particular and General, became prominent. The Particular Baptists were mainly the adherents of John Calvin (1509–1564) while the General Baptists followed closely the teachings of Jacobus Arminius (1560–1609).[9]

A Frenchman who became a Protestant reformer in Geneva, Switzerland, Calvin began his studies as a Roman Catholic, but sometime around 1533 converted to Protestantism. In time he became recognized as the father of Presbyterianism and also as a major influence on Puritanism.[10] The Puritans sought to cleanse or purify the Church of England of what they believed to be Roman Catholic beliefs and practices, and finally separated themselves from Anglicanism during the reign of Queen Elizabeth I (1558–1603).[11]

The Calvinists became convinced that the writings of John Calvin in his monumental work, *The Institutes of Religion*, were based on the theological concepts of the Apostle Paul plus Augustine (354–430), the Bishop of Hippo in Northern Africa. Augustine, based on his study of the New Testament, produced a clear-cut explanation of salvation by grace through faith along with the authority and supremacy of the church.[12]

In Holland, Jacobus Arminius, a Reformed pastor, reacted to the dogmatic concepts of the Calvinists and developed his own views. His teachings became known as Arminianism, particularly in stressing the part man plays in salvation. He opposed the strict teachings of Calvin on unconditional election for salvation

---

[7] Ibid., 67.

[8] Ibid., 68.

[9] Ibid., 66–72.

[10] Donald T. Kauffman, *The Dictionary of Religious Terms* (Westwood NJ: Fleming H. Revell Company, 1967) 95–96.

[11] Ibid., 363.

[12] Ibid., 96.

and irresistible grace and emphasized instead the freedom of man to choose or reject salvation in Christ.[13]

The basic tenets of Particular Baptists were the sovereignty of the grace of God, divine predestination of all events, election to eternal life (i.e., only the elect could be saved), eternal security of the believer, total depravity of the unbeliever, the supreme authority of Scripture, the necessity of the church,[14] baptism only by immersion based on a profession of faith,[15] and religious and civil liberties.[16]

At the same time, General Baptists also believed in religious and civil liberties but taught general or unlimited atonement, aggressive evangelistic practices, and that salvation came through a personal profession of faith.[17]

Of the two groups, General Baptists were the oldest. Their prominent leaders in the early years of the seventeenth century were John Smyth, Thomas Helwys, and John Murton. The leaders who helped in the formation of Particular Baptists were Henry Jacob (even though he never became a Baptist), John Lathrop, Henry Jessey, Samuel Eaton, and John Epilsbury. The first Particular Baptist church began in 1638 in London and may have been established as early as 1633.[18]

As the number of Baptist churches increased, efforts were begun to associate together for defense against ridicule and persecution by the Church of England and the monarchy. However, the deep differences over doctrine and church organizational polity caused General and Particular Baptists to devise their own laws in keeping with their firm convictions. General Baptists were so called mainly because of their belief in general atonement for all men while Particular Baptists were known primarily for their adherence to particular atonement for the elect only.[19]

The Particular churches were more interested in an informal arrangement for correspondence and fellowship, with the congregations being independent, while General Baptists wanted more structural organizational relationships with some degree of authority over the churches. In 1704 the Particular Baptists formed the London Baptist Association, composed mainly of Calvinist-leaning churches. It was the first Baptist Association and had national implications, but in a rather loose-knit arrangement. In comparison, the General Baptist congregations were becoming increasingly universalistic in their doctrinal pronouncements and somewhat controlling over their churches. In addition,

---

[13] Ibid., 43–44.

[14] Ibid.

[15] Ibid.; also Torbet, *History of the Baptists*, 62-64.

[16] Torbet, *History of the Baptists*, 75–83.

[17] Ibid., 66, 69–71, 75–83.

[18] H. Leon McBeth, *The Baptist Heritage* (Nashville TN: Broadman Press, 1987) 32–56.

[19] Vedder, *Short History of the Baptists*, 201–30.

more and more of their churches were turning to baptism by affusion. That practice alone was anathema to Particular Baptists and led to an increase of strong feelings between the two groups.[20]

Locating in the New World

While a people called Baptists were expanding in parts of Europe, especially England, a new development was transpiring across the Atlantic. In the 1500s and 1600s, ships from Spain, France, and England made their way across the Atlantic to a new world that became known as America. The British, the first to settle in large numbers in the new land, came seeking their fortunes, but also many came for religious and political freedom.

As colonies were being developed, the king of England granted charters to various corporations and land grants to settlers. He also appointed governors to oversee the operations. By 1617 Virginia had its own legislature, and by 1632 some 40,000 persons had located in the new territory.

Others were coming as well to settle in Maryland and across much of what became known as New England. Many young men and women arrived as indentured servants so as to pay for their passage by working in the tobacco fields until they had paid off their debt to the merchant ships and corporations. The British discovered tobacco in Virginia and learned to plant and harvest it. In time, a huge market for tobacco was created back in England and the supply was met by returning ships from the colony. Hundreds of additional workers were quickly needed to work the fields. A few native Africans came on a Dutch ship in 1619, most likely as indentured servants. By 1660 planters were bringing large numbers of African slaves to labor in the fields to add to or replace the indentured servants who had satisfied their debts.

As history records, America was founded on the principle that all people have a right to life, liberty, and the pursuit of happiness. In 1620 ninety-nine hopeful settlers reached Plymouth, Massachusetts, on the Mayflower. They called themselves Pilgrims but were, in fact, Separatist Puritans from the Congregational Church. They were fleeing England because of religious persecution and to seek a more prosperous way of life. The Puritans established the Massachusetts Bay Colony and built their own churches, strangely enough, in relationship to their Congregational Church back in England from which they were fleeing. In so doing, they maintained their own strict demands and expectations of each other and non-Christians, and soon their influence was widespread.

---

[20] Ibid., 237–40.

The New England settlers did not grow tobacco because of the rocky soil and because their farms were smaller than the large plantations in the South, where vast tracts of land were required for tobacco farming. Hence, more slaves were needed to work the fields in the southern regions than in the northern areas.

The settlers in America grew to love their freedom and intensely resented the economic controls and obligations placed on them by the British, both politically and religiously. In New England, particularly, the Puritans had become even more harsh and demanding on the people than back in old England, especially in matters of religious customs and practices. Additionally, in the northern colonies, the citizens were expected to support the Congregational Church and their pastor, while in the South, people paid to support the Anglican churches and their clergy. The monetary system of support for churches and ministers, in both North and South, was very unpopular as it was in addition to the heavy tax requirements already imposed on the colonists by the government of Great Britain.[21]

In Massachusetts, Roger Williams, who had been trained as an Anglican minister, spoke out against the political enforcement of Christian legalistic principles and religious tax practices on everyone, especially non-believers. He felt their freedoms were being violated. Williams learned about Baptists' resistance to what was happening and appreciated that resistance. No doubt he knew that in both England and in the new world of America, Baptists had always stood firmly for separation of church and state, and had paid a high price of being imprisoned, fined, beaten, or losing property because of their convictions about personal freedoms. He also proposed that the native Indians should be compensated for their land. Soon Williams was expelled from the Massachusetts Bay Colony, and he moved to Rhode Island where there was more freedom to think, speak, and worship.

In spite of rejection and persecution, Baptist churches grew in number and influence. By the nineteenth century, they were an established religious tradition in the colonies, dating back to 1639. In that year, Roger Williams founded a Baptist church in Providence, even though he apparently never became a Baptist himself. The church was the first Baptist congregation in America and was soon followed by a second church located in Newport, founded by a physician named John Clarke.[22]

In time, General Baptist beliefs and customs became identified more with the Separatists in the New World, who were pulling away from the oppressive Congregational church, while the Particular Baptists became known as the

---

[21] Allan Nevins, "History of the United States," *World Book Encyclopedia*, vol. 19 (Chicago: Field Enterprises, 1971) 86–92.

[22] Bill J. Leonard, *Baptists in America* (New York: Columbia University, 2005) 13–16.

Regular Baptists.[23] The well-known convictions and practices of the Separatists centered on Arminian theology fused with some tenets of Calvinism. They rejected creeds and confessions of faith and promoted evangelistic appeals, which often included Indians and black slaves, with warm-hearted, noisy, emotional worship services that incorporated spirited singing. They preached the sufficiency of Scripture alone and focused on salvation as the primary reason for starting churches, allowing for lay men and women to speak in the churches as exhorters of the gospel. They stressed separation of church and state and baptism by immersion based on a personal profession of faith.

The Regular Baptists, by contrast, believed and practiced a determined loyalty to Calvinism that centered on five points: total depravity, unconditional election, limited atonement, irresistible grace, and perseverance of the saints. In addition, they advocated educated ministers and preachers, church discipline, and adoption of creeds and confessions of faith. Their worship was solemn, rational, and formal, with singing restricted to the Psalms. Like other Baptists, they practiced baptism by immersion based on personal regeneration but allowed for few lay exhorters of the gospel.

Moving South

The Baptist preacher who is credited with introducing Regular Baptist traditions into the Southland was William Screven, who in 1696 relocated from Kittery, Maine, to Charleston, South Carolina.[24] The Baptist preacher who is recognized as the one who brought Separatist thinking southward from Holland, Connecticut, through Virginia to Sandy Creek in the Guilford area (now Randolph County) of North Carolina was Shubal Stearns, around 1755.[25]

Without question, the rapid growth and influence of Baptists in America was due in large measure to the Great Awakening during the middle years of the eighteenth century. Through the evangelistic preaching of Jonathan Edwards, Gilbert Tennent, John Wesley, and especially George Whitefield in New England, thousands "experienced religion" by coming to personal faith in Jesus as Savior and Lord. The simple, heartwarming appeal of the preachers was in sharp contrast to the quieter, emotionless preaching heard in numerous churches, particularly Congregational and Anglican.[26]

---

[23] William L. Lumpkin, *Baptist Foundations in the South* (Ashville NC: Revival Literature, 2006) 1–19.

[24] *A Noble Company: Biographical Essays on Notable Particular-Regular Baptists in America*, ed. Terry Wolever (Springfield MO: Particular Baptist Press, 2006) 208–25.

[25] Lumpkin, *Baptist Foundations*, 20–23.

[26] Torbet, *History of the Baptists*, 239–42.

The Great Awakening, promoted mostly by Methodists, Presbyterians, and Baptists, was not confined to any one area of the New World but throughout the colonies. However, Baptists were the chief religious heirs of the Awakening. It is known, for instance, that in 1700 there were some fourteen Baptist churches in America with around 6,500 members. By 1800 there were 1,200 congregations with about 100,000 members. Many congregations left their denominations, especially the Congregational church, and became Baptist. At the same time, a host of Baptist churches were started on their own by just a few local converts. A great number of Separatist Congregational churches became Baptist.[27]

Perhaps the primary reason so many Baptist churches sprang up is due to the appeal of conversion and the congregational polity of independence that characterized the Baptists. As new believers, they formed churches as they wanted to, without asking permission of any official ecclesiastical authorities. They simply followed the leading of the Spirit of God and the dictates of their convictions as they gathered in Jesus' name to launch new churches.[28]

Another direct result of the Great Awakening was the emergence of the New Lights. They were so called by many members of the established churches, who opposed the manner in which the new believers began to exercise their leadership roles and evangelistic zeal. Consequently, the conservatives of the older churches were called Old Lights in keeping with their resentment of revivalism and their commitment to the state church order. Without doubt, the Awakening was a people's movement, as informal groups sent out preachers who were devoid of formal training and who went into regional parishes without invitation or notice. Their love for evangelism and seeing lost sinners converted compelled them to do so.[29]

Yet another vitally important outcome of the Whitefield revivals in New England was the split that occurred between Regular and Separate Baptists. Of definite note is what occurred in the life of Shubal Stearns, a native of Stonington, Connecticut. He joined the New Light Separates from the Congregational church in 1745. Six years later, after a careful study of the Scriptures, he was baptized by immersion. Stearns was baptized by Wait Palmer, the pastor of the Baptist church at North Stonington. Stearns himself became a Baptist and was ordained in May 1751 by Wait Palmer and Joshua Morse. He then became the pastor of a new church being formed at Tolland, Connecticut, where he remained for three years. Stearns' co-laborer in the gospel ministry was his brother-in-law, Daniel Marshall, the husband of Stearns's sister, Martha. They

---

[27] William H. Brackney, *Baptists in North America* (Malden MA.: Blackwell Publishing, 2006) 24–25.

[28] Leonard, *Baptists in America*, 16–19.

[29] Lumpkin, *Baptist Foundations*, 6–7.

also became Baptists and then joined with Stearns in spreading the gospel message during the years to come. They were New Light Separate Baptists and were open to whatever the Lord had for them to do. Soon they would bring revivalist energy to the South and lay the foundation for Baptist expansion in that region of the emerging nation.[30]

Regular Baptists in the South, dating back to 1696 with William Screven in Charleston, gave birth to new churches in the lower section of what became South Carolina and over into south Georgia. Edmund Botsford (1745–1819) was an important Regular Baptist who started as an itinerant preacher out of Charleston and traveled across lower South Carolina, over into Georgia, and up toward what became Augusta. He helped give birth to several churches, including one in Burke County about 25 miles below Augusta. The church was called New Savannah at first, but afterwards assumed the title of Botsford's Old Meetinghouse. It was started in 1773 and was the second Baptist church in Georgia.[31] The first was the Kiokee church, located just above Augusta, which had been started a year earlier by the Separate Baptist Daniel Marshall.[32] Both churches are still in existence today.

The Separatists were much more aggressive in evangelism and church starting in the South than were the Regular Baptists, mainly due to the leadership and influence of Shubal Stearns and Daniel Marshall. Separates gained a reputation by other denominations as being "the only ones in the country who go far and wide preaching and caring for souls."[33] By the years just prior to the American Revolution, it was said that the Separates had pulled far ahead of the Regulars in starting new congregations, especially in Virginia, North Carolina, South Carolina, Georgia, Tennessee, and Kentucky.[34]

For many years Shubal Stearns has been known as the "Reverend Old Father" of Separatist Baptists. He left Tolland, Connecticut, in 1754 in search of new territory to preach the gospel. He traveled to Opequon Creek in Berkeley County, Virginia (now West Virginia), and discovered that Daniel Marshall and his family had arrived there also. However, they soon realized that they were off the beaten path. Stearns and Marshall learned about new and promising settlements in central and western North Carolina. Hence, the next year they made their way by horse-drawn wagon, sled, and pack saddles to Guilford

[30] Ibid., 20–23.

[31] Charles D. Mallary, *Memoirs of Elder Edmund Botsford* (Springfield MO: Particular Baptist Press, 2004) 29–30.

[32] David Benedict, *A General History of the Baptist Denomination in America and Other Parts of the World*, vol. 2 (Boston: Manning and Loring, 1813) 173.

[33] Lumpkin, *Baptist Foundations in the South*, 47.

[34] Ibid., 53–54.

County. Soon they started the Sandy Creek Baptist Church, and Stearns's organizational skills and preaching appeal caused an explosion of growth all across the region. Between November 1755 and January 1758, the farmer-pastor Shubal Stearns baptized some 900 converts, 590 of whom became members of his church, while the others went out to join the forty or so churches he had helped to organize. There is no way to determine the true influence of this diminutive preacher—with his piercing eyes, melodious speaking tones, and a loving character in the spreading of the gospel—with the rapid increase of Baptist churches all across the southern states of America, which continues to this day. He was an uneducated pastor but, like the prophet Jeremiah, he had "fire shut up in [his] bones" (20:9) to tell people about God's mercy and forgiveness.[35]

As time transpired, the designations of Regular (or Particular) and General (or Separatist) Baptists became blurred, especially as many Particular Baptists identified with the Separatists in the South due to their growth, passion, and focus.

For many years there was little Christian association and communion between the Regular and the Separates. The smallest trifles were sometimes allowed to keep them at an unhappy distance from each other. But at length a gradual amalgamation was effected, and the invidious titles by which they were designated have long since fallen into disuse.[36]

Emergence of Black Baptist Preachers and Churches

When slaves from Africa began to appear in the colonies in the mid-to-late 1600s, there were those white settlers, especially in the North and some in the South, who opposed the evil and inhumane practice. There were also those slave owners who had personal reservations about the unjust system of slavery but were motivated by economics and self-interest to have slaves.[37] It was realized that tobacco farming especially in Virginia, drove much of the need for more and more slave labor, because the same acres of land could not tolerate the planting of tobacco year after year. Thus, the king of England would grant large tracts of additional land to the colonists for planting purposes, or the farmers who could afford it would buy more land, which resulted in the emergence of huge plantations in the southern region. For years the primary slave port, which was easy to reach by sea, was at Charleston due to the fact that rice, and later cotton production, and tobacco had become so much in demand back in Europe that

---

[35] John Sparks, *The Roots of Appalachian Christianity: The Life and Legacy of Elder Shubal Stearns* (Lexington: University Press of Kentucky, 2001) 1–17.

[36] Mallary, *Memories of Botsford*, 27.

[37] Robert A. Baker and Paul J. Craven, Jr., *Adventure in Faith: The First 300 Years of First Baptist Church, Charleston, South Carolina* (Nashville TN: Broadman Press, 1982) 273–74.

boatloads of new workers were needed.[38] Nothing, however, could ever be a defense for the wretched practice of slavery anywhere, especially in the new, freedom-loving world called America.

The developments that led to the rise of black Baptist churches are most intriguing and have been documented for years although on a limited basis. However, specific information pertaining to the emergence of black ordained Baptist preachers is somewhat unclear when it comes to the certainty of several key facts. For sure, the locations, dates, and names of the first black Baptist preachers and the first black Baptist churches were closely intertwined. The primary locations included Burke County, Savannah, and Augusta in Georgia and Silver Bluff in South Carolina. The dates were framed between the 1740s to approximately the early 1800s. The principal names were George Galphin, Henry Sharp, George Liele (Leile, Lisle), Matthew Moore, Wait Palmer, David George, Jesse Peter, and Andrew Bryan.

George Galphin was born in 1710 in Ireland. He came to America, probably in the 1740s, to seek a more prosperous way of life. He arrived at Charles Town Landing, South Carolina, and went inland to begin a new settlement, which he named Silver Bluff, some 12 miles from present-day Augusta, Georgia. The settlement was in what became Aiken County, South Carolina. Galphin gained skill as a trader, especially with the Indians, and in time acquired large tracts of land. He also started other trading posts and secured additional land tracts, with some near Louisville, Georgia, the first capital of Georgia. Galphin's trading post in that area was at Queensborough in St. George's Parish which became Burke County in 1777.

George Galphin was an enterprising businessman who cared for people. He learned the language of local Indians and traded fairly with them. He did indeed own slaves to help with the work of his trading posts and on his plantation, but he had a reputation for kindness and compassion. Galphin became a wealthy and influential entrepreneur in the colonial times of South Carolina and Georgia. It was said of him at the time that he was "a gentleman of very distinguished talents and great liberality. The spirit of justice and kindness was manifest in all his dealings with the peoples of the weaker races who were daily about him. The Red man and the Black man alike saw in him a man of kindly soul."[39]

Near the same period of time that Galphin was becoming a well-known business leader in South Carolina and Georgia, Henry Sharp, a farmer and British Tory captain from Virginia, was relocating to St. George's Parish near Queensborough in 1764. He and his family brought with them nine slaves,

---

[38] Nevins, "History of the United States," *World Book Encyclopedia*, vol. 19, 86–92.

[39] H. Leon McBeth, *A Sourcebook for Baptist Heritage* (Nashville TN: Broadman Press, 1990) 583.

including a youth of about fourteen years of age known only as George. In time the young slave was called George Sharp, being given the last name of his master, as was often the case in those days.

According to historical accounts, Henry Sharp had his differences with the colonial governmental officials of Georgia. He would try to secure land but was turned down for rather obscure reasons. He traded with the Indians without a required permit and was arrested, tried, and publicly beaten. His main problem was that he was a Tory, and the colonists were leery of him. The town of Queensborough was rendered a fatal blow when two Indian uprisings left many of the settlers dead and the others fled, quite a few of whom relocated several miles to the east around Buckhead Creek.[40] It appears that Henry Sharp, his wife and children, plus his slaves made the move. Queensborough vanished completely after the Revolutionary War ended.

Henry Sharp also had his differences with area authorities over religious customs, because apparently he was not opposed to a church having non-white preachers. Prior to the onset of the war in 1775, Sharp possibly owned as much as 1,500 acres in St. George's Parish and was instrumental in helping to start a Baptist church in his locale. The church most likely met in Sharp's own house at first, as often happened in those times. Much to the consternation of the local population, the church was a Tory Baptist church, which meant that many of the members were in sympathy with the British.[41] It is possible that George Galphin and Henry Sharp knew each other because of their large landholdings.

Sharp's wife was Mildred Moore Sharp. She was the sister of a Baptist preacher by the name of Matthew Moore. It is unclear whether Reverend Moore came from Virginia with Sharp, but land grant records indicate that a Henry Sharp was given by the king of England 250 acres in 1767 and that a Matthew Moore was the recipient of 250 acres in 1769.[42] It also has been conjectured that Moore and his sister were brought to Georgia from Ireland by the assistance of George Galphin, who arranged for several boatloads of Scotch-Irish to settle in Georgia and South Carolina. Tradition has indicated that Moore was a good man who before and during the Revolutionary War lived with his sister as a devoted

---

[40] Albert M. Millhouse, *A History of Burke County, Georgia 1777–1950* (Spartanburg SC: Reprint Company, 1985) 6–9.

[41] Charles O. Walker, "Georgia's Religion in the Colonial Era, 1733–1790," *Viewpoints: Georgia Baptist History* 5 (1976): 33–34.

[42] *The Families of Burke County, a Census*, ed. Robert Scott Davis, Jr., and Silas Emmett Lucus, Jr. (Greenville SC: Southern Historical Press, Inc., 1981).

Loyalist.[43] It is not known whether or not he was ever married or had a family of his own, but it seems doubtful that he did.

In 1773 or 1774 Matthew Moore, a Baptist preacher, along with Henry Sharp, a Baptist deacon, began a Baptist church near Buckhead Creek.[44] The church did not have a name but was known simply as Matthew Moore's church.[45] Apparently it was customary in those years to refer to a church by the name of its pastor.[46] It was most likely the third or perhaps fourth Baptist church organized in Georgia, and might also have been referred to as the Baptist Church on Buckhead Creek.

Very little is actually known or recorded about the church except that it did not last for many years due to the war. Henry Sharp, as a British officer, lost his life in a battle on Tybee Island not long after the war began. His death must have had a profound effect on the continued life of the church and on Pastor Moore's decision not to keep the church alive. As a Loyalist, no doubt he feared for his life and also realized that the Revolutionists would not look with favor on the gathered church because of its reputation as a Tory congregation. After the war Moore left with the British to parts unknown.

The church was reorganized in 1787 after the conflict ended and adopted the name of Buckhead after the stream near its location. For many years, the church was called Big Buckhead, and a church a few miles away was known as Little Buckhead. Both churches disbanded many decades ago, but the Big Buckhead building still exists and is used periodically for community events, such as an Easter sunrise worship service each year. It is a stately structure even today.[47] It has the colonial architecture very similar to the First Baptist Church of Charleston, South Carolina, the first Baptist church established in the South.

Most probably Matthew Moore's church (or the Baptist Church on Buckhead Creek) would long since have been forgotten were it not for a defining action taken by the pastor and the members. That action was centered around Henry Sharp's slave George. Even though the church has received little recognition through the years by historians (perhaps because the pastor and Deacon Sharp were sympathetic to the British cause), it nevertheless played a key role in the eventual beginning of black Baptist preachers and churches in America,

---

[43] W. L. Kilpatrick, *The Hephzibah Baptist Association Centennial 1794–1894* (Augusta GA: Richards and Shaver Printers, 1894) 290–91.

[44] Alfred Lane Pugh, *Pioneer Preachers in Paradise* (St. Cloud MN: North Star Press, 2003) 5.

[45] Walter H. Brooks, *The Silver Bluff Church: A History of Negro Baptist Churches in America* (Washington DC: Press of R. L. Pendleton, 1910) 10.

[46] A. H. Newman, *A History of the Baptist Churches in the United States* (New York: Charles Scribner's Sons, 1894) 318.

[47] Kilpatrick, *Hephzibah Baptist Centennial*, 290–94.

especially across the Southland. In their tense and turbulent time, the decision made by Matthew Moore, Henry Sharp, and the members of their congregation to set apart the young slave man George to preach the gospel of Jesus Christ was remarkable and certainly courageous. These individuals were ahead of their time and no doubt drew the ire of their neighbors and local civic officials along with the disapproval of other churches. George himself proved to possess great courage and faith as he stepped onto the pages of church and American history. The story of Matthew Moore's church and George needs to be told and fully accepted as an act of God and as a valuable accounting of early American developments, which have had such lasting results through the years. There is a marker in front of the church that reads "Big Buckhead Church."

> This church, near Buckhead Creek, from which it derives its name, was probably organized before the Revolution by Matthew Moore, Baptist minister, whose Loyalist sympathies led him to leave with the British. Buckhead Church was reconstituted 11 September 1787 with James Matthews, pastor, and Sanders Walker and Josiah Taylor acting with him as presbytery. Four church buildings have stood on or near this site. The first was log followed in 1807 by a white frame one. A brick church was built in 1830. It was condemned and the present one was erected. Here, the Hephzibah Association was organized and plans to create Mercer University proposed.

When Henry Sharp moved to Georgia from Virginia and brought his slaves with him, what happened to the parents of George? Most accounts seem to indicate that they were left behind, while others believe that they also moved with the Sharp family. Their names were Nancy and Liele. Most probably they stayed in Virginia.[48]

For a number of years the slaves would attend the churches of their owners when permitted to do so. Sometimes they would sit in the same pews as their master and his family, or there would be a special section of the church reserved for the slaves.

Many slave owners were afraid for their slaves to attend church services by themselves lest plots be arranged for uprisings to occur when the whites were not around to listen. Also, some of the owners wanted their slaves in church to hear the white preacher justify slavery from the Bible, especially the Old Testament, which would perhaps help keep slaves docile and more accepting of their dire circumstances. Yet there were also those owners who were convicted of the conversion message of Christ and wanted their slaves to be in church for full

---

[48] Pugh, *Pioneer Preachers*, 3.

exposure to the gospel.[49] From all indications, that was the desire of Henry Sharp. For instance, when he and his family and slaves arrived in Georgia, there was a population of about 23,000 in the colony, including some 15,000 slaves. By the earlier adoption in 1753 of a slave code, they were not to be taught to read or write. But Sharp paid no attention to the law and permitted some of his slaves to learn the skills of reading and writing.[50]

As a young man, George Sharp (later called George Liele) attended Matthew Moore's church. At the same time, he was one of the slaves being taught to read and write by members of the Sharp family. He became an avid listener of the pastor's sermons and was greatly touched by the transforming power of what he heard about Jesus. George accepted the Lord as his personal Savior around 1774 and was immersed in baptism by Moore. The church baptized new believers at "Dipping Ford" on a cleared-out portion of Buckhead Creek, and doubtless that is where George was baptized. The area may have been so called by non-Baptists, especially Anglicans, who would show up for a Sunday afternoon baptizing in order to make light of those Baptists who practiced immersion. George then became a member in good standing of the church.[51] In a letter dated 18 December 1791 to the Reverend John Rippon in London, George wrote:

> I was born in Virginia; my father's name was Liele, and my mother's Nancy. I cannot be certain of much about them so I went to several parts of America when young, and at length resided in New Georgia. I was informed both by white and black people that my father was the only black person who knew the Lord in a spiritual way in that country (Virginia). I always had a natural fear of God from my youth, and was often checked in conscience with thoughts of death which barred me from many sins and bad company. I knew no other way at that time to hope for salvation but only in the performance of good works. About two years before the late war, the Rev. Mr. Matthew Moore one Sabbath afternoon, as I stood with curiosity to hear him, I was convinced that I was not in the way of heaven, but in the way of hell. This state I labored under for five or six months. The more I heard or read, the more I saw that I was condemned as a sinner before God, till at length I was brought to perceive that my life hung by a slender thread, and if it was the will of God to cut me off at that time, I was sure I should be found in hell, as sure as God was in heaven. I saw my condemnation in my own heart, and I found no way wherein I could escape the damnation of hell, only through the merits of my

---

[49] Emmanuel L. McCall, *The Black Christian Experience* (Nashville TN: Broadman Press, 1972) 21–24.

[50] Pugh, *Pioneer Preachers*, 4.

[51] Kilpatrick, *Hephzibah Baptist Centennial*, 290–91.

dying Lord and Savior Jesus Christ, which caused me to make intercession with Christ for the salvation of my poor immortal soul. I still recollect, I requested of my Lord and Master to give me a work, I did not care how mean it was, only to try and see how good I would do it. I felt such love and joy as my tongue could not express. After this I declared before the congregation of believers the work which God had done for my soul, and the same minister, the Rev. Matthew Moore, baptized me, and I continued in this church for about four years till the "vacuation" of Savannah by the British…. Desiring to prove the sense I had of my obligations to God, I endeavored to instruct the people of my own color in the word of God. The white brethren seeing my endeavors, and that the word of God seemed to be blessed, gave me a call at a quarterly meeting to preach before the congregation.[52]

It is understood that following the preaching of George Liele, Mr. Moore consulted with the church's congregants concerning George's abilities as one possessed of ministerial gifts, and it was their unanimous opinion to license him as a probationer. He then began to preach to the slaves on surrounding plantations on Sunday evenings when there was not a service being performed in the church to which he belonged.[53]

As previously noted, Henry Sharp was an unusual man. He held deep Christian principles and exercised his convictions by believing in the worth of those around him. He wanted his slaves to experience the grace and love of the Lord and to have acceptance in his church, which in those days would almost certainly have had more black members than white, as often was the case in many churches. Sharp was apparently a moral and religious man, kind and considerate. He obviously saw in George an aptitude for Bible study plus communication skills as a preacher, and he gave him permission to utilize his talents. Later events in George's life indicate that he had been a close observer of the spiritual sensitivities and the determined relating abilities of Baptist deacon Henry Sharp, and he modeled much of his actions after what he had observed and experienced. Undoubtedly, Sharp's interest in the spiritual development of his slaves set him apart as being most unusual from many other slave owners far and near.[54]

If Henry Sharp was an exceptional man and church member, so was his brother-in-law, the pastor Matthew Moore. He, too, was concerned about the salvation and spiritual growth of both whites and blacks. He preached, as made

---

[52] John Rippon, *The Baptist Annual Register for 1790, 1791, 1792, and part of 1793* (London: Vestry, 1793) 332–34.

[53] Ibid, 333.

[54] Pugh, *Pioneer Preachers*, 5–6.

clear in George's letter to John Rippon, an urgent message of redemption for all his hearers and invited anyone who responded by faith to be baptized as a believer in Jesus as Savior and Lord, and to then become an active member of the church. Moore was the catalyst in seeing in George his God-given gifts for functioning as a preacher, and he gave him opportunities to preach in the church.[55] How unusual that was in the mid-1770s and how daring![56] Soon the entire congregation recognized the talents and calling of George and agreed with their pastor and Deacon Sharp that George should be licensed and ordained as a Baptist minister. He was then given the freedom by his owner to travel to surrounding plantations to preach the gospel to other slaves wherever he could gather with them, perhaps in barns or houses or out in the open fields or under the shade trees.[57]

When Reverend Matthew Moore, Deacon Henry Sharp, and the members of the Baptist church on Buckhead Creek sent slave George Sharp out to preach Jesus to persons beyond their own congregation, they could not have known the significance of their actions or how far-reaching they would prove to be. They literally set in motion a movement of God which is alive and well all across the nation and many areas of the world right up to the present time. They were making history as George Sharp became the first black man to be ordained as a Baptist preacher anywhere in America, with thousands upon thousands to follow.[58]

When the Revolutionary War broke out in 1776, Henry Sharp went immediately to battle as a British officer. In time he made his slave George a freed man. Soon afterwards, George assumed as his last name the name of Liele (Leile, Lisle), the name of his father back in Virginia.[59]

It is rather ironic that at the same time Matthew Moore's church was being started in St. George's Parish in Georgia (later changed to Burke County, part of which was later split off into Jenkins County),[60] a Baptist church was also being started not too many miles away and over across the state line into South Carolina. That church was on the George Galphin Plantation at Silver Bluff. It was one of the sites where George Liele went to preach when he was still a slave,

---

[55] Rippon, *Baptist Annual Register*, 333–34.

[56] James Lowell Underwood and W. Lewis Burke, *The Dawn of Religious Freedom in South Carolina* (Columbia: University of South Carolina Press, 2006) 126–33.

[57] Pugh, *Pioneer Preachers*, 7–8.

[58] Torbet, *History of the Baptists*, 369.

[59] Walker, "Georgia's Religion," 34.

[60] Donald E. Perkins, "Big Buckhead Church," *The Millen News Centennial Edition*, August 24, 2005, 58–59.

perhaps because his owner knew Galphin. Liele was the first black minister to preach at the church.

The Silver Bluff Baptist Church was started for the slaves of George Galphin. He gave consent for the church to gather in his millhouse and to use the nearby stream for baptizing.[61] Galphin financially supported the needs of the congregation and attended the church services along with his family. They may have even been full and active members.[62] Galphin might also have been influenced to give permission for the founding of the church because of the purposes of the Society for the Propagation of the Gospel (Anglican) to evangelize and minister to black slaves and Indians.[63]

The beginning dates of the church are thought to be sometime around 1773.[64] It seems that Waitstill (Wait) Palmer (1711–1795),[65] the same Baptist pastor who baptized Shubal Stearns at a church in Preston, Connecticut, in March 1751, was the originating pastor of the Silver Bluff church. He served many of his adult years as an itinerant preacher, going from place to place and founding Separatist Baptist churches, often serving as the pastor to get the church started.

There is little question but that Wait Palmer stayed in contact with Stearns because of their friendship and because of their desire to spread the message of soul winning, the immersion of new believers, and the starting of Separatist congregations which were spreading like wildfire across much of the Southland. Palmer made a practice of going to areas that were often referred to as destitute regions as he went about his missionary endeavors.[66]

In his travels, Palmer somehow learned about the possibility of a church being started at Silver Bluff, and he approached George Galphin to inquire about the opportunity. He was given permission to start the church and did so, actually serving as its first pastor but having a strategy of training black members for leadership roles.[67] On one occasion, George Sharp (Liele) was the guest preacher. In the audience was a slave of Galphin's by the name of David George.

David George was older than George Liele and had know him since Liele was a boy. David George did not let this stop him from believing what Liele preached. The sermon was, "Come unto me all ye that labor and are heavy laden,

---

[61] McBeth, *Sourcebook for Baptist Heritage*, 583.

[62] Frank G. Roberson and George H. Mosley, *Where a Few Gather in My Name* (North Augusta SC: FGR Publications, 2002) 10.

[63] C. Eric Lincoln, "The Development of Black Religion in America" in *The Review and Expositor* (Louisville KY: Southern Baptist Theological Seminary; 1973) 302.

[64] McBeth, Ibid., 581.

[65] Sparks, *Roots of Appalachian Christianity*, 34, 41.

[66] Brooks, *The Silver Bluff Church*, 45–46.

[67] Ibid., 19–20.

and I will give you rest." When the sermon ended, David went to Liele and told him, "I am so."[68]

The Silver Bluff Baptist Church is regarded by most church historians as the first organized black Baptist church in America to be led by blacks. It was obviously the intent of Wait Palmer, and perhaps George Galphin, from the start to turn the church over as soon as possible to a black preacher if one could be secured. A pastor became available in the person of David George. He was ordained by Palmer, as was Jesse Peter, another slave member of the church. When David George became the pastor and Palmer departed, he became the first black Baptist pastor of a black Baptist church anywhere in America.[69]

Later in life, Reverend David George wrote to Baptist leaders in London and recalled his experiences at Silver Bluff:

> Brother Palmer formed us into a church, and gave us the Lord's Supper at Silver Bluff.... Then I began to exhort in the church, and learned to sing hymns.... Afterwards the church advised with Brother Palmer about my speaking to them, and keeping them together.... So I was appointed to the office of an elder, and received instruction from Brother Palmer how to conduct myself. I proceeded in this way till the American War was coming on, when the ministers were not allowed to come amongst us, lest they should furnish us with too much knowledge.... I continued preaching at Silver Bluff, till the church, constituted with eight, increased to thirty or more, and 'till the British came to the city of Savannah and took it.[70]

During the war, the Silver Bluff church was disbanded, as was Matthew Moore's church, and their leaders fled to safer territory. Where Moore located is not known. George Sharp, with his wife and four children, went to the Savannah area, where he preached for about three years at Brunton Land and at Yamacraw.

During the time at Yamacraw he was joined by David George, and together they engaged in farming and in preaching to black slaves. Several of the slaves had come from Silver Bluff with David George. While there they started a church in 1778 which was named the First Colored Baptist Church. At that time George Sharp was given his freedom by Henry Sharp, only to have his freedom challenged by the descendants of Henry Sharp, and George was placed in jail. However, he was able to produce his "free papers" and was released. He then sought ways to leave the country with his family by sailing in late 1782 to

---

[68] Roberson and Mosley, *Where a Few Gather*, 13.
[69] Ibid., 14.
[70] McBeth, *Sourcebook for Baptist Heritage*, 582.

Kingston, Jamaica, as an indentured servant of a British officer, Colonel Kirkland, from whom he had borrowed $700 for passage.[71]

Before leaving for Jamaica, George Liele baptized Andrew Bryan and his wife, Hannah, along with two other black women, Kate and Hagar. Bryan became the second pastor of the church, and even though he was severely beaten, abused, and twice imprisoned by his white persecutors, he managed to keep the church alive. It is reported that during one of his beatings as he was bleeding terribly, Bryan held up his hands and declared that he rejoiced over his whipping and that he would freely suffer death for the cause of Jesus Christ.[72]

George Liele made his way to Jamaica, a British slave-holding colony, and continued his ministry of preaching and starting churches. He was appalled by the terrible conditions of the slaves he discovered and began to preach to them at a racecourse. He was soon persecuted by adherents of the Church of England and by governmental officials. Liele was charged with preaching sedition and was jailed, loaded with irons and his feet placed in stocks. Eventually, he was released and continued with his preaching, even though he broke the law of the British Empire, which was against preaching the gospel to slaves. By 1791 there were some 500 Baptists in Jamaica, but within thirty years the number grew to nearly 20,000. Liele was sponsored by no church nor missionary society, and he supported himself and his family mainly by farming.[73] He was a true missionary of his Lord and was, in fact, the first Baptist missionary of all time, preceding by ten years William Carey, who sailed from Moulton, England, to Calcutta, India, in 1793 as the first acknowledged Baptist missionary in modern times.[74] Liele's influence eventually reached to Sierra Leone and Malawi in Africa, to the British West Indies, and to Canada.[75] His work even caught the attention in 1807 of William Wilberforce, the legal crusader who led efforts for the elimination of slave trading throughout the British Commonwealth.[76]

The ministerial companion and protégé of George Liele was indeed David George, first black pastor of Silver Bluff Baptist Church in 1775. David George

---

[71] Edward A. Holmes, Jr., "George Liele: Negro Slavery's Prophet of Deliverance," *Baptist History and Heritage* 1/1 (August 1965): 29–30.

[72] Benedict, *History of the Baptist Denomination*, 189–90.

[73] Holmes, "Prophet of Deliverance," 331–36.

[74] Sunil Kumar Chatterjee, *William Carey and Serampore* (Sheoraphuli, India: Lasterplus, 1984) 7–21.

[75] "Forgotten Missionary Pioneer George Liele," *Baptist World* 50/3 (July/September 2003): 17.

[76] F. A. Cox, *History of the Baptist Missionary Society from 1792 to 1842* (London: T. Word and Co. and Gand J. Dyer, 1842) 12–21.

was in sole charge of the church.[77] He, too, escaped when the Revolutionary War was raging, and in 1778 he and about fifty other slaves went to Savannah when that city fell to the British. Sometime later he made a move to Charleston, South Carolina, and then to Nova Scotia, along with some 500 white persons who were faithful to the British flag. There he preached and started a Baptist church at Shelburne for whites and blacks, the reported first Baptist church established in Canada. David George faced strong opposition and rejection by the government, though, and ten years later he moved to Sierra Leone in West Africa to start a church, quite possibly the first Baptist church on that continent expressly for blacks.[78]

When the Silver Bluff church ceased to meet because of the Revolutionary War, some of the slaves became identified with the British in seeking their freedom while others remained as they were. Reverend Jesse Peter (also known as Jesse Peter Galphin) did not venture any greater distance away than Savannah. He decided to return to Silver Bluff after the hostilities ended and resume his life as a slave on the Galphin Plantation, which by that time was being operated by George Galphin's son, Thomas. Like his father, Thomas Galphin was an indulgent and kind-hearted man. He gave Jesse Peter permission to be the pastor of the resurrected Silver Bluff Baptist Church and also the freedom to travel and preach at other locations, such as Augusta. Peters was evidently the Silver Bluff pastor from the years 1788 to 1792.[79]

From several reports, Jesse Peter was well thought of and highly respected by blacks and whites as a Baptist preacher.[80] By 1793 he helped to start the First African Baptist Church of Augusta and became the pastor.[81] Quite a number of the members were former slaves of the Galphin Plantation. Later the name of the church was changed to the Springfield Baptist Church, which is still in existence today. It has the distinction of being the oldest existing black Baptist church in America to still conduct its services at the original location.[82] Notably, the First African Baptist Church in Savannah, which was started in 1778 or 1779 by George Liele and assisted by David George, is today possibly the oldest sustained black Baptist church in the nation.[83]

---

[77] McBeth, *Sourcebook for Baptist Heritage*, 582.
[78] Roberson and Moley, *Where a Few Gather*, 14, 19–20.
[79] Brooks, *The Silver Bluff Church*, 24–26.
[80] Benedict, *History of the Baptist Denomination*, 193.
[81] McBeth, *Sourcebook for Baptist Heritage*, 585.
[82] Roberson and Mosley, *Where a Few Gather*, 26.
[83] McCall, *Black Christian Experience*, 29.

Summary

The two focus churches of this study, Matthew Moore's church and the Silver Bluff church, were followers of either the Separatist Baptist or Regular Baptist persuasion during their originating years. While it is ultimately unknown due to the scarcity of existing records, there are some clues which are noteworthy and rather intriguing.

Consider Matthew Moore's church (or the Church on Buckhead Creek or Big Buckhead Baptist Church). The church might not have been identified with either Separate or Regular Baptists in their early days, but that would have been unlikely due to the prevalence of the two Baptist traditions at that time. Certainly almost all Baptist churches would have been one or the other, or in some rare situations, a blend of the two in a kind of fraternal relationship.[84]

It has been suggested that the obscure church was at first a Separate congregation but, like others, changed after the war to being Regular Baptists, or blended in order to possess an evangelistic fervor like the Separatists along with a demand for education and orderliness like the Regulars (Particulars).[85] It seems impossible to know for certain. There are at least four indications, however, that the Matthew Moore church near Buckhead Creek was a Regular Baptist congregation:

First, Regular Baptists in America had stronger ties back to England than did the Separatists, and both Henry Sharp and Matthew Moore were strong British sympathizers.

Second, Reverend Edmund Botsford from the First Baptist Church of Charleston, South Carolina, a well-known Regular Baptist congregation, spent time in Georgia in the early 1770s helping to found churches. It is known that he came to Burke County in the area just south of Waynesboro to do his work. One of the churches he started bears his name to this day: the Botsford Baptist Church, or Botsford's Old Meetinghouse, as it is often called. That church is not far from the area where it is believed the Matthew Moore church was located. It is conceivable that Reverend Botsford, "the Flying Preacher," as he was known, had a part to play in the launching of the church near Buckhead Creek. If so, his influence as a Regular Baptist would have been substantial.[86] It has been said that Matthew Moore was assisted in George Liele's ordination service by other

---

[84] Newman, *History of the Baptist Churches*, 317.

[85] Robert G. Gardner, Charles O. Walker, J. R. Huddlestun, and Waldo P. Harris III, *A History of the Georgia Baptist Association 1784–1984* (Atlanta: Georgia Baptist Historical Society, 1988) 16.

[86] Mallery, *Memories of Elder Edmund Botsford*, 23–34.

Baptist pastors in the area.[87] It is not known who they were, but Reverend Botsford could possibly have been one of them.

Third, Regular Baptists believed in Church covenants much more than the Separatists. If Matthew Moore and Henry Sharp were Regular Baptists indeed, they would have taught young George Liele to also believe in the value of written covenants for theological convictions and for the church polity practices of the congregation. It is a matter of record that when Liele started his church in Jamaica, he put in place a lengthy covenant for the membership to follow.[88] Also, John Rippon, an avid Regular Baptist in London, sent financial help to Liele in Jamaica. It is doubtful that he would have done so if Pastor Liele had come from a Separatist background.[89]

Finally, four buildings were erected through the years on the several acres of land where it is believed Matthew Moore started the church. One of the later pastors, Reverend W. L. Kilpatrick, gave a careful description in 1894. He said, "On the present site, or very near by, four houses of worship have stood, inclusive of the one now occupied. The first was of logs; the second was framed and worth about $300, completed in 1807; the third, built of brick in 1830, cost about $4,000, but from some defect in its construction, it was deemed unsafe, and gave place to the present building. This last is a neat structure, costing $3,000."[90]

The Big Buckhead Baptist Church building is a handsome structure of old Southern architectural style. It is, as observed earlier, eerie how similar it is to the sanctuary building of First Baptist Church, Charleston, South Carolina, which was erected in 1822.[91] Again, could there have been a Regular Baptist connection between the two churches?

What about Silver Bluff? If Wait Palmer, the dedicated, aggressive Separate Baptist pastor that he was, led in the formation of the church on the George Galphin land in South Carolina, there can be no question but that it started out as a Separate Baptist church! Palmer would have arranged it no other way. In addition, a defining conviction of the Separatists was that everyone needed to hear about their Lord Jesus and be forgiven of their sins. That was their guiding principle, and there are numerous references that they preached their message of salvation with passion and zeal to slaves as well as to the free in keeping with the example set by their "Reverend Old Father" Shubal Stearns. It would not have been a personal battle at all for Wait Palmer to devote his best efforts to putting

---

[87] Pugh, *Pioneer Preachers*, 10–12.

[88] Ernest A. Payne, "Baptist Work in Jamaica before the Arrival of the Missionaries," *The Baptist Quarterly* 7/1 (January 1934): 20–26.

[89] Pugh, *Pioneer Preachers*, 27–31.

[90] Kilpatrick, *Hephzibah Baptist Centennial*, 293.

[91] Baker and Craven, *Adventure in Faith*, 217–18.

in place a Baptist church for black slaves, even though that was unheard of in those times. That would have been consistent with his Separatist beliefs about evangelism and church starting,[92] along with recognizing the spiritual gifts of potential preachers and granting them the license to preach, both slave and free.[93]

It is to note that after the war, the Silver Bluff church was revived by Jesse Peter as a Regular Baptist congregation.[94] There was an increasing trend of Separate Baptists learning from Regular Baptists over the years, which continues to this time, as well as Regular Baptists receiving helpful concepts from Separate Baptists.[95] What transpired at Silver Bluff might have come about due to the influence of George Liele or Jesse Peter if, in fact, Liele was a Regular Baptist.

It has been observed that Liele was an unusually gifted man. He has been described as a student of the Scriptures from his youth and a powerful preacher. He possessed common sense in being able to relate to whites and blacks with diplomacy and timeliness. He often knew when to wait and when to move forward. He cared deeply for his own race and wanted to lift their sights and give them hope. He loved the church and sought vigorously to spread the word that Jesus Christ is indeed the Savior of the world. George Liele has been called a prophet of deliverance and a pioneer missionary, yet one who has never received the full recognition due him by church historians and missionary societies, probably because of his race. It has even been stated that there has been an appearance of conspiracy against George Liele to keep him from receiving the honor he deserved for his courageous and unselfish labors for his Lord. For sure, he was one who opened doors of light in the darkness for others to walk through.

The Reverend George Liele—Baptist preacher, pastor, missionary, and skillful leader—died in 1828.[96] His legacy lives on and deserves to be told with national and international acclaim, acceptance, and gratitude.

---

[92] Sparks, *Roots of Appalachian Christianity*, 220.

[93] Benjamin Quarles, *The Negro in the Making of America* (New York: Collier Books, 1964) 57–58.

[94] Leah Townsend, *South Carolina Baptists 1670–1805* (Florence SC: Genealogical Publishing Co., 1935), 259.

[95] Brackney, *Baptists in North America*, 27–28.

[96] Holmes, "Prophet of Deliverance," 35.

Resources

Ashcraft, Robert. *Landmarkism Revisited.* Mablevale AR: Ashcraft Publications, 2003.

Baker, Robert A. and Paul Craven, Jr. *Adventure in Faith: The First 300 Years of First Baptist Church, Charleston, South Carolina.* Nashville TN: Broadman Press, 1982.

Baptist World, 50/3 (July/September 2003).

Benedict, David. *A General History of the Baptist Denomination in America and Other Parts of the World,* volume 2. Boston: Manning and Loring, 1813.

The Black Christian Experience. Edited by Emmanuel L. McCall. Nashville TN: Broadman Press, 1972.

Brackney, William. *Baptists in North America.* Malden MA: Blackwell Publishing, 2006.

Brooks, Walter. *The Silver Bluff Church: A History of Negro Baptist Churches in America.* Washington DC: Press of R. L. Pendleton, 1910.

Brown, Beverly. "George Liele: Baptist and Pan-Africanist 1750–1826." *Carribean Studies* (September, 1975), 58–66.

Chatterjee, Sunil Kumar. *William Carey and Serampore.* Sheoraphul, India: Lasterplus, 1984.

Cox, F. A. *History of the Baptist Missionary Society from 1792 to 1842.* London: T. Word and Co. and Gand J. Dyer, 1842.

The Families of Burke County, a Census, 1755–1855. Edited by Robert Scott Davis, Jr., and Silas Emmett Lucus, Jr. Easley SC: Southern Historical Press, 1981.

Gardner, Robert G., Charles O. Walker, J. R. Huddleston, and Waldo P. Harris III. *A History of the Georgia Baptist Association 1784–1984.* Atlanta: Georgia Baptist Historical Society, 1988.

Holmes, Jr., Edward A. "George Liele: Negro Slavery's Prophet of Deliverance," *Baptist History and Heritage.* 1/1 (August 1965).

Kauffman, Donald T. *The Dictionary of Religious Terms.* Westwood NJ: Fleming H. Revell Company, 1967.

Kilpatrick, W. L. *The Hephzibah Baptist Association Centennial 1794–1894.* Augusta GA: Richards and Shaver Printers, 1894.

Leonard, Bill J. *Baptists in America.* New York: Columbia University Press, 2005.

Lincoln, C. Eric. "The Development of Black Religion in America," *Review and Expositor* 70/3 (Summer 1973).

Lumpkin, William L. *Baptist Foundations in the South.* Ashville NC: Revival Literature, 2006.

Mallory, Charles D. *Memories of Elder Edmund Botsford.* Springfield MO: Particular Press, 2004.

McBeth, H. Leon. *The Baptist Heritage.* Nashville TN: Broadman Press, 1987.

McBeth, H. Leon. *A Sourcebook for Baptist Heritage*. Nashville TN: Broadman Press, 1990.

Millhouse, Albert M. *A History of Burke County, Georgia 1777–1950*. Spartanburg SC: Reprint Company, 1985.

Newman, A. H. *A History of the Baptist Churches in the United States*. New York: Charles Scribner's Sons, 1894.

A Noble Company: Biographical Essays on Notable Particular-Regular Baptists in America. Edited by Terry Woleven. Springfield MO: Particular Baptist Press, 2006.

Orchard, G. H. *A Concise History of Baptists from the Time of Christ Their Founder to the 18th Century*. London, 1838.

Perkins, Donald E. "Big Buckhead Church," *The Millen News Centennial Edition* (August 2005).

Pugh, Alfred Lane. *Pioneer Preachers in Paradise*. St. Cloud MN: North Star Press, 2003.

Quarles, Benjamin. *The Negro in the Making of America*. New York: Collier Books, 1964.

Rippon, John. *The Baptist Annual Register for 1790, 1791, 1792 and part of 1793*. London: Vestry, 1795.

Roberson, Frank G. and George H. Mosley. *Where a Few Gather in My Name*. North Augusta SC: FGR Publications, 2002.

Sparks, John. *The Roots of Appalachian Christianity: The Life and Legacy of Elder Shubal Stearns*. Lexington: University Press of Kentucky, 2001.

Torbet, Robert A. *A History of the Baptists*. Philadelphia: Judson Press, 1950.

Townsend, Leah. *South Carolina Baptists 1670–1805*. Florence SC: Genealogical Publishing Co., 1935.

Underwood, James Lowell and W. Lewis Burke. *The Dawn of Religious Freedom in South Carolina*. Columbia: University of South Carolina Press, 2006.

Vedder, Henry C. *A Short History of the Baptists*. Philadelphia: American Baptist Publication Society, 1907.

The Family Life of George Liele

VICTOR G. WILLIAMS

The fact that George Liele was a man of God has been well established. However, we do not know much about Liele's family life. For example, we will examine several aspects of his existence: the structure of his family, his provisions for family, and his Christian beliefs. And if we look at life as a drama, we must remember that Liele's drama was played out on a stage where slavery was the ominous backdrop. In spite of the harshness of slavery, the perils that were always present, and the defeatist mindset that could have resulted from slavery, George Liele triumphed. His focus was always on God's grace and man's salvation.

Slave Family Life

It is from the first experience of family that we learn what family means to us. Slavery was not a pro-family institution. The constant threat of being sold or having family members sold had a very negative impact upon family members. Physical and sexual violations of all types (i.e., seductions, rapes, and forced breeding) were common occurrences and had deeply hurtful effects on people and family life[1]. There were constant attempts to dehumanize the enslaved people. There were family separations as members of slave families were sold off to different plantations or left to heirs in the last will and testament of the slave owners[2]. Hurtful separations of children from mothers, husbands from wives, and brothers from sisters occurred frequently. The main reason for this disregard for families was because United States law did not legally recognize slave families. Marriages between enslaved persons required approval from the plantation owners. Sometimes married partners lived on different plantations and did not see each often. Despite these conditions, though, enslaved men and women struggled to preserve family life and protect their mates and children.[3] A succinct summarization of family life during slavery is stated here:

---

[1] Ruthe Winegarten, "Texas Slave Families," *The Texas Humanist* (March/April 1985), http://www.humanities-interactive.org/texas/rural/tx_slave_families.htm (accessed 18 June 2010).

[2] Ibid.

[3] Ibid.

Enslaved Americans were denied a secure family life. Because enslaved men and women were property and could not legally marry, a permanent family could not be a guaranteed part of an African American slave's life. They had no right to live or stay together, no right to their own children, and it was common for slave parents and children to live apart. Parents could not protect their children from the will of the master, who could separate them at any time. About one-third of slave families suffered permanent separation caused by the sale of family members to distant regions. This might occur to punish some infraction of plantation rules, to make money, to settle an estate after a death in the owner's family, or to pay back a debt.[4]

Given the above knowledge of slave family life, it is a marvel that George Liele could have a sustained family of his own. This is also a tribute to his owner, Henry Sharp, a deacon in his church. Sharp gave Liele his freedom so that Liele could go about the business of preaching more freely.[5]

Liele's Early Family Life

The first account of Liele's early family life was given by Liele himself in a letter to John Rippon, the British editor of the *Baptist Annual Register*. Quoting from the register, Edward A. Holmes gives us an account of Liele's own words: "I was born in Virginia, my father's name was Liele, and my mother's name Nancy; I cannot ascertain much of them, as I went to several parts of America when young, and at length resided in New Georgia; but was informed both by white and black people, that my father was the only black person who knew the Lord in a spiritual way in that country."[6] George Liele was born in Virginia in 1752, but lived much of his life as a slave in Georgia.[7] Separated from his parents, Liele knew very little of his mother, Nancy, but was informed by white and black that his father was a very devout man.

About being torn away from his mother and father by slavery, Liele simply stated, "I *went* to several parts of America when young...." A less positive, more self-centered person might have written, "I was *taken* to several parts of America...", but Liele said, "I *went*." What a revelation about the man! He lived

---

[4] "Countries Quest: African American Families under Slavery," 2004, http://www.countriesquest.com/north_america/usa/people/family_life/african_america n_families_under_slavery.htm (accessed 23 August 2010).

[5] Edward A. Holmes, "George Liele: Negro Slavery's Prophet of Deliverance," *Baptist Quarterly* 20 (1964): 340–51, 361.

[6] Ibid.

[7] "People & Events: George Liele, 1752–1825," *Africans in America: Part 2*, television episode, 1995, http://www.pbs.org/wgbh/aia/part2/2p49.html.

during slavery, but the spirit of slavery did not dwell within him. George Liele does not speak of the pain of separation from his parents. However, as has been noted, "When Africans were taken from their homes and forced into slavery they were separated from mothers, fathers, sisters and brothers and were torn from extensive kinship networks."[8] It *must* have been painful. One slave narrative describes a typical scene in which a child is being torn away from the mother after the child was sold:

> *While traveling in Delaware, a child of a slave was sold:* As the colored woman was ordered to take it away, I heard Fannie Woods cry, "O God, I would rather hear the clods fall on the coffin lid of my child than to hear its cries because it is taken away from me." She said, "Good bye, Child."
>
> We were ordered to move on, and could hear the crying of the child in the distance as it was borne away by the other woman, and I could hear the deep sobs of a broken-hearted mother. We could hear the groans of many as they prayed for God to have mercy upon us and give us grace to endure the hard trials through which we must pass.[9]

Family life for the whites was entirely different. One ex-slave, Harriet Robinson, described how white people wanted slaves to regard the white family. Robinson stated, "Whenever white folks had a baby born, den all de old niggers had to come th'ough the room, and the master would be over 'hind the bed, and he'd say, 'Here's a new little mistress or master you got to work for.' You had to say, 'Yessuh, Master,' and bow real low, or the overseer would crack you."[10]

The white families could fully celebrate new life being added to their family and expect the enslaved servants to celebrate the birth of the white baby, too. Slaves learned to hide their feelings and taught their children to hide their feelings also in order to escape punishment.[11] The structure of the white slaveholder family and that of enslaved persons varied. In fact, the structure of

---

[8] Nicholas Boston and Jennifer Hallam, "The Slave Experience: The Family," *Slavery and the Making of America*, television episode, 2004, New York, PBS Educational Broadcasting Corporation, http://www.pbs.org/wnet/slavery/experience/family/history.html (accessed 11 June 2007).

[9] "Black Christianity before the Civil War: Did You Know? Spiritual Memories of Slaves—in Their Own Words," *Christianity Today International/Christian History Magazine* (1999), http://www.ctlibrary.com/ch/1999/issue62/62h002.html (accessed 16 September 2009).

[10] Ibid.

[11] Boston and Hallam, *Slavery and the Making of America*.

the slave family varied from plantation to plantation.[12] On plantations requiring few slave hands (e.g., on tobacco farms), husbands and wives were probably on different plantations. Where there was a need for larger work forces (as with cotton), there was a better chance that husband and wife were on the same plantation. Children were with their mothers unless sold away.[13]

Liele's Wife and Children

George Liele earned a reputation as an upstanding family man who kept his word.[14] He was married, and his wife's name was Hannah Hunt Liele.[15] Colonel Kirkland of the British army befriended Liele after Sharp's heirs tried to re-enslave him. Colonel Kirkland advised Liele to leave the country with him when the British evacuated.[16]

George and Hannah Liele had four children—three sons and a daughter. When Liele left America, he took his family with him. To pay for their passage to Jamaica, Liele became an indentured servant to Colonel Kirkland.[17] Colonel Kirkland was in the Royal Militia, serving under the overall command of Colonel Thomas Fletchall. Because of his war activities, Colonel Kirkland left America after the evacuation by the British and sought refuge in Jamaica, where he settled in St. George's Parish.[18] It was in late 1782 that Colonel Moses Kirkland sailed from Tybee for Jamaica.[19] Both Liele and Colonel Kirkland sought refuge in Jamaica, each fleeing capture by separate would-be capturers. After two years, Liele paid off his debt to Colonel Kirkland. As soon as that debt was paid off, Liele obtained for himself and his family a certificate of freedom.[20] He was now free to establish a church in Jamaica and to provide for his family.

Rev. Love, quoting from Liele's letter of December 18, 1791, to Rippon, reveals information about Liele's life in Jamaica:

---

[12] Ibid.

[13] Ibid.

[14] Holmes, "Prophet of Deliverance," 340–51, 361.

[15] George Liele, Last Will and Testament (1830). See Appendix B.

[16] J. M. Simms, The First Colored Baptist Church in North America Constituted at Savannah, Georgia, January 20, A.D. 1788, with Biographical Sketches of the Pastors (Philadelphia: J. B. Lippincott Company) http://docsouth.unc.edu/church/simms/simms. html (accessed 15 September 2010).

[17] African American Religious History: A Documentary Witness, 2nd ed., ed. Milton C. Sernett (Durham NC: Duke University Press, 1999).

[18] Phil Norfleet, Biographical Sketch of Moses Kirkland, 1999, http://sc_tories. tripod.com/moses_kirkland.htm (accessed 15 September 2010).

[19] Elroy Christenson, Col. Moses Kirkland, 1998, http://www.next1000.com/family/ EC/kirkland.moses.html (accessed 15 December 2010).

[20] Sernett, African American Religious History.

I cannot tell what is my age, as I have no account of the time of my birth; but I suppose I am about 40 years old. I have a wife and four children. My wife was baptized by me in Savannah, and I have every satisfaction in life from her. She is much the same age as myself. My eldest son is nineteen years, my next son seventeen, the third fourteen, and the last child a girl of 11 years. They are all members of the church. My occupation is a farmer, but as the seasons in this part of the country are uncertain, I also keep a team of horses and wagon for the carrying of goods from one place to another, which I attend myself, with the assistance of my sons, and by this way of life have gained the good will of the public, who recommend me to business and to some very principal work for Government[21]

Providing a Living for His Family

While establishing the church at Jamaica, Liele did not take any pay from the church for his services. He did not want to be misunderstood and did not want to hinder the progress of the church of Christ. However, he did work hard outside the church to provide for his family. Liele was a farmer[22] and was determined to provide for his family even in the uncertain seasons in Jamaica. He kept horses and wagons that were used for employment by providing transportation for the government, which he did under contract. George Liele was a businessman who "kept the good will of the public."[23] In one article found in *The Journal of Negro History*, John W. Davis quotes Mr. Stephen Cooke as saying that Liele was "a very industrious man, decent and humble in his manners, and, I think, a good man."[24] In reference to Liele, Davis added, "His family life was pleasant."[25]

A pleasant family life, composed of husband and wife with children, must follow some organizational rules that yield that kind of pleasantness. There are responsibilities that each family member must adhere to if the life is to be pleasant. In examining the family life of George Liele, we will look at the

---

[21] E. K. Love, "History of the First African Baptist Church from Its Organization. January 20, 1788, to July 1st, 1888," *The Morning News Print.* http://www.reformedreader.org/history/love/toc.htm (accessed 15 September 2010).

[22] J. W. Davis, "George Liele and Andrew Bryan: Pioneer Negro Baptist Preachers," *The Journal of Negro History,* volume 3/2 (April 1918): 119–27, http://www.gutenberg.org/ebooks/20906 (accessed 5 February 2010).

[23] Ibid.

[24] Ibid.

[25] Ibid.

The Liele Family Tree

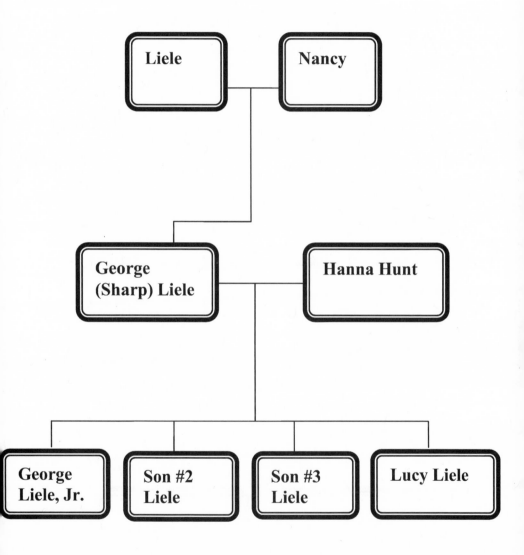

Liele — Nancy

George (Sharp) Liele — Hanna Hunt

George Liele, Jr.

Son #2 Liele

Son #3 Liele

Lucy Liele

Enslaved Members of the Liele Household

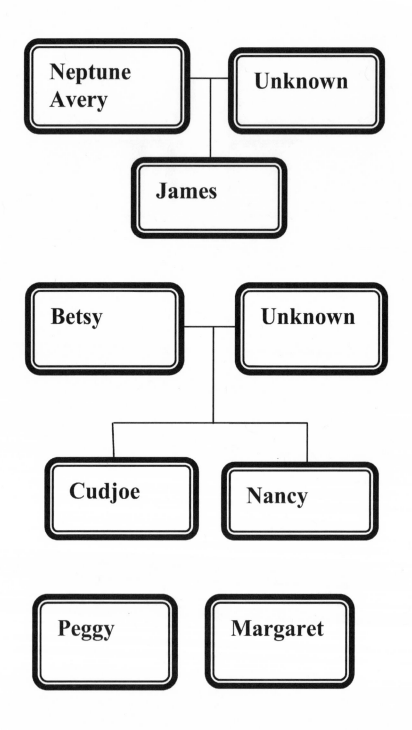

responsibilities of the husband. Dennis Rainey, president and cofounder of Family Life (a subsidiary of Campus Crusade for Christ), outlines the biblical responsibilities for the husband in a godly family. We will look at each of these responsibilities to see what kind of man headed the Liele family. Rainey only lists three responsibilities and supports each one with Scripture. Those responsibilities and a brief explanation of each are discussed here.

1. Be a leader. Divine appointment as leader in the family is given in 1 Corinthians 11:3, which states, "But I want you to understand that Christ is the head of every man, and the man is the head of a woman, and God is the head of Christ." God placed the husband there as leader. While not every husband will lead perfectly, he must care for his wife and family by "serving them with perseverance."[26] George Liele served his family with perseverance, even after death with his last will and testament.

2. Love your wife unconditionally. Citing Ephesians 5:25 Rainey notes, "Husbands, love your wives, just as Christ also loved the church and gave Himself up for her." There is no mention of loving the wife based upon her performance but instead based on her worth as God's gift to the husband. To love unconditionally means constant affirmation. Show that your wife is valued and respected. As stated earlier and emphasized here, George Liele spoke very highly and respectfully of his wife. Liele stated to Dr. Rippon, "My wife was baptized by me in Savannah, and I have every satisfaction in life from her."[27]

3. Serve your wife. Modeled after Jesus, this type of leadership involves serving. We see this type of servant leadership demonstrated in John 13:1–17 when Jesus washed his disciples' feet. Christ, the head of the church, took on the very nature of a servant when he was made in human likeness (Philippians 2:7). Rainey goes on to say, "Another way to serve your wife is to provide for her. This provision first involves assuming responsibility for meeting the material needs of the family."[28] First Timothy 5:8 tells us, "But if anyone does not provide for his own, and especially for those of his household, he has denied the faith, and is worse than an unbeliever." Providing for one's wife also means taking the initiative in helping meet her spiritual needs. This is done by modeling godly character, by praying with her, by spending time together in God's word, and by looking for ways to encourage her spiritually.[29] Liele encouraged his wife

---

[26] Dennis Rainey, *What Should Be the Husband's Role in Marriage*, from The Council on Biblical Manhood and Womanhood, http://www.cbmw.org (accessed 13 December 2010).

[27] Love, "First African Baptist Church," 35.

[28] Ibid.

[29] Ibid.

spiritually. In fact, his wife, Hannah, came to know Christ through Liele's preaching at Silver Bluff.[30]

George Liele was a leader, a lover, and a servant as he accommodated his life to the life of the gift God had given him—his wife.

George and Hannah: A Covenant Relationship

George and Hannah Liele, together and separately, seemed to follow the organizational structure of marriage and of family as set out in Scripture. As noted by Dennis Rainey, and according to 1 Corinthians 11:3, there is a hierarchy in the family. It states, "But I want you to know that the head of every man is Christ, the head of woman is man, and the head of Christ is God." From Ephesians we learn that men and women are to be submissive to each other and the emphasis changes in marriage. In marriage, a wife is to be submissive to her husband, as the church is to Christ. A man is to love his wife just as Christ loves the church (the bride of Christ) and gave himself up for her, so that he might sanctify her, as to the Lord who is the savior of the body (the church). William Hendriksen declared, "More excellent love than this is inconceivable."[31] A man is told to love his wife as his own body, nourishing and cherishing it just as Christ does the church, because a man and a woman (Christian men and women) are members of his body. The reference in Ephesians puts the ultimate responsibility with respect to the household on the shoulders of the husband.[32] The wife's duty is one of submission to her husband on a voluntary basis—only to her husband and not to every man.[33] Being "head" does not mean that the male should dominate and demand the female's total obedience to his every wish and command. The teaching of the New Testament clearly shows that women are to

---

[30] James Melvin Washington, *Frustrated Fellowship: The Black Baptist Quest for Social Power* (Macon GA: Mercer University Press) 9; Holmes, "Prophet of Deliverance, 340–51.

[31] William Hendriksen, *Exposition of Ephesians* (Grand Rapids MI: Baker Book House, 1967) 233.

[32] Ephesians 21–30 (NKJV): [21][S]ubmitting to one another in the fear of God. [22] Wives, submit to your own husbands, as to the Lord. [23] For the husband is head of the wife, as also Christ is head of the church; and He is the Savior of the body. [24] Therefore, just as the church is subject to Christ, so *let* the wives *be* to their own husbands in everything. [25] Husbands, love your wives, just as Christ also loved the church and gave Himself for her, [26] that He might sanctify and cleanse her with the washing of water by the word, [27] that He might present her to Himself a glorious church, not having spot or wrinkle or any such thing, but that she should be holy and without blemish. [28] So husbands ought to love their own wives as their own bodies; he who loves his wife loves himself. [29] For no one ever hated his own flesh, but nourishes and cherishes it, just as the Lord *does* the church. [30] For we are members of His body, of His flesh and of His bones.

[33] Hendriksen, *Exposition of Ephesians*, 233.

be respected and treated as equals with men. Therefore the woman is not to be viewed as a second-class citizen for, according to Galatians 3:28, all in Christ are one and the same.[34]

Scripture does more than assign leadership to the husband. The comparison that Paul makes of the husband with Christ reveals the sense in which the husband should be his wife's head. As the wife's head, he is interested in her welfare. He is her protector. He is her servant. His pattern is Christ, who, as head of the church, is savior and servant.

Looking at this Christian couple in the context of Scripture, we can also speculate, but with more certainty than doubt, that Hannah had to be a woman who would have respected her husband, neither resisting nor fighting his efforts of leadership. After all, the depiction that we have is of a family having a "pleasant" life.[35] Surely George appreciated the assistance of his helpmate when Hannah, along with others, worked side by side with her husband in establishing churches both in America and in Jamaica. It is significant to note that Hannah joined her husband in buying bonds to fund the property on which they lived. It was on that property that their first church was built.

In one of his letters Paul wrote (1 John 3:18), "Let us not love in word, neither in tongue, but in deed and in truth." One of the characteristics to be found in a Christian home is the presence of action—sacrificial action—that of a servant, akin to Christ as he is held up to be our role model. The missionary journey that George Liele carved out for himself occurred in the midst of religious, political and social change, wars, natural disasters, slavery, poverty, and persecution. In spite of a lot of the aforementioned circumstances, George Liele is depicted as a hardworking man who took care of his family as leader, lover, and servant.[36]

From America, George Liele took with him a covenant that he used in churches he organized. The covenant was entitled, "The Covenant of the Anabaptist church, begun in America, December 1777, and in Jamaica, December 1783." The first section of the covenant states, "We are of the Anabaptist persuasion because we believe [in the authority of the Bible]."[37] What Liele advanced in his covenant was a church of purity and simplicity—authority of the Scriptures, consisting only of people who are baptized by total immersion (non-

---

[34] Ibid.

[35] Davis, "Pioneer Negro Baptist Preachers," 119–27.

[36] Timothy Paul Erdel, "I Wish I'd Been There: Negro Slavery's Prophet of Deliverance," *Mennonite Historical Bulletin,* July 2001, Historical Committee & Archives of the Mennonite Church, http://www.mcusa-archives.org/MHB/Erdel-NegroSlavery'sprophet. html (accessed 10 February 2009).

[37] Ernest A. Payne, "Baptist Work in Jamaica before the Arrival of the Missionaries," *Baptist Quarterly* 1 (January 1934): 20–26.

baptism of infants but pastoral blessing); autonomy of the local church; a believer's church; religious liberty; democracy in voting on issues of the church; separation of church and state (no participation in government and no holding of public office); and nonviolence, including no participation in war.[38] Liele emphasized faith and mission as the primary focus of the church and the church as a source of renewal. He also espoused that "faith" came from an inner conviction and not from an external compunction. Moses Baker, a friend and fellow servant in the spreading of the gospel in Jamaica, wrote in a letter wherein he stated that the principles he had learned from Liele were Baptist principles. The term "Anabaptist" was not used.[39]

In terms of the covenant's relevance to George Liele's family life, it is important to look at the totality of information that we have before us. Justifiably, we start with the premise that George Liele was a God-fearing man who wanted to spread the gospel with every fiber of his being. In a letter written 18 December 1791 to John Rippon, coordinator of British Baptist evangelical efforts throughout the world, Liele stated that he well recalled that upon his conversion he requested "...my Lord and Master to give me a work. I did not care how mean it was, only to try and see how good I would do it."[40] Surely one can form a fairly accurate opinion of the man from his verbalizations, his actions, his writings, and even the company that he kept. We have all three. The covenant, certainly a symbol of what he believed, is a reflection of how he lived his life. First, the covenant tells the reader that the Bible was Liele's guide. In article 16, the covenant condemned the break up of families, which was a direct attack on the slave owners and plantation operators, who actively discouraged marriage and opposed family togetherness in every conceivable way.[41] But, as Liele believed, God created them male and female, so that through marriage they might reflect the communal love of the Holy Trinity.

As the infinitely loving bond between the Father and Son constitutes the Third Person of the Trinity, so, in a similar manner, a child embodies the love of a husband and wife. God's wonderful plan for marriage gives man and woman the opportunity to make up for deficiencies in the other, thereby completing each other (Gen. 2:18). This is complementarity—the mutual giving and receiving of

---

[38] Erdel, "Negro slavery's prophet of deliverance."

[39] David Alan Black, "The Anabaptists and State Religion," *The Covenant News* (10 November 2005), www.covenantnews.com/daveblack051110.htm (accessed 13 November 2010).

[40] Walter H. Brooks, *The Silver Bluff Church: A History of Negro Baptist Churches in America* (Washington DC: Press of R L Pendleton, 1910), http://docsouth.unc.edu/church/brooks/summary.html (accessed 29 December 2008).

[41] Payne, "Baptist Work in Jamaica," 20–26.

marital relations—and this unity is reflected in the crowning fruit of their union: children.

When we go beyond the marital union and look at the Liele children, we find that George Liele was an effective and loving father. He must have been proud to have written to John Rippon, "They are all members of the church."[42] When he for a time could not minister, his son stepped in to care for his flock. When he neared his death, he saw fit to remember his wife and children and his extended family (several slaves) as takers in his last will and testament.

Last Will and Testament

George Liele left a last will and testament, which expressed just how his estate should be handled after his death. Excerpts from that will show Liele's concern for his family. "In the name of God amen I George Liele the Elder of the City and Parish of Kingston in the County of Surry and Island aforesaid a free Black Man but shortly intending to depart the said Island for the United Kingdom of Great Britain and Ireland—having taken into mature consideration the Certainty of Death...." George Liele, the evangelist, the businessman, and the negotiator, was a family man whose provision for his family was a major consideration his entire life.

---

[42] Letter of December 18, 1791, in John Rippon, *The Baptist Annual Register* (London, 1793) 332-37.

Resources

African-American Religion: Interpretive Essays in History and Culture. Edited by Timothy E. Fulop and Albert J. Raboteau (New York: Routledge, 1997).

"Black Christianity before the Civil War: Did You Know? Spiritual Memories of Slaves—in Their Own Words." *Christianity Today International/Christian History Magazine* (1999). http://www.ctlibrary.com/ch/1999/issue62/62h002.html (accessed 12 December 2010).

Boston, Nicholas and Jennifer Hallam. *Slavery and the Making of America. The Slave Experience: The Family.* Broadcast by PBS Educational Broadcasting Corporation. 1995. http://www.pbs.org/wnet/slavery/experience/family/history.html (accessed 12 December 2010).

Christenson, Elroy. (1998). *Col. Moses Kirkland.* Retrieved from http://www.next1000.com/family/EC/kirkland.moses.html.

Countries Quest. (2004). "African American Families under Slavery." http://www.countriesquest.com/north_america/usa/people/family_life/african_american_families_under_slavery.htm (accessed 9 September 2010).

Davis, J. W. "George Liele and Andrew Bryan: Pioneer Negro Baptist Preachers," *The Journal of Negro History,* volume 3 (1918). http://www.gutenberg.org/ebooks/20906 (accessed 14 November 2007).

Holmes, Edward A. (1964). "George Liele: Negro Slavery's Prophet of Deliverance". *Baptist Quarterly* 20: 340–51, 361.

Liele, George. (1830). Last Will and Testament. (See Appendix B.)

Norfleet, Phil. (1999). *Biographical Sketch of Moses Kirkland.* Retrieved from http://sc_tories.tripod.com/moses_kirkland.htm.

Payne, Ernest A. "Baptist Work in Jamaica before the Arrival of the Missionaries." *Baptist Quarterly, New Series* 1 (January 1934): 20–26.

PBS. (1995–2008). "People & Events: George Liele, 1752–1825". Public Broadcasting Service (PBS) Africans in America: Part 2. Retrieved from http://www.pbs.org/wgbh/aia/part2/2p49.html.

Sernett, Milton C., ed. (1999). *African American Religious History: A Documentary Witness* Durham, NC: Duke University Press, 2nd Edition.

Simms, J. M. (1888). The First Colored Baptist Church in North America Constituted at Savannah, Georgia, January 20, A.D. 1788. With Biographical Sketches of the Pastors. Philadelphia, PA: J. B. Lippincott Company. Electronic Copy Retrieved from http://docsouth.unc.edu/church/simms/simms.html.

Winegarten, Ruthe. (1985). Texas Slave Families. The Texas Humanist, March–April. 1985. Retrieved from http://www.humanities-interactive.org/texas/rural/tx_slave_families.htm (accessed 12 December 2010).

George Liele: Apostle of Liberation and Faith

DAVID T. SHANNON, SR.
EDITED BY AVERETT P. SHANNON[1]

The purpose of this biographical work is to show an appreciation for the life and legacy of George Liele, the first African American officially ordained as a Baptist preacher and who is considered the father of the independent black church movement. George Liele's life is significant because it brings into focus the indisputable reality of God's action in the life and history of humankind. The background for understanding George Liele as well as his message to the people is found in the New Testament, John 13:13 *"Ye call me Master and Lord; and ye say well: for so I am."*[2] This phrase is the foundation of George Liele's theology and, therefore, the beginning of a "black theology of liberation."

A black theology of liberation is grounded in the African-American experience of slavery and other forms of oppression endured by blacks in America and other parts of the world. A black theology rests on the biblical concept of God's choosing the enslaved Israelites as his people. James Cone, an exponent of liberation theology, believes that God, manifested in Jesus Christ, becomes "the oppressed One."[3] Through the suffering of Jesus Christ, he makes humans understand that God is wherever humans experience oppression, humiliation, and suffering.[4] Thus a theology of liberation in America begins with George Liele's ministry, supported by his profound faith in and commitment to Jesus Christ.

The historical circumstances of Liele's birth and conversion provide the background for a theology of liberation. Like the biblical Hebrews, Liele and his family were the victims of chattel slavery. Born in Virginia in 1750 to parents known only as Liele and Nancy, George Liele began life in pre-Revolutionary

---

[1] Please note that Dr. David T. Shannon, Sr.'s, work has been compiled and edited after his unexpected death on 22 March 2008. The introduction and essay on George Liele found within this book accurately reflect his thinking and his writings.

[2] *Holy Bible*, ed. Russell L. Surls, King James Version (Iowa Falls IA: World Bible Publishers, 1986). Please note that all subsequent references to Scripture come from the KJV.

[3] James H. Cone, *A Black Theology of Liberation* (Jefferson NC: McFarland Press, 1970) 63–64.

[4] Ibid.

America in a slave-holding state. Perhaps his parents had already experienced some form of Virginia's harsh Slave Codes. For minor offenses, such as "insolence" or associations with free blacks, they could have been whipped, branded, or maimed.[5] In John Hope Franklin's book, from *Slavery to Freedom: A History of African Americans*, Franklin states that African Americans were not only poor and oppressed, but they had no identity.[6] Liele's parents had no last names. At first, Liele himself was known only by his first name, George. Later, as property of Henry Sharp, he became George Sharp. Eventually, he named himself George Liele after his father. As property of Henry Sharp, George Liele moved to Burke County, Georgia, near South Carolina. This is the approximate time that he married, since he estimated that he was twenty or twenty-one years older than the oldest of his children.

About three years after arriving in Burke County, Liele was converted and baptized by Matthew Moore, pastor of the white Baptist church where Henry Sharp (Moore's brother-in-law) was a deacon. Liele was allowed to attend services at the local white Baptist church. After six months of Bible study, prayer, and worship, he was baptized and accepted as a member of Sharp's church, Big Buckhead Baptist Church of St. George Parish, Georgia. In that Liele's father knew the Lord in a "spiritual way"[7] and that Liele professed a sense of morality, his ministry was firmly entrenched in his persona. George Liele would experience many difficulties in his ministry, but there is no record of his ever doubting his call to the ministry.

It is acknowledged that after Liele gave his personal testimony he was soon called to preach the gospel: "Desiring to prove the sense I had of my obligation to God, I endeavored to instruct...my own color in the Word of God: the white brethren seeing my endeavors...gave me a call at a quarterly meeting to preach before the congregation."[8] Moved by the sincerity of his sermon, church leaders granted Liele a probationary license to preach.[9] This made him the first African American to be officially ordained as a Baptist minister. Liele preached to both African Americans and Anglos. For two years, he preached in the slave quarters of plantations surrounding the Savannah River, including the congregation formed at Silver Bluff, South Carolina.

---

[5] John Hope Franklin and Alfred A. Moss, Jr., *From Slavery to Freedom: A History of African Americans* (New York: McGraw and Hill, 1994) 58.

[6] Ibid.

[7] Mechal Sobel, *Trabelin' on the Slave Journey to an Afro-Baptist Faith* (Princeton NJ: Princeton University Press, 1979) 104.

[8] Michael Thurmond, *Freedom Georgia's Antislavery Heritage 1733–1865* (Atlanta: Longstreet Press, 2002) 54.

[9] Ibid.

Liele's conversion to Christianity is one of the key experiences toward a liberation theology. Before his conversion, Liele's sense of right and wrong, instilled in him first by his father and second by Matthew Moore, a white Baptist minister, drove him to seek salvation. Although he joined Moore's church, engaged in Bible study, prayed, and did good work, it was his conversion that stimulated his deep love for Christ. He describes this important epiphany: "I felt such love and joy as my tongue was not able to express."[10] He testifies that he felt the need to teach the enslaved by "reading among them, encouraging the enslaved to sing, and sometimes explaining the most striking parts of them [the hymns]."[11] Liele's demonstrated love for the enslaved, as he endeavored to lift them up, is evidence of his love for Christ. By teaching other enslaved persons, Liele discovered his love for other enslaved people on the same plantation where he resided. His engagement with the oppressed enslaved people is also an example of liberation theology. The singing with the enslaved to help them escape their impoverished condition is a major aspect of commitment to the welfare of others. Just as Jesus shows love and humility by washing his disciples' feet, Liele demonstrates love and service by teaching and uplifting his people. Also, Liele's conversion allowed him to move to a salvation based on grace, rather than works alone.

George Liele's preaching among the enslaved is a continuation of the tenets of liberation theology. After he was ordained, Liele exercised his calling by preaching to the enslaved along the Savannah River from Silver Bluff, South Carolina, to Georgia. When the enslaved accepted Christ as their personal Savior, he baptized them in the river.

Because Liele's sermons that were delivered in the United States have not been located, one has to go to other sources to learn what he might have said in the content of his sermons. At first, the context of these sermons would have been close to "An Ante-bellum Sermon" by Paul Laurence Dunbar.[12] The following stanza of Dunbar's imaginative sermon to a group of enslaved people delivered by an enslaved preacher is representative of what Liele might have spoken to his enslaved flock at some point during his career.

We is gathahed hyeah, my brothahs,
In dis howlin' wildaness,
Fu' to speak some words of comfo't
To each othah in distress,

---

[10] Sobel, *Trabelin' on the Slave Journey*, 105.

[11] Ibid.

[12] *The Norton Anthology of African American Literature*, ed. Henry Louis Gates, Jr., and Nettie McKay (New York: W. W. Norton and Company) 891.

An' we chooses fu' ouah subjic'
Dis—we'll 'splain it by an' by;
"An' de Lawd said, 'Moses, Moses,'
An' de man said, 'Hyeah am I.'"[13]

In these few lines Dunbar imagines the place for a sermon is likely to be in the woods, in the brush arbor,[14] somewhere away from the Big House: "In dis howlin' wildaness."[15] The lines have double meaning; the howling wilderness suggests an antagonistic world known to the oppressed.[16] The first line suggests that this is a gathering of men ("my brothahs") who came to the place to speak some words of comfort to each other. There will be a sermon about "Moses," which will give the enslaved some hope of deliverance from "distress," which is the agony of slavery. Moses in the poem is the Hebrew who hears the call from God to lead the Israelites out of Egypt during Pharaoh's enslavement of the Hebrews. Although Liele believed in the New Testament gospel, he saw himself as a leader of God's people. The allusion to Moses suggests that the black preacher has the power and the ability to lead oppressed black people.

According to David T. Shannon in *Stony the Road We Trod*, the correlation of biblical situations to the enslaved people in their present condition indicates a mutuality that inspired hope: the African Americans and the Israelites shared a bondage. If Israelites also experienced divine redemption, so could African Americans. The focus of worship in the poem is God, the one who takes action, rather than God, an impersonal omnipotent being. In this sense, the biblical text becomes a tool of liberation and comfort for the oppressed.[17]

Paul Laurence Dunbar's "An Ante-bellum Sermon" represents a genre of the African-American sermon that was content laden. The sermons grew out of a situation in which the wounded was speaking to the wounded. Henri Nouwen suggests that we have a situation of the "wounded healer."[18] These sermons were remembered not only for their immediate effect, but also for their lasting value in

---

[13] Ibid., 891.

[14] An arbor made of brushwood, especially as a place for a camp meeting. See *Webster's Third New International Dictionary of the English Language Unabridged* (Springfield MA: G. & C. Merriam Co., 1981) 286, s. v. "brush arbor."

[15] "Howlin' wildaness" is a metaphoric representation of slavery. It was a condition of uncertainty, unpredictability, and danger.

[16] Ibid.

[17] David T. Shannon, "An Ante-bellum Sermon" in *Stony The Road We Trod, African American Biblical Interpretation*, ed. Cain Hope Felder (Minneapolis MN: Fortress Press, 1991) 104–105.

[18] Henri Nouwen, *The Wounded Healer* (Garden City NY: Doubleday, 1972).

empowering their hearers to live in the midst of the "howlin' wildaness" of oppression with faith, hope, and courage.[19]

The early African-American sermons of which Dunbar's poetic rendition is a remarkable remembrance makes a significant contribution to the development of an African-American hermeneutic in several ways. They address the issues of *contextuality, correlation, confrontation,* and *consolation.* These sermons affirm the full humanity of all persons in the sense of the Aristotelian notion of entelechy— that is, complete actuality as distinguished from potentiality.

Dunbar's poem is one example of African Americans telling their own story. It reflects the way in which one can view the style, content, and significance of the enslaved preacher. The language, method, and scope of the sermon provide a way of understanding the hermeneutical principles that the African-American enslaved preacher utilized in providing empowerment, hope, and consolation to the enslaved, who were faced with the daily and lifelong struggles of chattel slavery. The sermon also shows how the use of double entendre and the Bible gave immediate comfort to the hearers by affirming liberation from slavery.

The African-American preacher used the rhetorical device of double entendre to communicate with the enslaved without undue danger to the listeners. The use of this device yielded a cunning style of interpretation of the Bible in its fullest sense. The African-American preacher used the biblical text as a primary source to address the context of human slavery. The preacher drew a correlation (i.e., established the crossing point) between the Hebrew enslaved and the African-American enslaved. Confrontation grew out of the relevance of the biblical word in terms of divine creation and human liberation. The intent was to provide consolation, to empower the enslaved to deal with their daily insults and burdens, and to give them hope for ultimate deliverance. As an African-American Baptist preacher, George Liele used this strategy to significantly influence others.[20]

A Hermeneutical Analysis of Jesus as Lord and Master

George Liele based his theology on his conversion experience. His theology can be summarized in the statement "Jesus is my Lord and Master." In his letter to John Rippon, Liele gave his testimony, which began by stating, "I always had a natural fear of God from my youth, and was often checked in conscience with thoughts of death, which barred me from many sins and bad company. I knew no other way at that time to hope for salvation but only in the performance of my good works. I requested of my Lord and Master to give me work, I did not care

---

[19] James Weldon Johnson, *God's Trombones* (New York: Viking Press, 1927).

[20] Shannon, "Ante-bellum Sermon," 122–23.

how mean it was, only to try and see how good I would do it."[21] It seems clear that at first, Liele was unaware of the facts of salvation before his conversion. However, as he learned more about Christianity, he changed his way of thinking from a works-based salvation to that of grace-based salvation.

Liele's ministry in the United States ended in 1782, during the closing years of the Revolutionary War. While he is considered the father of a black theological liberation movement, he is only given credit currently for building a congregation of black Baptists, enslaved and free, including the Silver Bluff group of South Carolina that was led by David George. The First Colored Baptist Church began in December 1777, when George Liele constituted the congregation on the Yamacraw site, in Savannah, Georgia. The church was considered a source of strength and shelter during the peculiar institution of slavery and served as a source of protection all through the period of the Underground Railroad. Sometime before the American Revolution began in 1775, Henry Sharp manumitted Liele, providing him the freedom to plant the seeds of an international, "independent" black church movement. This he did with the assistance of David George and Jesse Peter, protégés of Liele's teaching. Andrew Bryan, one of Liele's Yamacraw converts, became the second pastor of the church that Liele had started in Savannah, after his ordination on 20 January 1788.[22]

However, when Henry Sharp was killed in battle in 1778, Liele lost his protection from re-enslavement. Savannah had fallen into the hands of the Patriots, and Henry Sharp's heirs attempted to re-enslave him. Fortunately, he was able to provide the papers granting him freedom. With the assistance of Colonel Kirkland, Liele was able to escape to Jamaica.[23] Liele continued his evangelism in Jamaica, which proved further that he was a proponent of what is known today as liberation theology.

George Liele was a man of great faith. His faith, like that of Apostle Paul, was greatly tested in Jamaica. Liele's mission work started in Kingston, Jamaica, when he first began preaching in a private home to a small congregation. Next, he organized a church on his own land with four other men who had come from America. The Jamaica Assembly permitted him to preach, and despite opposition from members of the white Anglican Church, he expanded his ministry to rural areas, gaining a large number of communicants. Liele built a church, taught a

---

[21] John Rippon, *The Baptist Annual Register, for 1790, 1791, 1792, and Part of 1793* (London: Dilly, Button, and Thomas, 1793), 332–37. John Rippon, *The Baptist Annual Register, for 1798, 1799, 1800, and part of 1801* (London: Button and Confer, 1801) 366–67.

[22] Rippon, *Baptist Annual Register 1793*, 332–37.

[23] *African American Religious History: A Documentary Witness*, ed. Milton C. Sernett (Durham NC and London: Duke University Press, 1999) 45–46.

free school, and gained a living as a farmer and hauler of goods. In exchange for a number of concessions, including inspection by authorities of every prayer and sermon, his ministry was tolerated, and he was allowed to preach to the poor and enslaved on plantations and in settlements. Liele resumed his missionary work among the island's enslaved and free black populations, but he was persecuted and tormented by local officials. In spite of this, though, Liele persevered and established the Windward Road Baptist Church in Kingston, Jamaica's first Baptist church. Liele faced persecution and imprisonment for his faith but stayed committed to his calling. Carey Robinson, a Jamaican historian, recognizes Liele as a father of the freedom movement that eventually led to the abolition of Jamaican slavery by the Emancipation Act of 1833.[24]

George Liele's work was never easy. He suffered from financial problems as he worked among a destitute enslaved population. Moreover, Liele was constantly suspected of preaching incitement to rebellion. He incurred the disfavor of the legally established Anglican Church by building up a body of dissenting believers. Liele was jailed twice—once on a charge of sedition, and once for debt incurred in building a chapel. He was freed of the first charge due to lack of evidence, but he remained in jail for the second charge until the debt was paid. To overcome his financial difficulties Liele attracted the support of men like Stephen A. Cook, a member of the Jamaica Assembly, who won permission from the assembly for the church to function and helped Liele solicit funds from English Baptists. Liele worked hard as a farmer and carried goods with a team of horses and wagons to support himself and his family.

Awareness of the accomplishments of African Americans has been sporadic throughout the study of missions. But there are some individuals who have indeed recognized and acknowledged George Liele's contributions. Gustav Warneck, for instance, is one of the few who stated, rightly, "The Baptist Mission began its work in Jamaica in 1813, following in the steps of an original Negro from Virginia, George Liele, who had labored in Kingston since 1783 and had gathered a congregation...."[25]

George Liele's steadfast faith and his ability to work well with others enabled him to draw significant numbers of blacks to the Baptist church in the United States as well as Jamaica, an achievement so great that its effects are still felt today.

---

[24] Christopher Brent Ballew, *The Impact of African-American Antecedents on the Baptist Foreign Missionary Movement, 1782–1825* (Lewiston NY: Edwin Mellon Press, 2004) 33.

[25] Gustav Warneck, *Time Outline of a History of Protestant Missions from the Reformation to the Present,* ed. George Robson, 3rd. English ed., trans. from the 8th German edition (New York: Fleming H. Revell Company, 1906) 203.

Understanding: A Comparison between Liele and Paul

Like the Apostle Paul, George Liele was a man of great faith who accepted Jesus as his Lord and Master and committed himself to spreading the gospel. Like Paul also, Liele's conversion was key to his understanding and faith. Some scholars suggest that the radical impact of Paul's conversion (call) is redefined by his relationship between God and the Jews and the Gentiles. Paul's experience with God led him to a new focus. This is an example of understanding how one's faith can be radically changed by one's experiences. Paul believed that Jesus would return in his lifetime to consummate the history of the world and reward those who had been faithful to him.

George Liele's faith was grounded in an intimate relationship with God. He used the study of the Bible as a source to overcome the negative and hostile experiences associated with enslavement. Liele, as other African-American people have done, strengthened his faith through Bible study. Bible study was a source for inspiration for their songs, sermons, prayers, testimonials, funerals, and rites of passages. This discipline became one of the roots that nurtured and sustained the tree of black spirituality. One example of how Bible study influenced their songs is in the text of the song "I Love the Lord." The words that make up this song demonstrate one of the fundamental affirmations of black Spirituality and faith. Both the enslaved and their children and grandchildren have expressed this belief in many songs and testimonies. They sang with enthusiasm and conviction songs that included words similar to those found in this epic song:

> "I love the Lord, he heard my cries,
> And pitied every groan:
> Long as I live, when troubles rise,
> I'll hasten to his throne."

Black Christians have affirmed their faith in God, who is omnipotent and omnipresent, meaning always available and able to effect life's circumstances. They sang this song as a statement of faith; to give expression to the depth of their understanding of God, to provide a rationale for faith, and as a determination to keep the faith. They expressed love of God in the sense of the text of Deuteronomy 6:5: "Love the Lord your God with all your heart and with all your soul and with all your strength." Jesus amplified this concept in the restatement of the proper human response to God in Mark 12:30: "Love your God with all your heart and with all your soul and with all your mind and with all your strength." This is a profound theological understanding of the centrality of commitment.

George Liele and Paul believed that their faith required them to submit totally to Jesus with a humble heart and an open mind. They realized that Jesus loved them and would accept and protect them. One of the basic truths that Paul brings to us today is associated with what he learned through many of his experiences: over and over again, Apostle Paul exclaimed that man is not justified by works, but by faith. Paul shows that man is on trial before the tribunal of God. As man stands there, he is condemned because we all have sinned. Yet Paul makes it clear in Romans 3:24 when he talks about "being justified freely by his grace through the redemption that is in Christ Jesus:" Faith means that we accept the fact that we are accepted by God without earning it.

Judgment

Judgment, motivated by one's feelings and leading to decision-making, undergirds both George Liele's and Paul's faith. Conversion leads to their exercising judgment and strengthens their faith in God. Liele utilized his critical faculties to say yes or no to God's assignment; Liele said yes to the assignment. This was his decision. For example, one may demonstrate judgment by affirming what one believes. Another example of judgment would be to adapt to what one believes. Therefore, reflection and insight can lead one to convert what one believes into something new and radical. Sometimes an experience does not confirm one's faith but confronts it with questions and challenges. Such behavior fits the case of Paul. Conversion is often thought of as a sudden dramatic reversal of a person's way of life, as it was for Paul. The description of Apostle Paul being knocked down on the road to Damascus is the standard model in Acts 9:3–4: "As he neared Damascus on his journey, suddenly a light from heaven flashed around him. He fell to the ground and heard a voice say to him, "Saul, Saul, why do you persecute me?"

Sometimes, conversion takes a longer period of time. The experience that provokes it may be sudden and dramatic, but the actual change to a new way of thinking or acting is usually slower. There are times when an actual experience calls for a decision and leads to direct action as a result. It points out the faith that is the source of principles as well as moral behavior. One can benefit most when one's faith is of an actual experience that has affirmed belief and displays relevance by demonstrating in everyday terms that what one believes is real and important to one's life.

Comparison Chart of Liele and Apostle Paul

Apostle Paul	**George Liele.**
1. Dual Lineage (Jewish and Roman)	1. Dual Lineage (African and American)
2. Radical conversion experience	2. Radical Conversion Experience
3. Commitment to evangelization	3. Commitment to Evangelization
4. Authenticated by church leaders (At Damascus) With Ananias	4. Authenticated by church leaders (At Silver Bluff) Palmer and Galpin
5. Challenged and educated other Christian disciples for evangelization Ex. Titus, Phoebe, Timothy, Mark	5. Challenged and educated other Christian disciples for evangelization Ex. David, George, Bryan, etc.
6. Started Churches	6. Started Churches
7. Spread gospel across the seas (From Asia Minor to Europe)	7. Spread gospel across the seas (From America to Jamaica)
8. Dual Vocations - Tent-maker/Evangelist - First Missionary	8. Dual Vocations Businessman/Church Builder First Missionary
9. Solicited Fundraisers for the spread of the gospel.	9. Solicited Fundraisers for the spread of the gospel
10. Wrote letters to encourage converts and fellow workers to continue the spread of the gospel. Reference letters to the churches in the New Testament. eg. Romans and Corinthians.	10. Wrote letters to encourage converts and fellow workers to continue the spread of the gospel. Reference letters from Liele to Executive Secretary of British Baptist, Dr. John Rippon; David George and others.

The effect of Liele's conversion differed from Paul's. Sometimes God breaks into life in a spectacular manner and sometimes conversion is a quiet experience. The right way to come to faith in Jesus is whatever way God brings you. As an example, when George Liele became acquainted with the method of salvation by our Lord Jesus Christ, he soon found relief, particularly at a time when he was earnestly engaged in prayer. "Yes," he said, "I felt such love and joy as my tongue was not able to express. After this I declared before the congregation of believers the work which God had done for my soul, and the same minister, the Rev. Matthew Moore, baptized me, and I continued in this church about four years."[26] This author believes that true conversion, or the call from God, comes from a personal encounter with Jesus Christ and leads to a new life in relation with him. Such was the case for Apostle Paul and George Liele.

Of course, the comparison of Liele's life with Apostle Paul is far more inclusive than the discussion of faith in this essay. Consequently, a chart is included to demonstrate the broader scope of the similarity between the two apostles.

Conclusion: Permanent Significance of the Crossing Points of George Liele's Life and Implications for the Twenty-First Century

The crossing points help one to reflect upon how one's belief or faith provides a basis for faith in the future. The biblical events that were narrated in the Bible and taught in Bible studies were adapted by people in their everyday life. The worshipers in Old Testament times were required to present an offering of first fruits as a symbol of their response to God. Each person is called upon to respond to God's acts of love as George Liele and his colleagues sought to do. This is the source of faith in the future. Faith is responding in love to God's outpouring of himself in Jesus, the Christ.

George Liele stayed encouraged and kept his faith as he continued to help the people in spite of difficult times. God calls us to commitment, not to comfort. He promises to be with us through suffering and hardship, not to spare us from it. Similarly, all humans (free and enslaved persons) have the opportunity to better relate to God's greatness, forgiveness, mercy, goodness, compassion, and love. It is imperative that humans in this present day heed God's call to remember his greatness, compassion, mercy, and love as people forge through daily living, which presents unique challenges. The manner in which George Liele lived his life is an indication of his belief that God promises that he is always with his people. In Psalm 34:7 it states, "The angel of the Lord encampeth round about

---

[26] Rippon, *Baptist Annual Register 1793*, 334.

them that fear him, and delivereth them." God is always in total control of every situation. Therefore, we have to believe, have faith, and be willing to respond to God's love.

The crossing points also provide an opportunity to focus upon God's relationship with individuals and groups. Black spirituality is rooted not only in one's faith in God, but also in one's understanding of God's purpose for his or her life. Each individual is important to God. Jesus emphasized this truth when he spoke of God's care, even for the sparrow (Matthew 6:26–34).

The process of making decisions invites one to be ready to draw upon one's spiritual reserve that addresses the experience. It is the foundation on which everything else rests. George Liele recognized that God was in charge of the lives of the enslaved people he encountered. Therefore, he chose to emphasize the Christlike dimension rather than Southern abstract laws that supported slavery. The liberation theme is in the foundation of the Bible. This theme combines man's experience in an indissoluble union with the Bible and all that it represents. This is a unique insight because it is promoting inclusive rather than exclusive behavior. The slave owner and the enslaved persons are a part of a higher order. The emphasis is not on personal integrity. It is on the community of people who love.

George Liele was able to establish the crossing point between the Hebrew slaves and the African slaves. The intent was to provide consolation, to empower the enslaved to deal with their daily insults and burdens, and to give them hope for ultimate deliverance. Liele's message was not only for the enslaved persons, but also for those who lived in the eighteenth century as well as those who live in the twenty-first century. George Liele was an unsung hero who allowed his faith to guide his life. The context of Liele's life and confession of faith depicts the individual's responsibility to respond to Christ's call and to humankind to respond to God's acts of love. Faith is responding in love to God's outpouring of himself in Jesus, the Christ. The key belief in the sovereignty of God and his saving and liberating action in history is the main crossing point between the Hebrew faith and Christianity.

The experiences of George Liele and the Apostle Paul were amazing and so unique that they left an unforgettable imprint on the lives of others. Liele and Paul do not challenge people to just rethink their previous understanding and practice; they actually challenge people to reflect upon a new faith. Liele and Paul became devout followers of Jesus Christ, the Way. Sometimes God breaks into a life in a spectacular manner, and sometimes conversion is a quiet experience. The right way to come to faith in Jesus is whatever way God brings a person or a people to having faith in the Savior. (See Acts 9:1–7.)

George Liele was a committed man of God who accepted Jesus as his Lord and Master, which was manifested by his sharing the liberation theology he believed was embodied in the teachings of Jesus. He dared to present to his listeners that Jesus was the Son of love and light to all humankind (both the enslaved persons and the owners). Liele was informing his listeners of the liberating power of Jesus' love. This is a profound trigger to transform the mind-set of enslaved people from bondage to the understanding that they could become a free people. Also, Liele's message may have changed the mindset of open-minded slave owners. George Liele made a significant impact on the course of history. It is tenable that he is "the father of the independent black church movement." He was an apostle of faith who sought to spread the gospel of Jesus Christ wherever he went.

Resources

African American Religious History, A Documentary Witness. Edited by Milton C. Sernett. Durham NC and London: Duke University Press, 1999.

Ballew, Christopher Brent, *The Impact of African-American Antecedents Baptist Foreign Missionary Movement, 1782–1825.* Lewiston NY: Edwin Mellon Press, 2004.

Cone, James H. *A Black Theology of Liberation.* Jefferson NC: McFarland Press, 1970.

Dunbar, Paul Laurence. "An Ante-Bellum Sermon." In *The Norton Anthology of African American Literature,* edited by Henry Louis Gates and Nellie McKay. New York: W. W. Norton & Company, 1997.

Franklin, John Hope and Alfred A. Moss, Jr. *From Slavery to Freedom: A History of African Americans.* New York: McGraw-Hill, 1994.

"Letters Showing the Rise and Progress of the Early Negro Churches and the West Indies." In *Journal of Negro History* 1, edited by Carter G. Woodson, 1916.

Nouwen, Henri. *The Wounded Healer.* Garden City NY: Doubleday, 1972.

Rippon, John. *The Baptist Annual Register, for 1790–1799, 1800, and Part of 1801.* London: Button and Confer, 1801.

Shannon, David T. "An Ante-bellum Sermon." In *Stony the Road We Trod, African American Biblical Interpretation,* edited by Cain Hope Felder. Minneapolis MN: Fortress Press, 1991.

Thurmond, Michael. *Freedom: Georgia's Antislavery Heritage 1733–1865.* Atlanta: Longstreet Press, 2002.

Warneck, Gustav. *Outline of a History of Protestant Missions from the Reformation to the Present Time.* Translated and edited by George Robson. New York: Fleming H. Revell Company, 1906.

The Literacy of George Liele as Revealed in His Writings

JULIA FRAZIER WHITE

The marvel of George Liele's success as a preacher in America is the fact that he was enslaved at the time. Because Liele was enslaved, the question of his literacy has been raised. Did Liele read and write or simply mimic? There may have also been other indicators of literacy. The ability to communicate that which was read is one of those measures, and we know that Liele was able to preach. "He often preached on Sunday evenings at the Kiokee Baptist Church, and his preaching was received by black and white alike. Liele was hesitant about seeking church membership because of his color, but his master encouraged him and was in fact even more delighted to discover that he seemed to have a gift for preaching."[1] In spite of his "gift for preaching," some might have questioned whether Liele read and wrote or simply mimicked others. These questions might be answered by examining his writings in his later correspondences and the reactions to his correspondences and sermons.

In Georgia, where Liele lived, slave literacy was a controversial matter. In fact, "The history of African American literacy is necessarily intertwined with the particularities of American slavery, with all of its various mechanisms of power and control. At times, slave codes impeded or altogether prohibited blacks' access to the printed word."[2]

Slave Literacy

Slave literacy was controversial because while there were those who believed that enslaved persons were capable and should be educated, others feared that enslaved persons "could not be enlightened without developing in them a

---

[1] Hughes Oliphant Old, *The Reading and Preaching of the Scriptures in the Worship of the Christian Church: The Modern Age* (Grand Rapids MI: Eerdmans, 2007) 585.

[2] Shevaun E Watson, "'Good Will Come of This Evil': Enslaved Teachers and the Transatlantic Politics of Early Black Literacy," *College Composition and Communication* 61/1 (September 2009): 66, http://proquest.umi.com/pqdweb?did=1869979801&sid=6&Fmt =3&clientId=77774&RQT=309&VName=PQD (accessed 19 December 2010).

longing for liberty."[3] Carter G. Woodson relates that many slaveholders maintained that the more brutish they were, the more pliant enslaved persons would become and that exploitation would be easier. Woodson further asserts, "It was this class of slaveholders that finally won the majority of southerners to their way of thinking and determined that Negroes should not be educated."[4] It was this kind of thinking that gave rise to several laws that forbade enslaved persons to read and write in spite of the knowledge that Negroes were talented and intellectual. As Woodson notes, that very early in the history of the colonies there were scholars and statesmen who did not hesitate to declare their belief in the intellectual possibilities of the Negro. These men agreed with George Buchanan that the Negro had talent for the fine arts and under favorable circumstances could achieve something noteworthy in literature, mathematics and philosophy. The high estimate placed upon the innate ability of the Negro may be attributed to the fact that early in the history of the country there was a goodly number of slaves who had managed to attain a certain intellectual proficiency in spite of the difficulties which had to be overcome.[5]

One effort in the early history of the colonies was the Charles-Town Negro School. It was the most sustained effort in early America that promoted slave literacy.[6] The school was backed by the Society for the Propagation of the Gospel in Foreign Parts (SPG), the missionary arm of the Church of England.[7]

The methods used by blacks to get an education during slavery were circuitous and often undercover. "For the better part of the twentieth century, historians, sociologists, and folklorists, among others, traced the perils and possibilities of black literacy through the paths of households, hush harbors, slave narratives, white and black churches, established and informal schools, antislavery and abolitionist organizations, southern plantations, northern cities, early American print culture, colonial experiments, antebellum reforms, and postbellum promises."[8]

In the first ten years or so, the SPG did not educate as many black people as they would have liked. They changed their approach to appeal to Christian slave owners. The church argued that literacy was crucial for slaves' salvation, and it

---

[3] Carter G. Woodson, *The Education of the Negro Prior to 1861: A History of the Education of the Colored People of the United States from the Beginning of Slavery to the Civil War* (New York: G. P. Putnam's Sons) 1915.

[4] Ibid.

[5] Ibid, 51-55; 68.

[6] Watson, "Good Will Come of This Evil," 180. Note that Charleston was pronounced and written "Charles Town" (and variations thereof) until its incorporation in 1783.

[7] Ibid.

[8] Ibid.

was the highest duty of Christian slave owners. "If it be said that no time can be spared from the daily labour of the Negroes to instruct them, this is in effect to say that no consideration of propagating the gospel of God, or saving the souls of men, is to make the least abatement from the temporal profit of the masters."[9]

However, the profit of the slave owners was a serious consideration. Slavery was a matter of economics: many slaveholders feared the regional economy would fail without the cheap labor of slavery.[10] But literacy prevailed in many cases. For example, by 1791 a colored minister had so distinguished himself that he was called to the pastorate of the First Baptist Church (white) of Portsmouth, Virginia. Benjamin Banneker's proficiency in mathematics enabled him to make the first clock manufactured in the United States. As the author says, "The instances of Negroes struggling to obtain an education read like the beautiful romances of a people in an heroic age."[11] In a poignant statement in an article that appeared in the 31 January 1997 issue of the *New York Times*, Stephen Holden states, "Lest we forget, knowledge is power, and for slaves in the antebellum South, learning to read was forbidden. Some slaves who dared to become literate were punished by having a finger chopped off in front of the whole slave community. Or worse."[12] On the subject of literacy, Janet Duitsman Cornelius states, "In the English-speaking Protestant tradition, reading scripture was necessary for true religious understanding; antebellum slaves, despite the fact that up to 90 percent of them were illiterate, agreed with this contention and wanted to learn to read."[13] Further, Cornelius asserts that there was tension in slaveholders' beliefs. Some believed that enslaved persons should be taught to read and write so that they could study God's word. Others were distrustful and afraid that slave literacy would give enslaved persons the ability to challenge authority because they would be able to tell when a white person was lying about the contents of written documents, including the Bible and newspapers.[14] There was also the fear that an enslaved person who could read and write would

---

[9] David Humphreys, *An Historical Account of the Incorporated Society for the Propagation of the Gospel in Foreign Parts, from Its Foundation to the Year 1728* (New York: Arno Publisher, 1969) 21–31.

[10] Winthrop D. Jordan, *White Over Black: American Attitudes Toward the Negro, 1550–1812* (New York: W.W. Norton & Company, 1968).

[11] Woodson, *The Education of the Negro Prior to 1861*, 3.

[12] Stephen Holden, *Literacy: A Weapon for a Slave* (New York: New York Times Company, 1997), http://query.nytimes.com/gst/fullpage.html?res=9A02E7D8173DF932A05752C0A961958260 (accessed 30 April 2008).

[13] Janet Duitsman Cornelius, *When I Can Read My Title Clear: Literacy, Slavery, and Religion in the Antebellum South* (Columbia: University of South Carolina Press, 1991) xiii plus 215.

[14] Ibid.

be able to forge documents that facilitated escape and run away to the non-slaveholding territories.[15]

How Enslaved Persons Obtained Literacy

Although most Southern states discouraged or even outlawed the teaching of reading and writing to enslaved persons, somehow many enslaved persons learned to read and write anyway.[16] As early as 1620, when the slave trade began, English clergymen expressed an interest in extending religious training to those who were enslaved. Approximately 100 years later, the Presbyterians gave formal training to blacks in an effort to develop religious leadership among those in Charleston, South Carolina, in 1740, and in Virginia in 1755.[17]

The method of obtaining literacy among enslaved persons varied from state to state and even from plantation to plantation. "Religious instruction of slaves...was a thorny question and slaves' acquisition of literacy a surreptitious process."[18] Enslaved persons learned to read from family members and other enslaved persons. Some were even personally taught by their slaveholders or tutors hired by the slaveholders because of the slaveholder's practical need for literate slaves to do jobs such as record-keeping. Some slaveholders encouraged Bible-reading among enslaved persons. Some even established plantation schools.[19] Often enslaved children were taught to read by white playmates.[20] An example of this was seen on the plantation owned by George Galphin. George Galphin's children taught the enslaved David George to read, and David George began preaching to the small congregation on Galphin Plantation.[21]

Some enslaved persons secretly taught themselves from spelling books perhaps by associating the words with the pictures therein. In a conversation with Brother Rippon of London and Brother Pearce in Birmingham, David George, a friend to George Liele since childhood, wrote:

---

[15] Heather Andrea Williams, *Self-Taught: African American Education in Slavery and Freedom* (Chapel Hill: University of North Carolina Press, 2005) 320.

[16] Cornelius, When I Can Read My Title Clear, 13.

[17] Jeffrey H. Richards, "Samuel Davies and the Transatlantic Campaign for Slave Literacy in Virginia," *Virginia Magazine of History and Biography* 3/4 (2003): 333–78, http://www.vahistorical.org/publications/abstract_richards.htm (accessed 13 August 2009).

[18] Cornelius, *When I Can Read My Title Clear*, 57–58.

[19] Kimberly Sambol-Tosco, *Slavery and the Making of America-The Slave Experience: Education, Arts, and Culture* (2004). Accessed 30 April 2008 http://www.pbs.org/wnet/slavery/experience/education/history2.html

[20] Cornelius, *When I Can Read My Title Clear*, 57–58.

[21] Edward J. Cashin, *Old Springfield: Race and Religion in Augusta, Georgia* (Augusta GA: Springfield Village Park Foundation, Inc., 1995).

> Then I got a spelling book and began to read. As master was a great man, he kept a white school-master who was a great man, to teach the white children to read. I used to go to the little children to teach me a, b, c. They would give me a lesson which I tried to learn, and then I would go to them, again, and ask them if it was right. The reading so ran in my mind, that I think I learned in my sleep, as readily as when I was awake, and I can now read the Bible, so that what I have in my heart, I can see again in the Scriptures.[22]

David George's words exemplify the depth of the desire to read—especially the Bible. But most plantations were not so receptive to enslaved persons learning to read.

On most plantations, enslaved persons were not allowed to teach their children how to read and write.[23] In spite of the dangers, though, many parents chose to violate those laws and taught their children how to read and write in hopes that such knowledge would contribute to their survival. Adults felt obligated to show their children how to "handle the inhumane acts and degradation by the whites without losing their own spirits"[24] On certain plantations, learning was encouraged. For example, "Some of the large planters established Sunday Schools as a means of implanting obedience through religious education. It was also the feeling of some religious leaders that literacy would save the system of slavery rather than stimulate revolt."[25] One of the most successful campaigns for slave literacy during the time that Liele lived (the eighteenth century) was led by a pastor named Samuel Davies. Davies expressed the strong belief that a person needed to read the scriptures for himself. Therefore, he reasoned, enslaved persons must be taught to read. Davies evangelized both enslaved persons and free congregants. Eventually, by 1753, he had really made his point of doing something about teaching enslaved persons to read and write in English.[26]

---

[22] David George, "Black Loyalist. An Account of Life of Mr. David George from S. L. A. given by himself. In a conversation with Brother Rippon of London and Brother Pearce in Birmingham," http://www.blackloyalist.com/canadiandigitalcollection/documents/diaries/george_a_life.htm (accessed 15 September 2009).

[23] Woodson, *The Education of the Negro Prior to 1861*, 5, 6, 49, 81.

[24] Adrian Bacariza, "Black Education in Antebellum America," *Antebellum Slavery: Paternalism and Black Education*, 1990, http://cghs.dadeschools.net/slavery/antebellum_slavery/paternalism/black_education.htm (accessed 13 April 2009).

[25] Cornelius, *When I Can Read My Title Clear*, 57–58.

[26] Richards, "Samuel Davies," 333–78.

Liele's Literacy: Written Sermons and Prayers

Although we do not have a record of *how* George Liele learned to read and write, we do have the record that he *did* learn to read and write. Any questions about George Liele's literacy are answered as we look at the letters he exchanged with others. For example, Liele exchanged letters with John Rippon of England. "Dr. Rippon was a great friend of missions, and his church gave large sums to the home and foreign Baptist missionary societies. He projected and edited the Baptist Annual Register, to give our brethren...an organ through which they might address each other."[27]

In a letter of 1791 to Dr. Rippon, Liele reported "500 converts, 400 of whom were already baptized."[28] Further, the letter stated, "We have together with well-wishers and followers in different parts of the country, about 1,500 people."[29]

Liele formed a church on his own land in Kingston, Jamaica. When Liele arrived in Jamaica, slavery was in full force. Enslaved persons were living and working in many parts of the island, but Kingston was the center of the slave trade in the British West Indies. Enslaved persons were treated very cruelly, and there were several and frequent insurrections.[30] The fear of insurrections created an atmosphere of distrust that could have hurt George Liele's ministry, but his ministry was tolerated because of concessions he made. For example, every prayer and every sermon was inspected by authorities before they were delivered. In other words, Liele's sermons and prayers had to be written out in advance so that they could be inspected. Written! Liele had to make many compromises to maintain his church. His sermons were read and edited by white authorities to be certain that he wasn't spreading a message of revolt. During the revolution, Liele's sermons were stopped entirely for fear that enslaved persons might learn too much from a traveling preacher with contacts in white Christendom. Literate and able to discern the meaning of Scripture, Liele preached in the style and conviction of an evangelist. In the words of Hughes Oliphant Old, "George Liele was a gifted evangelistic preacher who knew how to

---

[27] William Cathcart, "John Rippon: Baptist Cameos," *Cathcart's Baptist Encyclopedia, 1881*, http://www.reformedreader.org/rippon.htm (accessed 10 April 2009).

[28] Walter H. Brooks, *The Silver Bluff Church: A History of Negro Baptist Churches in America.* (Washington DC: Press of R L Pendleton, 1910), http://docsouth.unc.edu/church/brooks/summary.html (accessed 29 December 2008).

[29] Ibid.

[30] Clement Gayle, *George Liele: Pioneer Missionary to Jamaica* (Kingston, Jamaica: Jamaica Baptist Union, 1982).

present the gospel in the language of his people."[31] The church grew despite persecution from whites.

Liele used written letters as a primary means of communicating with church authorities in London and with other African Americans who had gone into the ministry. As is evident from the content of these letters, Liele sought support from London to establish his ministry and to help it grow. Some of those letters are quoted here. This is not an exhaustive representation of his letters. Rather, these are more examples offered as proof of Liele's literacy. In the centennial publication of the history of the First African Baptist Church (which was founded by Liele), Rev. E. K. Love (1888) included several of Liele's letters.[32] Rev. Love was a minister, missionary, and writer. Rev. Love wrote, "In early to mid-year 1791, Rev. Liele wrote to Dr. John Rippon, the British editor of the Baptist Annual Register:

> My occupation is a farmer, but as the seasons in this part of the country are uncertain, I also keep a team of horses and wagon for the carrying of goods from one place to another, which I attend myself, with the assistance of my sons, and by this way of life have gained the good will of the public, who recommend me to business and to some very principal work for Government. I have a few books, some good old authors and sermons, and one large Bible that was given me by a gentleman. A good many of our members can read and are all desirous to learn. They will be very thankful for a few books to read on Sundays and other days. I agree to election, redemption, the fall of Adam, regeneration and perseverance, knowing the promise is to all who endure, in grace, faith and good works to the end, shall be saved.
>
> There is no Baptist church in this country but ours. We have purchased a piece of land at the east end of Kingston, containing three acres, for the sum of £155, currency, and on it have begun a meeting-house, 57 feet in length by 37 in breadth. We have raised the brick wall eight feet high from the foundation, and intend to have a gallery. Several gentlemen, members of the House of Assembly, and other gentlemen, have subscribed towards the building about £40. The chief part of our congregation are slaves, and their owners allow them, in common, but three or four bits per week for allowance to feed themselves, and out of so small a sum we cannot expect anything that can be of service from them; if we did, it would soon bring a scandal

---

[31] Old, *Reading and Preaching of the Scriptures*, 586.

[32] E. K. Love, *History of the First African Baptist Church from Its Organization* (Savannah GA: Morning News Print, 1888) 36.

upon religion; and the free people in our society are but poor, but they are all willing, both free and slaves, to do what they can. As for my part, I am too much entangled with the affairs of the world to go on, as I would, with my design in supporting the cause. This has, I acknowledge, been a great hindrance to the gospel in one way; but as I have endeavored to set a good example of industry before the inhabitants of the land, it has given general satisfaction another way. And, Rev. Sir, we think the Lord has put it in the power of the Baptist Societies in England to help and assist us in completing this building, which we look upon will be the greatest undertaking ever was in this country for the bringing of souls from darkness into the light of the gospel. And as the Lord has put it in your heart to inquire after us, we place all our confidence in you to make our circumstances known to the several Baptist churches in England, and we look upon you as our father, friend and brother. Within the brick wall we have a shelter in which we worship until our building can be accomplished.[33]

In a letter dated Kingston, 18 December 1791, Rev. George Liele wrote to Dr. John Rippon again. In this letter, Liele states, "The more I heard or read..." He is *writing* to Dr. Rippon and speaks of his *reading*. Reading and writing is the greater part of literacy. George Liele was a literate man. In that letter, Liele also shows that he can express his emotions very well. The reader can almost agonize as Liele describes his grave concerns about his own salvation. In part, the letter reads:

I always had a natural fear of God from my youth, and was often checked in conscience with thoughts of death, which barred me from many sins and bad company. I knew no other way at that time to hope for salvation but only in the performance of my good works.... The Rev. Mr. Matthew Moore one Sabbath afternoon, as I stood with curiosity to hear him, he unfolded all my dark views, opened my best labor and good works to me which I thought I was to be saved by, and I was convinced that I was not in the way to heaven, but in the way to hell. This state I labored under for the space of five or six months. The more I heard or read, the more I [saw that] I was condemned as a sinner before God; till at length I was brought to perceive that my life hung by a slender thread, and if it was the will of God to cut me off at that time, I was sure I should be found in hell, as sure as God was in Heaven. I saw my condemnation in my own heart, and I found no way wherein I could escape the damnation of hell, only through the

---

[33] Ibid.

merits of my dying Lord and Saviour Jesus Christ; which caused me to make intercession with Christ, for the salvation of my poor immortal soul; and I full well recollect, I requested of my Lord and Master to give me a work, I did not care how mean it was, only to try and see how good I would do it. I felt such love and joy as my tongue was not able to express. After this I declared before the congregation of believers the work which God had done for my soul, and the same minister, the Rev. Matthew Moore, baptized me, and I continued in this church about four years, till the vacuation[34]

Dr. Rippon thought that the expression "til the vacuation" was unclear, so he sought information from persons who were in positions of mentoring Liele. From their explanation, Rippon added five words to Liele's statement which made it read like this: "I continued in this church about four years, till the vacuation—*of Savannah by the British*." In addition, Dr. Rippon noted that "Brother George's words are distinguished by inverted commas, and what is not so marked, is either matter compressed, or information received from such persons to whom application had been made for it."[35] Rippon explains that the "inverted comma" is the British name for quotation marks. Rippon drew that inference from one of George Liele's letter written the same year. In it Liele stated, "Our beloved Sister Hannah Williams, during the time she was a member of the church at Savannah, until the 'vacuation, did walk as a faithful, well-beloved Christian.[36] We see the inverted comma (quote mark) used with the word 'vacuation. Rippon said that this was typical of and peculiar to Liele's writing.

George Liele did not only write to Rippon. He also wrote to others in the ministry. Writing from the West Indies in 1791, Liele said to the Reverend Joseph Cook, of South Carolina, "Brother Jesse Gaulphin, another black minister, preaches near Augusta, in South Carolina, where I used to preach."[37] Also, in a letter to Rev. Cook, written from Jamaica in 1790, Liele refers to one of these members in the following manner: "Also I received accounts from Nova Scotia of a black Baptist preacher, David George, who was a member of the church at Savannah."[38] We can see from this exchange that Liele communicated freely back and forth with others in the ministry. Sometimes he wrote to answer queries about others.

---

[34] Brooks, *The Silver Bluff Church: A History*, 11.
[35] Ibid.
[36] Ibid.
[37] Ibid.
[38] Ibid.

In answer to questions, regarding Rev. Jesse Peter, Liele replied in a letter to his London correspondent as follows: "Brother Jesse Gaulphin, another black minister, preaches near Augusta, in South Carolina, where I used to preach. He was a member of the church at Savannah."[39] We see that Liele was a point of contact for other missionaries and ministers when church officials wanted to know about them. Liele built a network and kept in touch through letter writing.

Liele kept in contact with many other Baptist pioneers such as Andrew Bryan, who was baptized by Liele, and David George through letter writing and reading. Excerpts from one letter to Dr. Rippon appear in *African American Religious History: A Documentary Witness*. Liele wrote:

> The last accounts I had from Savannah were, that the gospel had taken very great effect both there and in South Carolina. Brother Andrew Bryan, a black minister at Savannah, has TWO HUNDRED MEMBERS, in full fellowship and had certificates from their owners of ONE HUNDRED MORE, who had given in their experiences and were ready to be baptized. Also I received accounts from Nova Scotia of a black Baptist preacher, Brother David George, who was a member of the church at Savannah; he had the permission of the Governor to preach in three provinces; his members in full communion were then sixty, white and black, the gospel spreading. Brother Amos is at Providence, he writes me that the gospel has taken good effect, and is spreading greatly; he has about THREE HUNDRED MEMBERS. Brother Jessy Gaulsing, another black minister, preaches near Augusta, in South Carolina, at a place where I used to preach; he was a member of the church at Savannah, and has sixty members.[40]

Collectively, Liele wrote about their ministries, saying that "a great work is going on."[41]

Not only did Liele write letters, sermons, and prayers, he also wrote out a covenant. Noted author Timothy Paul Erdel laments, "I wish I'd been there to query Liele about his insightful Covenant, which he probably started to compile in 1777 and completed by 1784. The document begins, 'We are of the Anabaptist persuasion, because we believe it agreeable to the Scriptures.'"[42] Erdel further notes that Liele's covenant is "filled with such trademark Anabaptist practices as

---

[39] Ibid.

[40] *African American Religious History: A Documentary Witness*, ed. Milton C. Sernett (Durham NC and London: Duke University Press, 1999) 48.

[41] Brooks, *The Silver Bluff Church: A History*, 39.

[42] Timothy Paul Erdel, "I Wish I'd Been There: Negro Slavery's Prophet of Deliverance," *Mennonite Historical Bulletin* (July 2001), http://www.mcusa-archives.org/MHB/Erdel-NegroSlavery'sprophet.html (accessed 14 December 2010).

believer's baptism, foot-washing, refusing to shed blood, not swearing at all, forgoing legal suits, plain dress, and church discipline, while still displaying Liele's own editorial voice and stamp throughout, including statements on anointing the sick, slavery, and sexual purity."[43]

Liele thought it was important that others learn to read and write. To that end, Liele envisioned and put his efforts behind a free school for black children taught by a black deacon. A few adult members of his congregation also learned to read. Liele wrote that "all are desirous to learn."[44]

The conclusion that one must draw about the literacy of Rev. George Liele is that Liele was a literate man who could both read and write. When the question of Liele's literacy is raised, we have only to point to the accounts of his letters to Dr. Rippon and others in the ministry as evidence to that end. Further, Liele's sermons had to be written out so that they could be inspected before being delivered. The purpose was to allow white authorities to read over and edit sermons and prayers to be certain he wasn't spreading a message of revolt. While that was the original purpose, this inspection activity provides further proof that Liele could read and write. Liele read the Bible and interpreted Scripture to black and white congregates. He was a literate man and wanted others to be literate, too.

---

[43] Ibid.
[44] Love, *History of the First African Baptist Church*, 36.

Resources

African American Religious History: A Documentary Witness Edited by Milton C.
    Sernett. Durham NC: Duke University Press, 1999.

Bacariza, Adrian. "Black Education in Antebellum America." *Antebellum Slavery:
    Paternalism and Black Education*. 1990.
    http://cghs.dadeschools.net/slavery/antebellum_slavery/paternalism/bla
    ck_education.htm (accessed 13 April 2009).

*Black Loyalist. An Account of the Life of Mr. David George from S. L. A. given by
    himself. In a conversation with Brother Rippon of London and Brother Pearce in
    Birmingham*. 2000.
    http://www.blackloyalist.com/canadiandigitalcollection/documents/diari
    es/george_a_life.htm (accessed 15 September 2009).

Brooks, Walter H. *The Silver Bluff Church: A History of Negro Baptist Churches in
    America*. Washington DC: Press of R L Pendleton, 1910.
    http://docsouth.unc.edu/church/brooks/summary.html (accessed 29
    December 2008).

Cashin, Edward J. *Old Springfield: Race and Religion in Augusta, Georgia*. Augusta
    GA: Springfield Village Park Foundation, Inc., 1995.

Cathcart, William. "John Rippon: Baptist Cameos." *Cathcart's Baptist Encyclopedia,
    1881*. http://www.reformedreader.org/rippon.htm (accessed 10 April
    2009).

Cornelius, Janet Duitsman. *When I Can Read My Title Clear: Literacy, Slavery, and
    Religion in the Antebellum South*. Columbia: University of South Carolina
    Press, 1991.

Erdel, Timothy Paul. "I Wish I'd Been There: Negro Slavery's Prophet of
    Deliverance," Historical Committee & Archives of the Mennonite Church.
    Mennonite Historical Bulletin (July 2001). http://www.mcusa-
    archives.org/MHB/Erdel-NegroSlavery'sprophet.html (accessed 13 August
    2009).

Gayle, Clement. *George Liele: Pioneer Missionary to Jamaica*. Kingston, Jamaica:
    Jamaica Baptist Union, 1982.

Holden, Stephen. *Literacy: A Weapon for a Slave* (1997).
    http://query.nytimes.com/gst/fullpage.html?res=9A02E7D8173DF932A057
    52C0A961958260 (accessed 30 April 2008).

Jordan, Winthrop D. *White Over Black: American Attitudes Toward the Negro, 1550–
    1812*. New York: W. W. Norton & Company, 1968.

Love, E. K. *History of the First African Baptist Church from Its Organization. January
    20, 1788, to July 1st, 1888*. Savannah GA: *The Morning News Print* (1888).

http://www.reformedreader.org/history/love/toc.htm (accessed 19 January 2009).

Old, Hughes Oliphant. *The Reading and Preaching of the Scriptures in the Worship of the Christian Church: The Modern Age*. Grand Rapids MI: Eerdmans, 2007.

Richards, Jeffrey H. "Samuel Davies and the Transatlantic Campaign for Slave Literacy in Virginia," *Virginia Magazine of History and Biography*. 111/4 (2003). http://www.vahistorical.org/publications/abstract_richards.htm (accessed 13 May 2009).

Sambol-Tosco, Kimberly. *Slavery and the Making of America: The Slave Experience: Education, Arts, and Culture*. (2004). Accessed 30 April 2008. http://www.pbs.org/wnet/slavery/experience/education/history2.html.

Williams, Heather Andrea. *Self-Taught: African American Education in Slavery and Freedom*. Chapel Hill: University of North Carolina Press, 2005.

Wilson, Kenneth G. "Inverted Commas." In *The Columbia Guide to Standard American English*. New York: Columbia University Press, 1993. http://www.bartleby.com/68/12/3412.html (accessed 10 December 2010).

Woodson, Carter G. *The Education of the Negro Prior to 1861: A History of the Education of the Colored People of the United States from the Beginning of Slavery to the Civil War*. New York: G. P. Putnam's Sons, 1915.

George Liele and Phillis Wheatley:
Pioneering Preacher and Poet

George Liele (1750–1825) and Phillis Wheatley (1755–1784) are two African-American geniuses born during the eighteenth century, when America was struggling for its identity as a country. The nation was attempting to free itself from dependence on England. After the beginning of the Revolutionary War in 1775, and its ending in 1783, a new republic was formed. Both Liele and Wheatley developed their talent during the turbulent period before the national struggle. Although they were enslaved, the circumstances of war and enslavement did not prevent them from becoming pioneers who contributed to American culture in their respective areas—Liele in religion and Wheatley in poetry.

Converted to Christianity, George Liele became a well-respected evangelist and leader in the Baptist movement in the United States and Jamaica. Born in Africa and brought to America as a slave, Phillis Wheatley became a renowned poet in America and England. How did these humble African Americans rise to prominence under the conditions of slavery and war? What circumstances thwarted or contributed to their success? Above all, what is their legacy to America today?

Before determining how George Liele and Phillis Wheatley became prominent, a brief discussion of American unrest during the revolutionary period will shed some light on their milieu. The rumblings of the Revolutionary War, and later its occurrence, put the country in turmoil for some time. Some of the key events that signaled war were the Boston Massacre (1770) and the death of Crispus Attucks, the first person to shed blood in the cause of freedom during this period. This event was recognized widely in Boston and commemorated by one of Wheatley's non-extant poems: "On the Affray in King-Street, on the Evening of the 5th of March." The Boston Tea Party (1773) and the Minutemen's clash with British soldiers (1775)—"the shot heard 'round the world," celebrated in Ralph Waldo Emerson's poem, "The Concord Hymn"—gave the Patriots the courage to declare war. Finally, the Battle of Bunker Hill, an early major battle after the official declaration of war, strengthened the Patriots' resolve to expel the British from the colonies. These events created much tension in the country among the people. There were Loyalists (Tories) who kept their allegiance to Great Britain, and there were Patriots fighting for American independence. Then there were the indentured servants and African Americans who were not so concerned with either country's politics, but rather, their own individual freedom. Since African Americans were excited by the ideas of "liberty," "freedom," "unalienable rights," and "created equal," they became Patriots or Loyalists. Seeking a life different from human bondage, enslaved people realized that their loyalty was not to a particular place or to a particular people, but to a principle. Liele and Wheatley certainly set their hearts on the ideals of freedom.

Despite the bleak conditions caused by slavery and war in Colonial America, Liele's and Wheatley's religious and intellectual environment shaped the talents responsible for their successful contributions to American culture. Because their pioneering work in religion and literature is little known and sparsely appreciated, this comparative study of the two aims to enrich the existing knowledge in these areas. Therefore, in this essay, I discuss similarities and differences in Liele's and Wheatley's religious and intellectual development from their status of enslaved persons to that of contributing citizens.

The conditions of servitude for George Liele and Phillis Wheatley were different, yet similar. George Liele, the son of enslaved parents Nancy and Liele, was born in Virginia. He knew very little about his early life except that he lived in several parts of the country and finally settled in New Georgia.[1] Liele became the property of Henry Sharp, a prosperous businessman who settled in Burke County, Georgia, near Augusta on the Savannah River. At the time Sharp settled in Georgia (1765), it was not a slave-holding territory. Because of this fact, one Georgia historian speculates that Sharp may have freed George Liele to avoid being prosecuted under the Slave Act of 1770.[2] Whatever the reason for his decision, Henry Sharp is believed to have emancipated Liele between 1773 and 1779; however, Liele accompanied Sharp into battle against the Patriots and remained with him until Sharp's death in 1779.

Whereas George Liele was born in slavery, Phillis Wheatley (1755–1784) was neither born in America nor in slavery. Life began for her in the Senegal-Gambia area of West Africa. Wheatley's arrival in Boston from Africa is described in

---

[1] John Rippon, *The Baptist Annual Register for 1790–1793; 1794, 1797, and part of 1793* (London) 332–44, 540–43. John Rippon first published Liele's letters in *The Baptist Annual Register 1790–1793*. I have used the republished version found in "Letters Sharing the Rise and Progress of the Early Negro Church of Georgia and the West Indies," *The Journal of Negro History* 1 (January 1916): 69–92. This issue, edited by Carter G. Woodson, furnishes a clear printing of the letters. The 1791 letter will be documented as "Liele to Rippon, 18 December 1791."

[2] Christopher Brent Ballew, *The Impact of African American Antecedents on the Baptist Foreign Movement 1782–1825* (Lewiston NY: Edwin Mellen Press, 2005) 5, 9. Georgia's Slave Act allowed religious services among slaves, but they were restricted, and masters were fined if restrictions were violated.

detail by one of her biographers, William Robinson. According to him, on July 1761, a slave ship named the "Phillis" sailed into Boston Harbor, carrying commercial goods along with a small group of slaves. The slaves were advertised in Boston as "a parcel of likely Negroes," imported from Africa, "cheap for cash or short credit."[3] It was from this cheap, bedraggled group of human cargo that Susanna Wheatley chose Phillis Wheatley, a small, frail, half-naked child clad only in a piece of dirty carpet. Susanna Wheatley was looking for a young girl whom she could train as a personal servant. She chose Phillis (despite her sickly appearance), because of the little girl's "modest demeanor" and "interesting facial features." With two front teeth missing, Phillis Wheatley's biographers estimate her age to have been seven or eight and noted that Mrs. Wheatley called her Phillis, the name of the ship that brought her to America.[4]

As in the case of George Liele, there is very little information about Wheatley's parents or how she became a slave or what her life had been like in Africa. Similar to Liele, Wheatley seems not to have remembered much about her life before being enslaved; however, John Shields believes that Phillis Wheatley never forgot Africa.[5] Indeed, one is inclined to agree with Shields when Wheatley writes these lines taken from "To the Right Honorable William, Earl of Dartmouth:"

From Native clime, when seeming cruel Fate
Me snatch'd from Africa's fancy'd happy seat
Impetuous—Ah! What bitter Pangs molest,
What sorrows labour'd in the parent's breast?
That, more than stone, never soft compassion mov'd.
Who from its father seiz'd his much beloved.
Such, such my case. And can I then but pray
Others may never feel tyrannic sway?[6]

Written in 1772, the entire poem praises the desire for freedom in the colonies, but Phillis Wheatley skillfully uses the above lines to state her own situation, perhaps. These lines suggest that she was abruptly and unexpectedly taken from Africa (snatch'd). Further, the poet remembers her father's agony

---

[3] William Robinson, *Phillis Wheatley and Her Writings* (New York: Garland Publishing, 1984) 5.

[4] Ibid., 5.

[5] John C. Shields, *Phillis Wheatley's Poetics of Liberation: Background and Contexts* (Knoxville: University of Tennessee Press, 2008) 97–99.

[6] Julian D. Mason, *The Poems of Phillis Wheatley* (Chapel Hill: University of North Carolina Press, 1989) 148–50.

(bitter pangs), the close relationship with her father (siez'd his much beloved), the abductor's lack of compassion, and, at the same time, the heavy burden that must have lingered in her father's heart after her abduction (that more than stone ne'er soft compassion mov'd). If Wheatley imagined the whole scene, she definitely wants the reader to have a vivid picture of what her experience might have been. The abduction is more personalized by the poet's use of "I," "me," "my" and the phrase "such, such, my case." This poem is one of the clearest suggestions of Wheatley's African entry into slavery. Notice there is only a reference to the father in the poem; Wheatley's first biographer, Mary Odell, though, reports that the poet's only memory of Africa was seeing her mother "pour out water before the rising sun every morning."[7] This poem's beginning "Hail happy Day/when smiling like the morn" very well may be an example of Wheatley's memory of her mother performing a religious ritual. The image of the morning and the sun are recurring themes in Wheatley's poetry, which help establish the fact that Phillis Wheatley retained thoughts of her African home.[8]

Liele and Wheatley both were influenced heavily by their Christian environment. This environment included a religious home life and the influence of the Great Awakening evangelist George Whitefield. During Whitefield's numerous visits to America between 1738 and 1770, he traveled throughout the South and New England colonies, preaching the gospel of Jesus Christ. Both Liele and Wheatley would have been influenced indirectly or directly by him.

Liele was probably introduced to Christianity by his religious father. In the 1791 letter published by John Rippon, Liele reports that he was told by everyone who knew his father that "he was the only Black person who knew the Lord in a spiritual way."[9] In the same letter, Liele relates the beginnings of his moral consciousness and deep religious inclinations: "I always had a natural fear of God from my youth, and was often checked in conscience with thoughts of death, which barred me from many sins and bad company." At first, Liele thought that doing "good works" was his key to salvation, but this view changed when he heard a sermon by the Reverend Matthew Moore, a white Baptist preacher on the Galphin Plantation in South Carolina. Liele testifies, "I was convinced that I was not in the way to heaven, but in the way to hell." Thus, the young Liele seriously petitions Christ in prayer for the "salvation of his immortal

---

[7] G. Herbert Renfro, *Life and Works of Phillis Wheatley*. Reprint (Miami FL: Mnemosyne Publishing, 1969). For a 1773 letter in which Phillis recalls the Middle Passage, see Michael Harper and Anthony Walton, *The Vintage Book of African American Poetry* (New York: Vintage Books, 2000) 172–73.

[8] Shields, *Poetics of Liberation*, 101.

[9] Liele to Rippon, 18 December 1791, Kingston, Jamaica. Perhaps the "spiritual way" means the father was converted to Christianity.

soul," and soon afterwards, becomes converted to the Christian faith.[10] Converted in Moore's church, Liele describes his joy: "I felt such love and joy as my tongue was not able to express. After this, I declared before the congregation of believers the work which God had done for my soul, and the same Rev. Matthew Moore baptized me and I continued in this church about four years till the vacuation."[11] Although a slave, at least part of the time that he was with Sharp, it is clear that Liele was allowed to hear preaching. His conversion and baptism by the Reverend Matthew Moore suggest that Liele's foundation in faith started in his home environment. Henry Sharp was the Reverend Matthew Moore's brother-in-law, and his plantation in Georgia was near the South Carolina border. Both Sharp and George Galphin allowed their slaves to attend church and religious meetings.[12]

Similar to Liele, Phillis Wheatley's religious training began in her home environment. She was introduced to Christianity by Susanna Wheatley, who became a surrogate mother to her. Embracing the teachings of Christ, Susanna promoted charities to uplift Indians and blacks, even though she kept slaves.[13] Nevertheless, Bible study and learning to read and write were firm components of Phillis Wheatley's acculturation to Boston and New England. She attended Boston's Old South Meeting House with the Wheatleys. For much of the poet's youth, the Reverend George Sewell was the pastor and religious monitor in her efforts to become a Congregationalist and a member of the Old South Congregational Church. Although Sewell, who died in 1769, was Wheatley's monitor, he did not baptize her. John Shields makes an interesting observation explaining why Sewell did not perform this ritual of acceptance, which would have made Wheatley a full-fledged member of the church. Shields suggests that Phillis Wheatley's readings and use of classical writings might have caused Sewell to think that his protégé was not ready for baptism.[14] In the poem "Atheism" (1767), written when she was thirteen or fourteen, Wheatley raises questions that suggest her unbelief and her passion for classical symbols.

Where now shall I begin this Spacious Field
To Tell what Curses—Unbelief doth Yield,
Thou That Doest, daily, feel his hand & rod,

---

[10] Ibid.

[11] Ibid.

[12] Carter G. Woodson, *The History of the Black Church* (Washington DC: Associated Publishers, 1921) 42–44.

[13] Mason, *The Poems of Phillis Wheatley*, 5.

[14] Shields, *Poetics of Liberation*, 129.

And dar'st deny the Essence of a God...[15]

As Shields notes, this early poem might have resulted from a catechism assignment in which the learner tries to convince herself and teacher that there is a God and there are consequences associated with being an atheist.[16]

Contrary to Liele's account of his acceptance of Christian dogma when he was young, Wheatley seems to have had trouble with Christian concepts in her youth. She could not resist her love for classical paganism. Even her awareness of the existence of God, as seen in this poem, does not deter her use of references to the pagan gods of the sun and moon.

Look thou above and see who made ye Sky
Nothing more Lucid to an Atheist's eye...
Mark rising Phebus [the sun] when he spreads his ray,
And his commission is to Rule ye day,
At Night keep watch & see a Cynthia [the moon] bright,
And her Commission is to rule the Night.[17]

Concluding her poem with the names Phebus and Cynthia, Greek pagan gods, could not have pleased the Reverend Sewell or perhaps some other Christians of the day, especially most of the strict Congregationalists. But finally, in 1771, Phillis Wheatley, at sixteen, was baptized by the Reverend Samuel Cooper, with whom she was well acquainted as the pastor of a neighboring church. Cooper was a friend of the Wheatley's and substitute pastor of the Congregationalist Old South Church after Sewell's death.[18]

Perhaps other reasons for the differences in Liele's and Wheatley's attitudes toward Christianity lay in the differences in their intellectual environment. Compared with the plantation life of Liele, Wheatley's Boston was certainly more cosmopolitan. While Liele's early mentors were Baptist preachers influenced by the exhortations of Wesley and Whitefield, Phillis's early influences, other than the Wheatleys, were prominent, well-educated neighbors who were ministers, poets, and politicians. Some of these were the Reverend Ebenezer Pemberton, the

---

[15] John Shields, *Collected Works of Phillis Wheatley* (New York: Oxford University Press, 1988) 197. This is variant 1, the earliest of several versions of the poem. For a full discussion of this poem, see Sondra O'Neale's "A Slave's Subtle War: Phillis Wheatley's Use of biblical Myth and Symbol" in *Early American Literature* 21 (1986) 145–63. O'Neale argues that Wheatley protested slavery in her poetry by the subtle use of biblical and classical imagery.

[16]Shields, *Poetics of Liberation*, 129–30.

[17] Shields, *Collected Works*, 199.

[18] Mason, *The Poems of Phillis Wheatley*, 5.

Scottish-Presbyterian; the Reverend John Moorehead, the eloquent, poetry-writing Patriot; the Reverend Samuel Cooper, who baptized Wheatley; the very influential clergyman and friend Matthew Byles; and Thomas Hutchinson, governor of the Massachusetts Colony.[19] Although Mrs. Wheatley and her daughter taught Phillis Wheatley how to read and write, recent critics believed that Matthew Byles taught her language of Latin and literature and cultivated her love for the classics.[20]

Clearly, Liele and Wheatley were shaped by different cultural and religious environments. It is interesting, however, that both of them found common ground, of a sort, in George Whitefield's teachings. Whitefield and John Wesley, both fiery evangelists from England, are associated with the Great Awakening, a religious movement of the eighteenth century. The Awakening of Whitefield's day emphasized preaching as opposed to ritual and liturgy, salvation by faith rather than good works alone, and a sense of responsibility for the religious development of Indians and slaves.[21] Liele became acquainted with Whitefield's ideas through the preaching of Matthew Moore and Wait Palmer, both ardent followers of Whitefield. Thus, Liele's conviction that confession and conversion, and not works alone, are the keys to salvation, is a reflection of Whitefield's thinking. Also, Liele's teaching slaves how to read and write is what Whitefield attempted to do in Georgia and South Carolina.

Phillis Wheatley had a more direct relationship with George Whitefield than Liele. The evangelist visited Boston between 1763 and 1765, several years after Phillis became a member of the Wheatley family. Therefore it is very logical to conclude that she would have met and perhaps conversed with Whitefield on more than one occasion. Although enslaved, Wheatley's creative ability as a poet would have been reason enough for this introduction. Because Susanna Wheatley was a great admirer of Whitefield and became engaged in the mission work with which the evangelist was associated, it is most probable that Wheatley could have heard him preach as well.[22] These speculations are given even more credibility when one considers the elegy she wrote in honor of Whitefield's death

---

[19] Robinson, *Phillis Wheatley: Writings*, 19.

[20] Shields, *Poetics of Liberation*, 128.

[21] Alfred L. Pugh, "The Great Awakening and Baptist Beginnings in Colonial Georgia: The Bahama Islands and Jamaica 1739–1833," *American Baptist Quarterly* 26/4 (Winter 2007): 358.

[22] Shields, *Poetics of Liberation*, 116; Mason, *The Poems of Phillis Wheatley*, 3. According to Shields and Mason, Wheatley had several opportunities to meet Whitefield. After visiting the Old South Meeting House (the church the Wheatleys attended) and seeing posters of Whitefield and Wheatley prominently displayed at the entrance, I am convinced that the poet heard Whitefield preach.

in 1770. "On the Death of the Rev. Mr. George Whitefield" begins by addressing him as a saint who has ascended to an "immortal home." The speaker refers to his sermons as if she were a listening observer: "Thy sermons in unequall'd accents flow'd;/And every bosom with devotion glow'd." Then Wheatley launches into the core of the poem by letting us hear a mock sermon:

"Take him, ye wretched, for your only good;"
"Take him, ye starving sinners, for your food;"
"Ye thirsty, come to this life-giving stream;"
"Ye preachers, take him for your joyful theme;"
"Take him my dear Americans, he said"
"Be your complaints on his kind bosom laid;"
"Take him, ye *Africans*, he longs for you;"
"*Imperial Savior* is his title due;"
"Washed in the fountain of redeeming blood,"
"You shall be sons, and kings and priests of God."[23]

Here, Wheatley preaches a sermon as she memorializes the evangelist who reached all people. One cannot overlook Wheatley's reference to Africans and the impartiality of the Savior (Jesus Christ), which is reminiscent of the Great Awakening. Each line is enclosed by quotes, suggesting that Wheatley was an apt listener who might have repeated some phrases that she heard directly from Whitefield. Later in the poem, the poet expresses condolences to the "Countess" on behalf of New England: "Great Countess, we Americans revere thy name and mingle in thy grief sincere." These words must have been exceedingly touching to the countess, as well as this line: "[T]he Orphans mourn...their more than father will no more return." The passage refers to Whitefield's request that the countess take over the orphanage that he established in Georgia. The poem, dedicated to the Countess of Huntingdon and reproduced on a broadside, was sold in America and England. It gained Wheatley much popularity in both places. Although Liele and Wheatley never met and did not share the same religious faith, their religious experience was united somewhat by Whitefield's preaching. As enslaved persons, they were encouraged by the principles of personal and spiritual freedom found in Christ. Although Whitefield did not share Wesley's profound antipathy to slavery, he did recognize the innate intellectual equality of Africans, which was a different view from the prevailing ideas of Anglicans and other Christians.[24]

---

[23] Shields, *Collected Works*, 22.
[24] Sylvia R. Frey and Betty Wood, *Come Shouting to Zion* (Chapel Hill: University of North Carolina Press, 1998) 92.

The general idea about black people during the eighteenth century was that Africans and African Americans were intellectually inferior. The thinking was that slaves probably had souls, but they did not have brains. Phillis Wheatley understood this view when she wrote the poem "On Being Brought from Africa to America," one of her earliest works:

Some view our sable race with scornful eye;
"Their Colour is a diabolic dye";
Remember Christians, Negros, black as Cain,
May be refin'd and join the angelic train.[25]

A young Phillis penned these bold lines at the age of fourteen. She realized that blacks were not accepted by some Christians, who believed that blacks did not have souls, morals, or good minds. But Wheatley refutes this notion, and by referring to Cain, suggests that black people have souls and that they can be redeemed.

Wheatley shared Whitefield's and Wesley's view that Africans had the capabilities to be educated. Hence, Whitefield insisted that all children, including those enslaved, were sinners from birth but were "naturally capable" of being improved. Despite this epistolary written in 1740, by the mid-1740s, Whitefield advocated legalizing slavery in Georgia and eventually owned slaves himself.[26] Even though the Great Awakening saw religious reform that invited more participation of slaves, C. Eric Lincoln reports that when the Colonial Era ended, most blacks were "untaught and unchurched." He contends that those slaves who were allowed to attend or join white churches were given no opportunity to realize the complete Christian dignity and personal freedom inherent in the whole gospel. In the white churches, they were assigned a "place," and even in churches in Massachusetts, they had no vote.[27] The conditions for black Christians cited above were the general circumstances under which Liele and Wheatley began their careers in America. Luckily, both Liele and Wheatley had the extraordinary support of their owners, who allowed them to develop their talents as evangelist and poet. Henry Sharp permitted Liele to travel with him to preach to people on other plantations and to be baptized and ordained. The Wheatleys taught Phillis to read and write, allowed her to be baptized, to travel to England, and to associate with Boston intellectuals. These kinds of privileges were denied the average bondperson.

---

[25] Shields, *Collected Works*, 18.
[26] Frey and Wood, *Come Shouting*, 93.
[27] C. Eric Lincoln, "The Development of Black Religion in America" in *African American Religious Studies*, ed. Gayraud S. Wilmore (Durham NC: Duke University Press, 1989) 19.

Liele's ministry began immediately after his conversion and baptism by the Reverend Matthew Moore, who became his guide. Liele's career in the ministry can be divided into two phases: his work in the United States and in Jamaica. This essay focuses on his American experience.

George Liele began as a probationary minister in Silver Bluff, South Carolina. Desiring to prove to himself that he had been called to preach and that he understood his obligation to God, he began to instruct other enslaved persons in the word of God.[28] Seeing his good work among his own people, Liele's white brethren invited him to deliver a trial sermon. This group was composed of the men who would decide whether or not Liele should be ordained as a Baptist minister. In addition to the Reverend Matthew Moore and Liele's owner, Henry Sharp, the group probably included other Separatist Baptists in the area, such as Wait Palmer, Daniel Marshall, and his son, Alexander Marshall.[29] After the successful sermon, George Liele was ordained and became the first black ordained Baptist minister in the world. Liele preached and baptized mostly slaves in the area along the Savannah River between Augusta and Silver Bluff, South Carolina. Walter H. Brooks stated that the Silver Bluff Church that Liele helped establish is important because it proves that blacks in the South were the first to start their own churches, rather than the blacks in the North, who have been credited with this accomplishment. The Silver Bluff Church was established in 1774, long before any black church in the North was founded.[30]

Unfortunately, the dearth of information about Liele's important ministry at Silver Bluff makes it difficult to judge the effect of his preaching directly. Nevertheless, one of his protégés, the Reverend David George, gives valuable insight about the impact of his sermons and his counseling: "His sermon was very suitable [on the subject] 'Come unto me all that labor and are heavy laden and I will give you rest.'" Recounting the effect of the sermon, George indicates that the words seemed exclusively for him: "When it [the sermon] was ended, I went to him [Liele] and told him I was so; that I was weary and heavy laden, and that the grace of God had given me rest." Indeed his whole discourse "seemed for me."[31] The Scripture that George describes is taken from the New Testament (Matthew 11:28), and David George's account of the effect gives us a glimpse of the powerful impact Liele must have had on those who heard him, especially the

---

[28] Liele to Rippon, 18 December 1791.

[29] Pugh, "The Great Awakening," 369.

[30] Walter H. Brooks, *The Silver Bluff Church: A History of Negro Baptist Churches in America* (Washington DC: Press of R.L. Pendleton, 1910). Brooks contends that there were no black churches in the North until the beginning of the nineteenth century, even though there were black Baptists in Rhode Island before 1774.

[31] Ballew, *Impact*, 17.

enslaved. They would have been encouraged, most likely, by Liele's sermon as opposed to a typical plantation sermon preached to the slaves in Maryland in 1743: "I now come to lay before you your duties to your master and mistresses on earth. And for this you have one general rule always to carry in your minds: and that is, to do all services for them as if you did it for God himself."[32]

The plantation preacher continues, accusing the enslaved persons of their bad habits of lying, stealing, and of being wasteful, impudent, and stubborn. The sermon states specifically that these abominations or faults were against God, who put "masters and mistresses" over the enslaved to stand in for Him.[33] Obviously, Liele's sermons did not take the same tone. More than likely, Liele would have continued the Matthew Scriptures with the verses "take my yoke upon you and learn of me, for I am meek and lowly in heart and ye shall find rest unto your souls" (Matthew 11:29).[34] The slaves would have identified with the Savior and found hope in these words, and some, as David George and Jesse Peters were, would have been inspired. David George and Jesse (Galphin) Peters became ministers as a result of their contact with Liele. On other occasions, George heard Liele preach "in a corn field" in Silver Bluff. After being ashamed to pray in public and "pouring his heart out to the Lord" about the matter, David George asked Brother George Liele for "instructions." Liele's advice was this: "In the intervals of service, you should engage in prayer with the friends."[35] The friends were the enslaved, and Liele himself was strengthened and inspired by extensive contact with his people. At another time, when Liele was preaching, David George was spiritually moved to pray: "I felt the same desire, and after he had done, I began in prayer—It gave me great relief, and I went home with a desire for nothing else but to talk to the brothers and sisters about the Lord."[36]

Although David George was influenced by Liele, he was baptized by Wait Palmer, whose ministry at Silver Bluff seemed to have coincided with Liele's. Palmer baptized eight people, including Jesse (Galphin) Peter, David George, and his wife at the Mill stream on or near the Galphin Plantation.[37]

Liele faced some difficulties with his ministry in America. Although Henry Sharp allowed Liele to preach freely to slaves on the Galphin plantation, Liele and one of his mentors, Wait Palmer, ran into trouble. In 1775 planters became wary of plantation preachers and Galphin was no exception. Liele and Palmer

---

[32] Lincoln, "The Development of Black Religion," 18.

[33] Ibid.

[34] "New Testament," *Holy Bible, King James Version,* Riverside Large Print Reference Edition (Nashville TN: Royal Publishers, Inc., 1971) 14.

[35] Ballew, *Impact,* 18.

[36] Ibid.

[37] Brooks, *The Silver Bluff Church: A History,* 3–8.

were no longer permitted to preach there. Having been baptized and made an elder, David George became the leader after Liele left. He states that he acted in that capacity until the war, "when the ministers were not allowed to come amongst us, lest they should furnish us with too much knowledge."[38] Planters were afraid of itinerant preachers because of the possibility of financial loss if their slaves were to run away to the British. Liele would have been suspected since Sharp, his owner, and probably Wait Palmer were Loyalists. The meeting in the cornfield with David George referenced above certainly suggests that Liele and Palmer lost the privilege to preach at Galphin Plantation.[39]

The Revolutionary War interrupted Liele's evangelistic efforts at Silver Bluff and Savannah and, eventually, he left the country. When the British arrived in Savannah in 1778, the Revolutionary War intensified in Georgia, and there were far more battles between the Loyalists and the Patriots than before. Henry Sharp, Liele's owner and a long-time Loyalist, became a major in the British army in charge of Burke County, Georgia. In 1779 a bloody battle occurred between the Loyalists and the Patriots, and Sharp was killed. During the British and Patriot occupation of Augusta, Liele, freed from slavery in 1777 by Sharp, went to Savannah, and so did David George. Liele and George worked together in Savannah, and Liele established the first Baptist church there. Liele's statement in the letter published by Rippon that he preached in "Brountonland [Brampton] and Yamacraw near Savannah"[40] authenticates his efforts in that area. Ballew believes that Brampton Plantation was the exact place because "Brountonland" cannot be found on the map. The Brampton plantation seems logical also because Jonathan Bryan, the last proprietor of the plantation, was the owner of Andrew Bryan, who became a prominent minister in Savannah after he was baptized by George Liele. An account of the baptism and Liele's last performance of evangelism in America is reported by Johnny Clarke and published by Rippon:

> Brother Andrew was one of the black hearers of George Liele.... Prior to his departure to Jamaica, he came up from Tybee river where departing vessels frequently lay ready for sea and baptized our Brother Andrew, with a wench by the name of Hagar, both belonging

---

[38] Ibid.

[39] Walter H. Brooks, "The Priority of the Silver Bluff Church," *Journal of Negro History* 1 (January 1916): 69–92. Referring to a letter from Stephen Bull to Col. Henry Laurens, president of the Council of Safety, Charleston, South Carolina, 14 March 1776, Brooks reports that Negroes along the Savannah River were abandoning their masters, in "scores and hundreds" to the detriment of their owners and the cause of American Independence.

[40] Ballew, *Impact*, 15, and Liele to Rippon, 18 December 1791.

to Jonathan Bryan. These were the last performances of Brother Liele in these quarters.[41]

W. L. Kilpatrick, tracing the history of the first black church in Savannah, observes that George Liele worked "efficiently" among his own color, collecting material for the organization of a church.[42] Before baptizing Bryan, Liele's ministry in Yamacraw yielded quite a number of converts. Yamacraw was originally an area with a large Indian population. During the time that Liele was there, it is conceivable that some Indians or their descendants were still in the vicinity even though it was described as being predominately black. The Yamacraw and Brampton experience was very important to Liele, perhaps because Sharp had liberated him by then, or perhaps, because Liele was comfortable in British territory and again felt free to preach. At any rate, Liele's evangelism in America came to an end in 1782 when the British fled Savannah. To escape re-enslavement by Sharp's relatives, Liele was befriended by Moses Kirkland, a British colonel who paid Liele's passage as an indentured servant on a British ship bound for Jamaica. Once they reached Jamaica, Kirkland was responsible for procuring employment for Liele with the governor of Jamaica. When the allotted years of his indenture ended, Liele, true to his word, repaid Kirkland.

Because Wheatley began writing poetry at a young age, one might conclude that she was a born poet. However, we may say that her career began when she received national recognition with the publication of the elegy honoring Whitefield discussed earlier in this paper. She wrote proposals for three books of poetry, but only one collection was ever published. As in the case of Liele's ordination, Phillis Wheatley's proposal for a book of poetry had to undergo the scrutiny of a panel of white citizens in Boston. Different from Liele's panel of clergymen, who judged his oral ability to preach the gospel, the group judging Phillis Wheatley was not there to critique the merit of her poetry, but rather, to validate the fact that Phillis, a black teenager, was capable of writing the poems. In other words, as Henry Louis Gates puts it, the panel was there to answer the big question: Was a Negro capable of producing literature?[43] As the young poet sat before eighteen men answering questions about her writing, she must have wondered if she would have to produce a poem on the spot, as she had done for Thomas Woolridge, the emissary of the Earl of Dartmouth, who wrote this account after visiting Wheatley's mistress:

---

[41] Ballew, *Impact*, 28.

[42] Ibid., 14 (note 44).

[43] Henry Louis Gates, Jr. *The Trials of Phillis Wheatley* (New York: Basic Civitas Books, 2003) 16.

I found by conversing with the African that she was no impostor; I asked if she could write on any subject? She said yes; we had just heard of your Lordship's appointment; I gave her your name, which she was acquainted with. She immediately wrote a rough copy of the enclosed address and letter.... I was astonished and could hardly believe my own eyes. I was present while she wrote and can attest that it is her production.[44]

The eighteen men who met with Phillis Wheatley were as equally as impressed with her as Woolridge, but certainly not astonished. Several of them were her Boston neighbors, who not only knew of her capabilities but helped cultivate them. Nevertheless, they obliged the printer, who needed their distinguished signatures to authenticate Wheatley's writings. The panel composed a note and each one of them signed it. A portion of the note follows:

We whose Names are underwritten, do assure the World, that the poems specified in the following pages were...written by Phillis a young Negro girl, who was but a few years since brought an unculti-vated Barbarian from Africa...and now under the disadvantage of serving as a slave in a Family in this Town. She has been examined and is thought qualified to write them.[45]

When the 1772 proposal advertised in the Boston *Censor* from February to April failed to attract the 300 subscribers necessary for a Boston publication, Susanna Wheatley and her friends began efforts to have Wheatley's poems published in England. Susanna's contacts with Selena Hastings, the Countess of Huntingdon, and other prominent Methodists in London were most helpful in getting a 1773 proposal to a British press. Needless to say, there were some changes made to make the book attractive to a British audience. Julian Mason notes that some of the poems were too political (i.e., supportive of the Revolution) and others carried prominent names recognizable by Americans but not by the British. The 1773 edition includes the dedication to the Countess of Huntingdon along with more religious poems than were first proposed.[46] Finally, on 1 April 1773, *Poems on Various Subjects, Religious and Moral* was published in London by Archibald Bell Bookseller. Although Phillis Wheatley visited London and was well-received by British and American statesmen, including Benjamin Franklin, she did not meet the Countess. Her prearranged visits to meet the countess and the Queen of England were canceled because Wheatley had to return to Boston to attend her dying mistress. Nevertheless, the young poet's trip

---

[44] Robinson, *Phillis Wheatley: Writings*, 329.
[45] Shields, *Collected Works*, Preface.
[46] Mason, *The Poems of Phillis Wheatley, 186–87*; Shields, *Poetics of Liberation*, 8–10.

to England paid off; her book was published there, and she received her freedom from the Wheatleys in 1773, undoubtedly as a result of international sentiments and pressure.

Since its publication, *Poems on Various Subjects* has generated much critical response. Gates and Shields point out that much of Wheatley's criticism in the eighteenth century and later was not literary but socio-anthropological.[47] Publishing at a time when the thinking of Hume, Kant, Locke, and Jefferson were much respected, Wheatley and her poetry were used to prove or disprove the innate ability of blacks to produce high art. Writing poetry was considered the highest intellectual act; if blacks could create poetry, then they belonged to the same species as whites. Consider Hume's statement: "I am apt to suspect the Negroes...to be naturally inferior to the whites...no ingenious manufacturers amongst them, no arts, no sciences."[48] Kant's ideas were even worse: "The Negroes of Africa have by nature no feeling that arises above the trifling. So fundamental is the difference between these two races of man, and it appears to be as great in mental capacities as in color."[49] Although Benjamin Rush cited Phillis's poetry as proof of the mental ability of Africans to equal Europeans, Thomas Jefferson disagreed: "Religion indeed has produced a Phyllis [*sic*] but it could not produce a poet. The compositions published under her name are beneath the dignity of criticism."[50] Despite Jefferson's unkind review, some of Wheatley's early critics believed her book praiseworthy. Voltaire called her poems very good English verse. President George Washington praised her poems, and Gilbert Imlay even goes so far as to challenge Jefferson to show him a white person who had written more beautiful lines than those found in Wheatley's poem "On Imagination."[51] One needs to read at least one stanza of "On Imagination" to gain some recognition of Phillis Wheatley at her best:

Imagination! Who can sing thy force?
Or who describe the swiftness of the course?
Soaring through the air to find the bright abode?
Th' empyreal palace of the thund'ring God,
We on pinions can surpass the wind
And leave the rolling universe behind:
From star to star the mental optics rove,

---

[47] Gates, *The Trials of Phillis Wheatley*, 23–24. Shields, *Poetics of Liberation*, 8–10.
[48] Gates, *The Trials of Phillis Wheatley*, 23–24.
[49] Ibid.
[50] Mason, *The Poems of Phillis Wheatley*, 30.
[51] William H. Robinson, *Critical Essays on Phillis Wheatley* (Boston: G. K. Hall and Co., 1982) 47–48.

Measure the skies, and range the realms above.
There in one view we grasp the mighty whole
Or with new worlds amaze th' unbounded soul.[52]

George Liele's and Phillis Wheatley's contributions to religious leadership and American letters are phenomenal when one thinks of the time period and circumstances under which they labored. First, both were slaves, and even though their Loyalist owners assisted in their development, Liele and Wheatley were bereft of the basic opportunity of personal freedom. Second, their lives were chained until they found freedom as a result of accepting Jesus Christ as their "Lord and Master." For Wheatley, artistic expression through poetry was a liberating force for her as well. Pugh and others claim that after Liele's baptism, he was never the same because he had a new interpretation of the term "master." Knowing Christ allowed him to realize that Sharp might have owned his body but not his soul.[53] In Jamaica he would prove his allegiance to Christ by enduring persecution from the people and the Jamaican government.[54] Similarly, Phillis Wheatley's acceptance of Christ through New England Congregationalism, a long-delayed baptism, and Whitefield's teaching was a spiritual achievement. Her ability to merge a classical and African consciousness with that of Christianity became a source of personal liberation for her.[55] As for their contributions and legacy, both Liele and Wheatley should be remembered for their deep and consistent faith in God through Jesus Christ and their intellectual genius, which made it possible for them to become pioneers in religion and art. Although the Revolution ended Liele's American leadership with the Baptist Church, his flight to Jamaica became a prosperous venture for him. In addition to his Baptist ministry, he became a farmer and successful businessman; he even traveled to England, where he met Rippon. On the other hand, the American Revolution and its aftermath destroyed Phillis Wheatley and the opportunities for promoting her poetry. The proposal for a second book of poetry and letters was never published, nor has the manuscript ever been found. Although Phillis Wheatley was manumitted by John Wheatley before his death, her relationship with the Wheatleys, who had been her benefactors, ended. Susanna and John Wheatley died and the Wheatley children left Boston; one of them even moved to England. Phillis Wheatley's husband, John Peters, a black businessman, was imprisoned because of debt. Consequently, Phillis Wheatley, the renowned poet,

---

[52] Shields, *Collected Works*, 66.

[53] Pugh, "The Great Awakening," 367.

[54] "Notices of the First Baptists in Jamaica, and of the Commencement of the Mission," *History of the Baptist Missionary Society*, ed. J. A. Cox. 13–14.

[55] Shields, *Poetics of Liberation*, 40–42.

went to work as a maid in order to earn a living. She lost three children and was found dead in a Boston rooming house in 1784, at age thirty-one. She was buried with one of her children in an unmarked grave somewhere in Boston. Neither Phillis Wheatley's grave nor George Liele's burial place has ever been located, according to twentieth- and twenty-first century scholars.

George Liele's and Phillis Wheatley's impact on the world cannot be overlooked today. Liele's Baptist leadership and legacy are far reaching. Not only is he credited with establishing the first black Baptist churches in the United States and Jamaica, he is also praised for creating a free school for enslaved and free children in Jamaica. As an evangelist, Liele inspired hundreds of people to become Christians. Among these converts were David George, Jesse Peters, Moses Baker, Andrew Bryan, and Amos Williams (known as Brother Amos). David George helped organize and pastor the church at Silver Bluff, and he assisted Liele in establishing the first African Baptist Church in Savannah. David George also founded the first Baptist churches in Nova Scotia, Canada, and Sierra Leone, Africa. Jesse Peters became pastor of the first Baptist church in Augusta, Georgia. Andrew Bryan, baptized and mentored by Liele, succeeded him as pastor of the church in Savannah; and he built his own church at Yamacraw near Savannah. Amos Williams, after leaving Savannah, established the first black Baptist church in the Bahamas. Baptists in the United States and throughout the black diaspora, especially, owe much appreciation to the sacrifices and successes of George Liele.

Quite similar to Liele's trailblazing in religion, Phillis Wheatley paved the way for an African-American literary canon. Her book *Poems on Various Subjects, Religious and Moral* (1773), both praised and denounced in America but well received in England, is the first book published by an African American. Initially seen as a mere imitator of eighteenth-century poets, such as Alexander Pope and other neo-classicists, Wheatley is now acknowledged as a brilliant wordsmith and certainly the best poet in American literature during the eighteenth century. Her greatest contribution is her ability to use biblical "myth and symbol" combined with classical and African images. During her time, she successfully honed her poetic skill to wage "a subtle war" on the dehumanizing system of slavery. Today, Phillis Wheatley is called the "mother of African-American literature," whose poetry is the vanguard of African-American literary criticism.

Resources

Ballew, Christopher Brent. *The Impact of African-American Antecedents on the Baptist Missionary Movement 1782–1825*. Lewiston NY: Edwin Mellen Press, 2004.

Brooks, Walter H. "The Priority of the Silver Bluff Church," *Journal of Negro History* 7 (April 1922): 172–96.

Brooks, Walter H. *The Silver Bluff Church: A History of Negro Baptist Churches in America*. Washington DC: R. L. Pendleton, 1910.

Cox, F. A. "Notices of the First Baptists in Jamaica, and of the Commencement of the Mission." In *History of the Baptist Missionary Society*. Edited by F. A. Cox. London: T. Ward and Co., 1842) 2–77.

Frey, Sylvia R. and Betty Wood. *Come Shouting to Zion*. Chapel Hill: University of North Carolina Press, 1998.

Gates, Henry Louis, Jr. *The Trials of Phillis Wheatley*. New York: Basic Cisrtas Books, 2003.

Lincoln, C. Eric. "The Development of Black Religion in America." In *African American Religious Studies*. Edited by Gayraud S. Wilmore. Durham NC: Duke University Press, 1989.

Mason, Julian D., Jr. *The Poems of Phillis Wheatley*. Chapel Hill: University of North Carolina Press, 1989.

O'Neale, Sondra. "A Slave's Subtle War: Phillis Wheatley's Use of Biblical Myth and Symbol," *Early American Literature* (Winter 1986): 145–63.

Pugh, Alfred L. "The Great Awakening and Baptist Beginnings in Colonial Georgia," *American Baptist Quarterly* 26/4 (Winter 2007): 357.

Rippon, John. *The Baptist Annual Register. for 1790, 1791, 1792, and Part of 1793*. London: Vestry, 1793.

Robinson, William H. *Critical Essay on Phillis Wheatley*. Boston: G. K. Hall and Co., 1982.

Robinson, William H. *Phillis Wheatley and Her Writings*. New York: Garland Publishing, 1981.

Shields, John C. *Phillis Wheatley's Poetics of Liberation*. Knoxville: University of Tennessee Press, 2008.

Wheatley, Phillis. *Collected Works of Phillis Wheatley*. Edited by John H. Shields. New York: Oxford University Press, 1988.

Woodson, Carter G. *The History of the Black Church*. Washington DC: Associated Publishers, 1921.

Woodson, Carter G. "Letters Sharing the Rise and Progress of the Early Negro Church of Georgia and the West Indies," *The Journal of Negro History* 1/1 (January 1916): 69–92.

Pioneer George Liele in Jamaica, the British Colony

WINSTON A. LAWSON

George Liele was born around 1750 in slavery to enslaved parents, who belonged to the family of Henry Sharp in Virginia. As part of the Sharp family, he moved to Georgia prior to 1770. Henry Sharp, his master, was a Loyalist supporter of the British and a deacon in the Buckhead Creek Baptist Church of Burke County, Georgia, where the Reverend Matthew Moore was pastor.

Liele provides important biographical and vocational information in a well-known letter to the general secretary of the British Baptist Missionary Society, Dr. John Rippon, dated 18 December 1791 and sent from Kingston, which reads as follows:

> I was born in Virginia, my father's name was Liele, and my mother's name Nancy; I cannot ascertain much of them, as I went to several parts of America when young, and at length resided in New Georgia; but was informed both by white and black people, that my father was the only black person who knew the Lord in a spiritual way in that country: I always had a natural fear of God from my youth, and was often checked in conscience with thoughts of death, which barred me from many sins and bad company. I knew no other way at that time to hope for salvation but only in the performance of my good works. About two years before the late war, the Rev. Mr. Matthew Moore one Sabbath afternoon, as I stood with curiosity to hear him, he unfolded all my dark views, opened my best behavior and good works to me, which I thought I was to be saved by, and I was convinced that I was not in the way to heaven, but in the way to hell. This state I laboured under for the space of five or six months. The more I heard or read, the more I saw that I was condemned as a sinner before God; till at length I was brought to perceive that my life hung by a slender thread, and if it was the will of God to cut me off at that time, I was sure I should be found in hell, as sure as God was in heaven. I saw my condemnation in my own heart, and I found no way wherein I could escape the damnation of hell, only through the merits of my dying Lord and Saviour Jesus Christ; which caused me to make intercession with Christ, for the salvation of my poor immortal soul; and I full well recollect, I requested of my Lord and Master to give me a work, I did

not care how mean it was, only to try and see how good I would do it.[1]

With this dramatic conversion experience in 1774, Liele was soon baptized by his pastor, and exhibiting a passion for the souls of his fellow people of color on the Sharp plantation, he engaged them in singing hymns and studying Scripture. Impressed with his abilities, Liele's church offered him a call to preach before the entire congregation at their quarterly meeting. They became so convinced by his ministerial talents and the success of his ministry with his own people that they unanimously issued him a license as a probationer preacher.

Between 1774 and 1775, Liele was busy in the work of ministry between Augusta, Georgia, and across the Savannah River into South Carolina, where he preached to what became the historic first black Baptist Church at Silver Bluff. In 1778 he moved to Savannah, Georgia, and by 1782 formed the second black Baptist Church in America.

At the end of the Civil War, in which Liele's master, Henry Sharp, was killed, Sharp's children attempted to re-enslave Liele, and he was jailed for some time but was able to regain his freedom by producing his "free papers" to the authorities. He had to borrow $700 from Colonel Kirkland (a British officer) to pay the passage for him and his family, and with that, left Savannah with the colonel as an indentured servant, bound for Jamaica, on board one of the ships that evacuated British troops in 1782.

Liele spoke of this new adventure in the 1791 letter to Rippon, saying:

> At the vacuation of the country I was partly obliged to come to Jamaica, as an indented servant, for money I owed him, he promising to be my friend in this country. I was landed at Kingston, and by the Colonel's recommendation to General Campbell, the governor of the Island, I was employed by him two years, and on his leaving the island, he gave me a written certificate from under his own hand of my good behaviour. As soon as I had settled Col. Kirkland's demand on me, I had a certificate of my freedom from the vestry and governor, according to the act of this Island, both for myself and family. Governor Campbell left the Island.
>
> I began, about September 1784, to preach in Kingston, in a small private house, to a good smart congregation, and I formed the church with four brethren from America besides myself, and the preaching took very good effect with the poorer sort, especially the slaves. The people at first persecuted us both at meetings and baptisms, but, God be

---

[1] John Rippon, *The Baptist Annual Register for 1790, 1791, 1792 and Part 1793*, vol. 1 (London: n.d.), 332–33.

praised, they seldom interrupt us now. We have applied to the Honourable House of Assembly, with a petition of our distresses, being poor people, desiring to worship Almighty God according to the tenets of the Bible, and they have granted us liberty to worship him as we please in Kingston.[2]

Liele's adjustment to the Jamaican society into which he was now introduced, was no doubt exceedingly difficult. For, as Beverly Brown astutely observes, "he was a non-native, a Black American southerner, free, literate, deeply religious and ardently committed to his race. This at once made his position precarious as he could hardly be grouped with the local slaves or for that matter with the slightly more privileged free coloureds; and he had experienced a slave society somewhat different from the one he was encountering in Jamaica."[3]

Orlando Patterson describes the difference between the North American colonies and Jamaica then, by emphasizing how "loosely integrated"[4] plantation Jamaica was, except for its brutal system of exploitation of the enslaved Africans. Then he adds, that "the men who ruled the country and made its laws were themselves the planters who were the masters of the slaves.... Jamaica is best seen as a collection of autonomous plantations...than as a total social system."[5]

Given that, and the fact that all authority was derived from Britain, which also established values and policies, both financial and political, it is not surprising that Liele walked a dangerous line in an environment of unrivaled inequality and brutality everywhere.

Full of commitment to his people and possessed of great charisma, Liele immediately attracted the attention of the blacks and was thus also suspect to the whites, who not knowing him, never trusted him, even with his connection to the governor for whom he worked right at the beginning. The Church of England in Jamaica held the authority to decide who should or should not preach in the island. And the magistrates had the legal right to grant or withhold licenses to preach from anyone other than Church of England clergymen. So the island authorities, both ecclesiastical and civil, had authority to prosecute Liele for any infraction of their laws, and he was indeed prosecuted for sedition, when at one of his first services in Kingston he preached on the text Romans 10:6: "Brethren, my heart's desire and prayer to God...is that they may be saved." The speed with which he overcame these challenges and obstacles to his ministry testifies to

---

[2] Ibid, 334.

[3] Beverly Brown, "George Liele: Black Baptist and Pan-Africanist 1750–1826," *Mona: Savacou Publications* 11/12 (September 1975): 59.

[4] Orlando Patterson, *The Sociology of Slavery* (London: Macgibbon and Kee, 1967) 70.

[5] Ibid.

his political skills, his experience in America, his mature survival instinct, and his new-found community's need for leadership.

George Liele succeeded beyond anyone's wildest imagination, between the Scylla of being an outsider to his own people and the Charybdis of suspicion by the planter class, by skillfully working at his transportation trade in the day and preaching, with due caution, at night. So he reported to Rippon on his efforts to gain converts to Christianity, saying,

> I have baptized four hundred in Jamaica. At Kingston I baptized in the sea, at Spanish Town in the river, and at convenient places in the country. We have nigh THREE HUNDRED AND FIFTY MEMBERS; a few white people among them, one white brother of the first battalion of royals, from England, baptized by Rev. Thomas Davis. Several members have been dismissed to other churches, and twelve have died. I have sent enclosed an account of the conversion and death of some. A few of Mr. Wesley's people, after immersion, join us and continue with us. We have, together with well wishers and followers, in different parts of the country, about fifteen hundred people.[6]

Liele met for the first few years at Kingston's racecourse and then in a private house. They then decided to build a house of worship in 1789. Of this he reported to his potential benefactor, Dr. Rippon in England, at the Baptist headquarters, as follows:

> There is no Baptist church in this country but ours. We have purchased a piece of land, at the east end of Kingston, containing three acres, for the sum of 155 pounds, and on it have begun a meeting-house, fifty-seven feet in length by thirty-seven in breadth. We have raised the brick wall eight feet high from the foundation, and intend to have a gallery. Several gentlemen, members of the house of assembly, and other gentlemen, have subscribed towards the building about 40 pounds. The chief part of our congregation are slaves, and their owners allow them, in common, but three or four bits per week for allowance to feed themselves; and out of so small a sum we cannot expect anything that can be of service from them; if we did it would soon bring a scandal upon religion; and the FREE PEOPLE in our society are but poor, but they are all willing, both free and slaves, to do what they can.[7]

Having made clear their precarious situation, Liele proceeded to appeal to Dr. Rippon to use his good offices and seek support from the British Baptist

---

[6] Rippon, *The Baptist Annual Register*, 334–35.
[7] Ibid., 336.

churches toward the completion of their new building, writing, "And as the Lord has put it into your heart to enquire after us, we place all our confidence in you, to make our circumstances known to the several Baptist churches in England; and we look upon you as our father, friend, and brother. Within the brick wall we have a shelter, in which we worship, until our building can be accomplished."[8]

Liele's appeal to the British Baptists was soon supported significantly by a letter written in November 1791 by Stephen Cooke, a member of the Jamaica House of Assembly. Rippon had written to Cooke and others in Jamaica to provide character references for this new person on the scene. Cooke was unusually forthcoming and fulsome in his praise of Liele, starting his reply by saying he had much pleasure "to find that you had interested yourself to serve the glorious cause Mr. Liele is engaged in!"[9] He then proceeds to give the account of his character that Rippon sought, the report of the progress of his Church work, the composition of the congregation, the view the planters had of his activity in seeking to convert the enslaved workers to Christianity, and, importantly, how Liele differed in his approach from the Methodists. Liele's pragmatism and survivalist skills, born of his experience in America, no doubt, shone through in Cooke's important evaluative letter, in which he says to Rippon:

> He has been for a considerable time past very zealous in the ministry; but his congregation being chiefly slaves, they had it not in their power to support him, therefore he has been obliged to do it from his own industry; this has taken a considerable part of his time and much of his attention from his labours in the ministry: however, I am led to believe that it has been of essential service to the cause of GOD, for his industry has set a good example to his flock, and has put it out of the power of enemies to religion to say, that he has been eating the bread of idleness, or lived upon the poor slaves. The idea that too much prevails here amongst the masters of slaves is, that if their minds are considerably enlightened by religion or otherwise, that it would be attended with the most dangerous consequences; and this has been the only cause why the Methodist ministers and Mr. Liele have not made a greater progress in the ministry amongst slaves. Alas! How much is to be lamented, that a full QUARTER of a MILLION of poor souls should so long remain in a state of nature; and that masters should be so blind to their own interest as not to know the difference between obedience enforced by the lash of the whip and that which flows from religious principles. Although I much admire the general

---

[8] Ibid., 337.

[9] Rippon, *The Baptist Annual Register*, 338.

doctrine preached in the Methodist church, yet I by no means approve of their discipline set up by Mr. Wesley, that reverend man of God. I very early saw into the impropriety of admitting slaves into their societies without permission of their owners, and told them the consequences that would attend it; but they rejected my advice; and it has not only prevented the increase of their church, but has raised them many enemies. Mr. Liele has very wisely acted a different part. He has, I believe, admitted no slaves into society but those who had obtained permission from their owners, by which he has made many friends; and I think the Almighty is now opening a way for another church in the capital, where Methodists could not gain any ground: a short time will determine it, of which I shall advise you.[10]

In later correspondence, Liele's gratitude, and that of the entire Jamaica Baptists, is clearly expressed concerning the generous and needed support of their English fellow Baptists, in the completion of the Church in 1793. This was to be known as the Windward Road Chapel, at the corner of Victoria Avenue and Elletson Road. It was the first Baptist Church on the island.

Even with Liele's commendably cautious and pragmatic approach to religion in a plantation society, he quite regularly ran into trouble. For example, while he awaited his fellow Baptists' gifts from England his creditors became impatient. And when the help he received was not enough to satisfy them, they had him thrown in jail. He refused to plead bankruptcy, as they suggested, but instead served his prison term until friends assisted him in paying off his obligations. Then, of course, in spite of his judicious and conservative approach to evangelizing the enslaved population, always (unlike the Methodists as Cooke pointed out) seeking planter permission, there were those who never trusted him. They always saw in the gospel that he preached the seeds of resistance and rebellion, for which Jamaica was later to be known.

Efforts were frequently made to undermine his work and to disturb his worship activity. One incident is well known, when on one occasion, as the church prepared to celebrate Holy Communion, an old drunken planter rode a horse into the building and stopped in front of the pulpit, calling out, "Come, old Liele, give my horse the sacrament!" Liele with characteristic composure and firmness is said to have replied, "No, sir, you are not fit yourself to receive it!" Disarmed, the disruptive and insolent intruder rode out after remaining there for some time.

Given the oppressive nature of Jamaican plantation society, it was only a matter of time before unrest among the enslaved Africans would erupt into widespread resistance, disruption, and rebellion. One such period is referred to

---

[10] Ibid.

by Liele in a November 1792 letter to Rippon, in which he explained his delay in replying to him, saying:

> I would have answered your letter much sooner, but am encumbered with business—the whole island is under arms; several of our members and a deacon were obliged to be on duty, and I being trumpeter to the troop of horses in Kingston, am frequently called upon. And also by order of the government, I was employed in carrying all the cannon that could be found lying about this part of the country.[11]

He was obviously a well respected and reliable member of society, even if he was not trusted in some planter circles.

Acknowledging the mostly hostile environment in which he was privileged to serve as a minister, Liele did everything he could to establish his conservative and orthodox theological credentials. Thus, as a pragmatic survivalist and to allay the fears of some of the whites, he promoted a covenant, to which all his members needed to assent and by which they were expected to abide. This covenant was called notably "the Covenant of the Anabaptist Church began in America in 1777 and in Jamaica 1783." The twenty-one clauses spell out clearly, with appropriate biblical texts to support each principle, his fundamental understanding of the relationship of the church to the society as a whole. The pacifist, play-it-safe theological and ethical principles evidently commended him and his followers to the majority of the planter class. It reads as follows:

> We are of the Anabaptist persuasion because we believe agreeable to the Scriptures. (*Matt. 3:1–3; 2 Cor. 6:14–18*)
>
> We hold to keep the Lord's Day throughout the year in a place appointed for Public Worship, in singing Psalms, hymns and Spiritual songs and preaching the gospel of Jesus Christ. (*Mark 16:2, 5, 6; Col. 3:16*)
>
> We hold to be baptized in a river or in a place where there is much water, in the name of the Father, and of the Son, and of the Holy Ghost. (*Matt. 3:13, 16, 17; Mark 16: 15, 16; Matt. 28:19*)
>
> We hold to receiving the Lord's Supper in obedience according to his commands. (*Mark 14:22–24; John 6:53–57*)
>
> We hold to the ordinance of washing one another's feet. (*John 13:2–17*)
>
> We hold to receive and admit young children into the church according to the Word of God. (*Luke 2:27–28; Mark 10:13–16*)
>
> We hold to pray over the sick, anointing them with oil in the name of the Lord. (*James 5:14–15*)

---

[11] Rippon, *The Baptist Annual Register*, 104.

We hold to labouring one with another according to the Word of God. (*Matt. 18:15–18*)

We hold to appoint Judges and such other officers among us to settle any matter according to the Word of God. (*Acts 6:1–3*)

We hold not to the shedding of blood. (*Genesis 9:6; Matt. 26:51–52*)

We are forbidden to go to law one with another before the unjust, but to settle any matter we have before the Saints. (*1 Cor. 6:1–3*)

We are forbidden to swear not at all. (*Matt. 5:33–37*)

We are forbidden to eat blood for it is the life of a creature and from things strangled, and from meat offered to idols. (*Acts 15:29*)

We are forbidden to wear any costly raiment such as superfluity [*sic*]. (*1 Peter 3:3, 4; 1 Timothy 2:9–10*)

We permit no slave to join the Church without first having a few lines from their owners of their good behaviour. (*1 Peter 3:3, 4; 1 Timothy 2:9–10*)

To avoid fornication we permit no one to keep each other, except they be married according to the Word of God. (*1 Cor. 7:2; Heb. 13:4*)

If a slave or servant misbehaves to their owners, they are to be dealt with according to the Word of God. (*1 Cor. 7:2; Heb. 7:4*)

If any of this Religion should transgress and walk disorderly and not according to the Commands which we have received in this Covenant, he will be censored according to the Word of God. (*Luke 12:47–48*)

We hold, if a brother or sister should transgress any of these articles written in this Covenant so as to become a swearer, a fornicator or adulterer; a covetous person, an idolater, a railer, a drunkard, an extortioner or whore-monger; or should commit any abominable sin, and do not give satisfaction to the Church according to the Word of God, he or she, shall be put away from among us, not to keep company or to eat with him. (*1 Cor. 5:11–13*).

We hold if a Brother or Sister should transgress and abideth not in the doctrine of Christ and he, or she after being justly dealt with agreeable to the 8th article and be put out of the Church, that they shall no right or claim whatsoever to be interred into the Burying-ground during the time they are put out, should they depart this life, but should they return in peace, and make a confession so as to give satisfaction according to the Word of God, they shall be received into the Church again and have all privileges as before granted. (*2 John 1:9, 10; Gal. 6:1, 2; Luke 18:3, 4*)

We hold to all other Commandments, Articles, Covenants, Ordinances and Ordinances [*sic*], recorded in Holy Scriptures as are set forth by our Lord and Master Jesus Christ and his Apostles, which are not written in this Covenant, and to give them as nigh as we possibly can, agreeable to Word of God. (*John 15:7–14*)[12]

It is noteworthy that in this document, which formed the foundation of the church's operation principles, (a) the master/slave relationship is accepted as the norm, as reflected in article 15; and (b) the enslaved must be approved by the master for membership in the church based on "good behaviour." Consider, too, article 17, where misbehavior would signify Liele's penchant for playing it safe and not rocking the boat of this corrupt and dehumanizing social system. And yet, as Brown correctly points out, the covenant also "contained a subtle criticism of the norms of the society."[13] In article 16, the covenant condemned the breakup of families, which was a direct attack on the owners and plantation operators who actively discouraged marriage and opposed family togetherness in every conceivable way. The covenant also established a system of law and governance within the church for its members, which strategically bypassed the civil authorities, who are categorized as "the unjust" in articles 9 and 11. The appointment of such judges and church officers created, in embryonic form, the leadership that would later become the organizational base for the class leadership system that evolved into that vital core of counterculture deacons, such as Sam Sharp in Montego Bay and Paul Bogle in Morant Bay, who challenged and changed the social order dramatically in 1831 and 1865 respectively.

But in consolidating leadership prerogatives, Liele included a cultural sanction to which the African enslaved person was especially sensitive. In articles 18 and 19, the transgressor of covenant rules would be censored or excommunicated. In addition to this being made known to "the master," who had earlier sanctioned church membership and now would at least hold the excommunicated member suspect, the excommunication would involve the loss of burial rites, as spelled out in article 20. This, to an African whose spirit in death would have neither resting place nor the possibility of return to the ancestral land, was the ultimate negation.

This double-edged sword of a covenant engendered both consistent standards of conduct by members while cultivating a key cadre of lay leadership and allaying the fears of the owners, whose cooperation and approval were always critical to Liele's survival as their leader. Another significant method of control of his fellow Africans and cooperation with the plantocracy was the use of a bell on the church steeple. Liele pointed out in a letter to Dr. Rippon that the

---

[12] Ernest A. Payne, "Baptist Work in Jamaica before the Arrival of Missionaries," *Baptist Quarterly* 7/1 (January 1934): 24–26.

[13] Ibid., 63.

bell was used not only to summon members to worship but also "more particularly to give notice to the owners of slaves...that they may know the hour at which we meet, and be satisfied that their servants return in due time."[14] Moreover, since the bell in use at the time was small, Liele asked Dr. Rippon to "send me out, as soon as possible, a bell that can be heard about two miles distance, with the price...."[15]

While all of this might at first appear conformist by Liele, the historical context, not just his personality, plus the history before coming to Jamaica and his conservative theology, must be taken into account. The Jamaican plantocracy made no bones about strictly maintaining "law and order" in society. In 1702, as dissenting church growth occurred, the Jamaican Assembly passed "an Act to prevent preaching by persons not duly qualified by law."[16] Violation of this legislation would entail imprisonment at hard labor for a free person and imprisonment plus whipping for enslaved individuals.

Even though this harsh measure was initially vetoed by the King of England in 1804, it was reintroduced and intensified in its severity in 1807, forbidding anyone not specifically authorized by the laws of Britain and Jamaica from preaching or teaching Africans, on penalty of fine, imprisonment, or whipping, depending on their status. To this, the Jamaica Assembly added clauses that specified that the instruction of the enslaved be carried out only by the planter-friendly Anglican Church.[17]

So Liele's apparent conformist and cooperative strategy, assuring planters that he would not use church attendance or instruction as opportunities to plan revolts, derived, no doubt, from his belief that to have half a loaf is better than having no loaf at all. No wonder he was well spoken of by most of the planter class, as historian W. J. Garner[18] attests. In fact, Liele carried his appeasement strategy-with-a purpose forward by enunciating the aforementioned covenant, not only as a strict religious guideline for members, but as an agreement of loyalty and cooperation with the Jamaican legislature. So the preamble to the covenant stated: "We bind ourselves, under an affirmation, to do duty to our King, country and laws, and to see that the affixed rules are duly observed."[19]

---

[14] Edward A. Holmes, "George Liele: Negro Slavery's Prophet of Deliverance," *Baptist History and Heritage* 1/1 (1965): 27–36.

[15] Ibid.

[16] Winston Lawson, *Religion and Race: African and European Roots in Conflict: A Jamaican Testament* (New York: Peter Lang, 1996) 75.

[17] Ibid., 75.

[18] Ibid.

[19] Ibid., 76.

In historical hindsight, to understand this unusual tactic of survival, almost at any price, as it might at first appear, one must remember that Liele had been commended by his master in America, Henry Sharp, as a "good slave."[20] Because of this assessment, he was allowed to instruct those enslaved by Sharp and thus began his notable career as evangelist and, later, pioneer of the Baptist Church in Jamaica.

Realizing the complexity and magnitude of the task before him, in ministering to the enslaved population in Jamaica, Liele began efforts to appeal to the English Baptists. This time it had to do with their sending missionaries to enhance the work so successfully already underway in Jamaica. He saw the need for added assistance to that of George Gibbs, a convert who came with him to Jamaica, and Moses Baker, a barber and enslaved person converted under Liele's preaching. These two colleagues of Liele's were to become major players in the expansion of the Church's witness in Kingston and its environs and to the Western areas around Montego Bay.

It would not be long, however, before Liele's appeasement strategy and philosophy caused several of those very colleagues to break away in protest to form "Native Baptist"[21] churches. This break was indicative of a different theological, cultural, and political calculus. It pointed to an alternative approach to the existing social reality and especially to a determined and unapologetic search for freedom and fulfillment.

On the one hand, Liele's survivalist approach was consistent with the conformist and pragmatic attitude that would later typify the go-along-to-get-along posture of the Baptists and other missionaries to Jamaica. On the other hand, however, the native Baptists exemplified a more transformist, liberation theological posture, as they explicitly affirmed their historic cultural norms and values as a legacy from their African ancestors. By their actions they appear to have been rejecting Liele's theological and ethical conformity model and especially the degrading cultural repression.

Even Moses Baker, who was baptized by Liele in 1787, at first had difficulty with Liele's ethical position. So historian Gardner said Baker did not identify with Liele and his God between 1783 when he came to Jamaica and 1787 when he was baptized. In fact, Gardner used the following tell-tale description of Baker that during those years he "lived in utter disregard of religion,"[22] which could mean that he was already involved in native, African religious practices. The

---

[20] Ibid.

[21] Philip Curtin, *Two Jamaicas: The Role of Ideas in a Tropical Colony 1830–1865* (New York: Atheneum, 1970) 36.

[22] W. J. Gardner, *A History of Jamaica: From Its Discovery by Christopher Columbus to the Year 1872* (London: Frank Cass and Co. Ltd., 1873) 344.

negative comments by European missionaries as to Baker's "strange system"[23] and his associates' "monstrous superstition"[24] reflect their biased dismissal of African emphases on trances and spirit possession as clearly unorthodox comingling with "heathen" practices.

After his baptism by Liele, Baker left his profession as a barber in Kingston to take up the offer of a Quaker. In 1786, this man, Isaac Lascelles Winn, from the western parish of St. James, bought slaves belonging to Liele's church and employed Baker as their instructor in religious and moral principles. But even Moses Baker's position proved unattractive to significant numbers on Winn's plantation in St. James, where he found them "living in grossest immorality and all firm believers in obeah."[25] To them, Baker's preaching was unacceptably culturally nihilistic, and so they refused to replace the gods of their ancestors with that of their masters, even when that God was commended to them by a brother!

In spite of all these internal and external challenges, however, success, at least in numerical terms, attended the labors of Baker, Liele, and their colleagues. As early as 1806 they made their first contact with the Baptist Missionary Society in London, asking for missionary assistance. There obviously were those who wanted to live cautiously with a pragmatic survivalist ethic as advocated by Liele and even Baker, who felt comfortable with the owner class's good favor.

William Knibb, the most famous of the missionaries who came to Jamaica as a result of Baker's pleas, writes this in his journal:

> Mr. Moses Baker, a gentleman of color, had for some years been communicating a knowledge of the Christian religion to the Negroes around him, many of whom, renouncing their heathen principles and practices, embraced the Gospel and were baptized.... Mr. Baker being advanced in years, wrote England in 1813 for help, in answer to which Mr. John Rowe...obtaining the concurrence of the Bristol Education Society, and being approved by the Committee of the Baptist Missionary Society, was solemnly set apart on the 8th December.[26]

On the 23 February 1814, Mr. Rowe landed at Montego Bay with the same instructions that were later given to his fellow missionaries, Mr. Compere, Mr. Coultard, Mr. Tinson, the Knibb brothers, James Phillippo, Thomas Burchell, and

---

[23] Hope Waddell, *Twenty Nine Years in the West Indies and Central Africa: A Review of Missionary Work and Adventure, 1829–1858* (London: Frank Cass and Co. Ltd., 1863) 26.

[24] Ibid.

[25] Ibid.

[26] William Knibb, History of the Baptist Church, Falmouth, Jamaica, page 1 of journal, MS in Falmouth church archives.

a whole line of propagators of the doctrine of abstemious noninvolvement in social affairs. They had been instructed and warned:

"Do not intermeddle with politics. Remember that the object of your mission is not to teach the principles and laws of an earthly kingdom, however important a right understanding of these may be, but the principles and laws of the Kingdom of Christ. Maintain toward all in authority a respectful demeanor. Treat them with the honor to which their office entitles them. Politics and party discussions avoid as beneath your office."[27]

The unfortunate outcome of such instruction was that the total transforming potential social impact of the Christian gospel was evidently never brought to bear on Jamaican society as, in later reflection, some would say it might have been. These missionaries should not be blamed unduly for this, however, when they were bound by mandates saying:

> You are going to people in a state of slavery and require to beware lest your feelings should lead you to say or do anything inconsistent with Christian duty. Most of the servants whom the Apostle Paul addressed in his epistles to the churches were slaves, and he exhorts them to be obedient to their own masters in singleness of heart, fearing God, and this, not only to the good and gentle, but also to the forward, etc.... These exhortations must be your guide, and while you act upon them, no man can justly be offended with you.[28]

This neutralist policy, laid down for them by their Missionary Societies and casting them in the impossible role of disinterested purveyors of religious truth as in a vacuum, inevitably made them suspect to both slave and planter alike. For the slaves saw them as equally "colonial" in their outlook and relations to them, while the establishment feared them as a constant potential threat to their position and practices.

Liele paid a visit to England in 1822, as the missionaries began to establish themselves as leaders of the church in Jamaica. He returned and carried on his mission until his death, probably in 1826, since William Knibb noted that he was present at his funeral, having arrived in Jamaica in February 1825. There is no record of where Liele was buried, but in 1983, on the 200th anniversary of the start of Baptist witness in Jamaica, a monument in his memory was erected at the East Queen Street Baptist Church, near the location where Liele originally began his life's work in Jamaica.[29] Moses Baker, on the other hand, was buried in the

---

[27] Lawson, *Religion and Race*, 78.

[28] Ibid.

[29] Clement Gayle, *Pioneer Missionary to Jamaica: George Liele* (Nashville TN: Bethlehem Book Publishers, 2002) 61–62.

old Salters Hill Baptist Church in St. James, the western parish from which a Native Baptist deacon, Sam Sharp, would lead the definitive "Baptist War" of a rebellion against slavery in 1831. This momentous occurrence, grounded in a rudimentary liberation theology that defiantly quoted John's gospel "Whom the Son sets free is free indeed" and Matthew's "No one can be a slave to two masters," culminated in emancipation in 1834 as a great tribute, even if unintended, to George Liele, the pioneer.

Resources

Brown, Beverly. "George Liele: Black Baptist and Pan-Africanist 1750–1826," *Mona: Savacou Publications* 11/12 (September 1975).

Curtin, Philip. *Two Jamaicas: The Role of Ideas in a Tropical Colony 1830–1865*. New York: Atheneum, 1970.

Gardner, W. J. *A History of Jamaica: From Its Discovery by Christopher Columbus to the Year 1872*. London: Frank Cass and Co. Ltd., 1873.

Gayle, Clement. *Pioneer Missionary to Jamaica: George Liele*. Nashville TN: Bethlehem Book Publishers, 2002.

Holmes, Edward. "George Liele: Negro Slavery's Prophet of Deliverance." *A Baptist History and Heritage* 1/1 (1965): 27–36.

Knibb, William. *History of the Baptist Church, Falmouth, Jamaica*. Unpublished manuscript. Archives of Falmouth Baptist Church.

Lawson, Winston. *Religion and Race: African and European Roots in Conflict: A Jamaican Testament*. New York: Peter Lang, 1996.

Patterson, Orlando. *The Sociology of Slavery*. London: MacGibbon and Kee, 1967.

Rippon, John. *The Baptist Annual Register for 1790, 1791, 1792 and Part of 1793*. Volume 1. London: Vestry, 1793.

Waddell, Hope. *Twenty-Nine Years in the West Indies and Central Africa: A Review of Missionary Work and Adventure, 1829–1858*. London: Frank Cass and Co. Ltd., 1863.

George Liele, Native Baptists, and the Revival Church

NOEL LEO ERSKINE

The Afro-Christian witness in Jamaica dates from the end of the American Revolution, when several hundred Loyalists migrated with their slaves to Jamaica from Savannah, Georgia, in the United States of America. These Afro-Christians seized the opportunity to preach their version of Christianity in Jamaica and found ways of merging their understanding of Christianity with local and indigenous expressions of religion. This was the beginning of the Native Baptist movement in Jamaica. The best known of these Afro-Christians was George Liele, who was born in Virginia about 1751 to a slave couple, Liele and Nancy. George Liele later became the property of Henry Sharp of Savannah, Georgia, where he was licensed to preach about May 1775.

George Liele migrated to Jamaica in 1783 and in 1784 founded the first Baptist church there, which he named the Ethiopian Baptist Church. It must have been a curious sight for enslaved people in Jamaica to see a person of African ancestry preaching Christianity in 1783. Prior to the arrival of Liele in Jamaica, enslaved people there adapted the religions they brought with them from Africa to the Jamaican context. As Afro-Jamaicans adapted their religion to the Jamaican context, two forms of this religion emerged on Jamaican soil: obeah and myalism. In Ashanti the word for wizard is *obayifo*, and in Jamaica this became "obeah." Afro-Jamaicans believed that the person who had the power of obeah had the ability to leave his or her body, fly at night, and cause great harm to befall the enemy. Leonard Barrett explains how obeah flourishes contextually, yet dangerously.

He suggests that in Africa, although witchcraft exists and the sorcerer is one of the religious functionaries of the religious system, his work is considered dangerous to society. If he is caught, he is killed and driven out of the community. There are built-in controls by which his polluting influence can be counteracted. In the social and religious system, the power of the sorcerer is always in conflict with the powers of the traditional priest. If the society is in equilibrium, that is, when the society is under proper control, there is little need for witchcraft. On the contrary, when the society is in an unstructured state, whenever there is cultural confusion or social disorientation, witchcraft is likely to flourish. This being the case, it is easy to see why witchcraft became dominant in the slave societies.[1]

Barrett is helpful in helping us understand why obeah flourished in slave society. It flourished not only because the society had lost its equilibrium and was in a state of disorientation, but because there was a void for a religious practitioner. The traditional African priest had lost his power in this alien society, and as he joined forces with the obeah practitioner, they became a formidable force to reckon with in slave society. So powerful was the role of obeah in Jamaican society that there were laws prohibiting Jamaicans to engage in this practice. The obeah man was able to offer Jamaicans protection against the cruelty of the master, who had the right to whip, mutilate, or sell any slave at will. Leonard Barrett calls attention to the Maroon rebellion of 1760 led by the Ashanti warrior Tacky. This rebellion was one of the bloodiest revolts staged by Afro-Jamaicans. Led by obeah man Tacky, the warriors prepared for war by mixing rum with gunpowder and grave dirt. Blood drawn from the arm of each participant was added and then the mixture was drunk in turn by each warrior. The drinking of this mixture meant that the covenant to fight until death was sealed by each participant. After this rebellion, the fear of the obeah man was so pervasive that the Jamaican legislature passed a law against him. The sum of the law was that anyone convicted of practicing obeah would face the possibility of being sentenced to death. This did not solve the master's problems, though, as Afro-Jamaicans believed "Massa can't kill obeah man."[2]

In West Africa, the worship of gods was organized in cult groups, often esoteric, which used drums, dancing, dreams, and spirit-seizure as part of organized worship. An aspect of this survived in Jamaica through the ritual referred to as myal. Perhaps the real difference between obeah and myal is that whereas the obeah man is usually a private practitioner, hired by a client for a specific purpose, the myal practitioner is a leader of a group, devoted to an organized religious life. But, as illustrated in the scenario of Tacky calling on warriors to blend rum, blood, and grave dirt together and then drink in establishing a covenant, the lines between obeah and myal are often blurred.

Winston Lawson informs us that myalism embodied African-derived cosmology and is the first documented religion cast in the African mold on Jamaican soil. At the heart of myal rituals is the myal dance. The myal dance was observed in honor of the minor deities or the ancestors who were feared. An important ingredient of this dance was spirit-possession. It was widely believed

---

[1] Leonard E Barrett, *Soul-Force* (Garden City NY: Anchor Press/Doubleday,1974) 64–65.
[2] Barrett, *Soul-Force*, 66–67.

by participants in myal that the dance gave them the ability to elude capture when they escaped or made them invincible to bullets.[3]

It is worth noting that during the 1790s there was a fusing of myalists beliefs with that of Native Baptists. Leonard Barrett points out that the Native Baptists were the first church to reach out to enslaved Jamaicans, and one reason for this was the loose structure of the Baptist Church, which enabled them to use the newly converted lay leaders to supervise African converts. This flexibility allowed the inclusion of African traditional practices, such as drumming, dancing, and spirit-seizure; in short, the practices of myal.

George Lewis was another leader of the Native Baptists who migrated with Liele from the United States. Lewis rejected the missionary version of Christianity in favor of his own, more African style. Lewis "had been born in Africa and taken to Virginia as a slave. After the American Revolution he was brought to Kingston, where his mistress let him work as a peddler in return for a monthly fee. He mixed peddling with preaching along his route in the parishes of Manchester and St. Elizabeth and spread his doctrine through the southwest part of the island."[4] Other leaders from the United States in the tradition of George Lewis were George Gibbs and Moses Baker. According to the church historian W. J. Gardner, for four years (1783–1787) Baker "lived in utter disregard of religion."[5] Of course, by religion Gardner meant the Christian religion. Philip Curtin provides clues of the organizational structure of Native Baptist churches:

> The organizational basis...was the "leader system," an adaptation of the English Wesleyan practice of dividing the church members into classes for teaching. Possibly, the native Baptists picked it up from the few White missionaries who were already at work in Jamaica, but more likely it was their American training. In any case the leader system underwent some strange transformations. The class-leaders became something more than just a teacher of new converts. They were real spiritual guides, taking a position equivalent to leadership of a myal cult group, and their power over the classes was authoritarian to the point of tyranny.[6]

---

[3] Winston Lawson, *Religion and Race* (New York: Peter Lang, 1996) 25.

[4] Philip D. Curtin, *Two Jamaicas* (New York: Atheneum, 1970) 33.

[5] W. J. Gardner, *A History of Jamaica* (London: T. Fisher, 1873) 344.

[6] Curtin, *Two Jamaicas*, 33. The practice of classes with leaders still occurs in Jamaica. Some years ago, when I served as pastor of a congregation in rural Jamaica, several of my deacons functioned as class leaders. They would conduct funerals, discipline wayward members, and christen babies. The truth is that they had much more power than I had in relation to the congregation.

The class leaders had power to refuse applications for baptism, and at times even expelled members. Needless to say, it was not long before the class became the basis for founding new churches. It is important to note that from 1783, when George Liele and his fellow African Americans arrived in Jamaica and started to interpret Christianity from an African perspective, they were unhindered by European theological traditions until about 1814, when Baptist missionaries arrived from Great Britain. We must also make allowance for European cultural adjustments in order to attain adequate numbers to deal with the vast number of enslaved persons who were on the island at that time. The important fact to remember is that for twenty-eight years the native Baptists were unhindered by Europeans as they constructed a theology that would speak to the enslaved situation. Native Baptists adopted a doctrinal position that elevated "the spirit" and neglected the written word.

The followers of Baker and Gibb were required to be possessed of "the spirit" before baptism was administered. This meant that the spirit had to descend on the applicant in a dream, which was then described to the leader. If the dream was satisfactory the applicant could enter the class. There evolved a regular technique and ceremony for bringing on spirit-possession, which included a fast according to a set canon followed by a trip into the bush alone at night to wait for the spirit to descend.[7]

Under the aegis of the spirit, the leaders of the Native Baptists were free to make the theological connections they saw fit. In the system of slavery, which denied them political power, they carved out space in their church under the aegis of the spirit. In this church, John the Baptist was seen as leader, since he baptized Christ and accepted Christ into his church, so to speak. It is not surprising that European missionaries later found this theological position shocking and untenable. As the Native Baptists merged African perspectives with Christian beliefs, they formulated a reinterpretation of Christianity, which would endure even under the impact of European ideas and beliefs. "By 1830 the doctrine and organization of the Native Baptist had become a thoroughly integrated part of Negro culture—another religion competing with the Christianity of European missionaries."[8] On the religious state of black people in Jamaica in the 1830s, a missionary organization comments that:

> [A]ll the Negroes in Jamaica now call themselves "Christians"—
> generally "Baptists," though their religion differs little from their old
> African superstitions. The bulk of them are enrolled in Classes under
> some Black Teacher as ignorant as themselves; and they are connected
> by the purchase of a ticket with the Baptist congregation in the nearest

---

[7] Ibid.
[8] Ibid.

Town, where they go, and receive the sacrament once a month, or once a quarter; but they are utterly ignorant of the simplest and plainest of God's commandments. They are too ignorant to understand and profit by the Public Preaching on the Sabbath; and they never see the Missionary at any other time; for they live far away from him and he has thousands attending him whom he does not know. They are perishing in their sins, and stand in need of instructions as the Zooloos.[9]

It is quite clear that the arrival of the missionaries did not slow down the Africanization of Christianity along myal lines.

It was not until 1824 that a potentially strong leader, Thomas Burchell, came to join Baker. Baker urged his followers to accept Burchell's leadership, but cultural barriers of communication and a predilection for Africanized, religious celebration made many of them abandon Baptist orthodoxy for native-led forms of expression.[10]

The missionary churches that adopted the class-leader system watched their numbers grow as Afro-Jamaicans flocked to those churches. What is interesting is that the masses that attended the missionary church contended they could not understand what the missionary said, and would meet after church with a class-leader who was referred to as "Mammy" or "Daddy" to have the missionary sermon explained. Afro-Jamaicans would attend the missionary church without any intention of hearing or understanding the sermon. The truth is that this system of class-leader became one reason for the failure of the missionary. It must be remembered that the missionary did not choose the class-leader. The class-leader was chosen by the people, and it was the task of the missionary to accept this person. Because class-leaders had the people base, they were free to break with the missionary and at times stand against him. This was what precipitated the rebellion of 1831, which was led by class-leader Sam "Daddy" Sharp.

Native Baptists Press for Freedom

The Baptist war of 1831 led by class-leader Sam ("Daddy") Sharp of the Native Baptists signaled the beginning of the end of slavery in Jamaica. The Baptist war, as the rebellion of 1831 in and around Montego Bay, is said to have brought to a climax the long struggle of Afro-Jamaicans for freedom from imperial rule. The struggle over the years took the form of running away, many, as in the case of the Maroons of Jamaica, fleeing to the hills and organizing

---

[9] Robert J. Stewart, *Religion and Society in Post-Emancipation Jamaica* (Knoxville: University of Tennessee Press,1992) 124–25.

[10] Lawson, *Religion and Race*, 31.

periodic attacks on the British. The focus of this war was Afro-Jamaicans organizing to withdraw their labor, with its emphasis directed on the institution of the plantation. A total of 120 buildings on the estate were torched as Afro-Jamaicans insisted that because they were human beings who had a right to freedom, they also had a right to withdraw their labor and attack the institutions that kept them in slavery.

The Baptist war "differed from earlier uprisings, such as Tacky's Coromantis…from Africa and that of the King of the Ebos with his small band of plantation slaves, in that more than 20,000 African-Jamaicans were involved. The call was to slaves everywhere, not a call to arms but a call to withdraw labor, and it was issued to people who were determined to win their freedom."[11] Edward Hylton, one of Daddy Sharp's followers, tells of a time he was in the hills and received a message from Daddy Sharp to attend a gathering at Johnson's house on Retrieve Estate in St. James. The gathering took the form of a prayer meeting. After the meeting Daddy Sharp, William Johnson, who became one of the leaders of the Baptist war, Hylton, and a few others remained behind.

After a while Sharp spoke to them in a low, soft tone so that his voice would not be heard outside. According to Hylton, he kept them spellbound while he spoke of the evils and injustices of slavery, asserted the right of all human beings to freedom, and declared on the authority of the Bible that the white man had no more right to hold the blacks in bondage than the blacks had to enslave the whites.[12]

The meeting went on late into the night as they agreed on a strategy to overturn slavery. They covenanted not to work after the Christmas holidays but to seize their right to freedom in faithfulness to each other. "If backra [master]would pay them, they would work as before. If any attempt was made to force them to work as slaves, they would fight for their freedom. They took the oath and kissed the Bible."[13] It seems as if what Daddy Sharp intended was a nonviolent protest, which would be expressed as a labor strike. The plan was that the day after the Christmas holiday an overseer or a driver would go to "busha" on each estate and inform him that the slaves would not work until the agreed to pay wages. The bushas were to be kept on the estate until they agreed to pay wages for work. The leadership of the Native Baptists had organized themselves into a trade union arm of the Native Baptist Church, advocating and negotiating wages for the slaves. Philip Curtin suggests that what in fact was happening was that the Native Baptists had skillfully taken the Baptist

[11] Hazel Bennett and Philip Sherlock, *The Story of the Jamaican People* (Kingston Jamaica: Ian Randle Publishers, 1998) 212.
[12] Ibid., 214.
[13] Ibid.

missionary organization from white missionaries and were using the Baptist organization as a European trade union leader might use the bargaining power of workers.[14] This seems to be the case as later developments attest.

On 27 December William Knibb, visiting Moses Baker's chapel at Crooked Spring (now Salter's Hill), tried to persuade the slaves that rumors about freedom having been granted were untrue, but his words were received with evident dissatisfaction by many of the slaves present, several of whom left the chapel offended. Others remarked: "The man ...must be mad to tell us such things."[15]

Further, missionary Knibb stated:

> I am pained—pained to the soul, at being told that many of you have agreed not to work any more for your owners, and I fear this is too true. I learned that some wicked person has persuaded you that the King of England has made you free. Hear me! I love your souls and I would not tell you a lie for the whole world; I assure you that this is false, false as hell can make it. I entreat you not to believe it, but go to work as formerly. If you have any love for Jesus Christ, to religion, to your ministers, or to those kind friends in England who have helped you build this chapel, and who are sending a minister for you, do not be led away. God commands you to be obedient....[16]

Fired by the spirit of the Native Baptists, Daddy Sharp responded, "We have worked enough already, and will work no more; the life we live is too bad, it is the life of a dog, we won't be slaves no more, we won't lift hoe no more, we won't take flogging anymore."[17]

Daddy Sharp and his compatriots Thomas Dove, Linton, and Dehaney and other freedom fighters seized the right to fight for justice and interpreted the message of liberation through the hermeneutic of freedom. They were already able to view themselves from the perspective of freedom. The price paid by Daddy Sharp and his people was very high. In the aftermath of the Baptist war, some 600 African Jamaicans were killed by British forces. In their defense they killed fourteen whites. But the seeds for the destruction of slavery were sown. On 1 August 1834 a partial freedom was granted with the abolition of slavery 1 August 1838.

---

[14] Curtin, *Two Jamaicas*, 86.

[15] Bennett and Sherlock, *Jamaican People*, 216.

[16] John Howard Hinton, *Memoir of William Knibb* (London: Houlston and Stoneman,1847) 118.

[17] Trevor Munroe and Don Robothan, *Struggles of the Jamaican People* (Kingston Jamaica: E. P. Printery,1977) 6.

The Emergence of Revivalism in Jamaica

It is quite clear that the Baptist movement that George Liele initiated in Jamaica went in directions he could not have imagined. It seems that perhaps a central distinction between the position that Liele advocated and that which was practiced by the Native Baptists had to do with perspective. While Liele benefited from being a part of a Christian community in Georgia and earlier in Virginia, he was able to interpret the world, slavery, and African religions from a Christian frame of reference. For example, one of the first sermons he preached while in Jamaica was from Romans 10:1: "Brethren, my hearts desire and prayer for Israel is that they might be saved." In this sermon he compared the plight of Afro-Jamaicans with that of the children of Israel in Egypt. This sermon was regarded by the authorities as incendiary and as a consequence he was imprisoned. The laws in Jamaica made it extremely difficult for Liele to practice his version of Christianity, with its claim that Afro-Jamaicans, like the children of Israel, needed to be set free. In 1802 a law was passed stating that if a free black person was found guilty of preaching sermons advocating the freedom of enslaved persons, he should be committed to prison and kept at hard labor. If the preacher were a slave, he should be put to hard labor for the first offense.[18]

In 1807 this law was made firmer when an ordinance was passed in Jamaica stating that persons not authorized by the laws of Great Britain and Jamaica could not preach or teach in Jamaica.[19] This was very difficult for Liele, as he did not wish to return to prison. First he assured the planters and the legislature that he would cooperate with them by promising that Afro-Jamaicans would not use church attendance as occasions to plan and plot revolts. Liele then attached a bell to the Baptist church in his charge. The purpose of the bell was not to inform Afro-Jamaicans what time church service would commence but, rather, to inform the masters of the time when worship began and ended[20] This was one way in which Liele opted to work with the system of slavery and thereby leave open the possibility of affecting slavery from within the system.

It seems that the converse was the case for the Native Baptists, who, while committed to Baptist freedom and organization, opted to work outside the system engineered by the plantocracy. They interpreted the world and Christianity from an African perspective inspired by myal, as was the case with Daddy Sharp, who challenged both the Christian church and the state in the quest for freedom.

---

[18] Gardner, *History of Jamaica*, 348.

[19] Ibid., 349.

[20] J. P. Gates, "George Liele," *The Chronicle* 6/3 (July 1943): 118–29.

I would like to conclude this section by calling attention to the Revival Church in Jamaica, which is an outgrowth of the Native Baptist witness in Jamaica and home of revivalist figures such as Alexander Bedward and Marcus Garvey.

It is generally agreed that Revivalism received its name from the Great Revival, which swept Jamaica from 1860 to 1861. Leonard Barrett provides the following important information about Revivalism:

> How can this Great Revival be interpreted? Was it really a revival of Christianity? The answer is no. There was no Christianity to revive among the slaves. What actually happened was a result of the confused state in which the Blacks found themselves after the emancipation of 1838. Their expectation that emancipation would result in freedom and self-betterment was disappointed and instead they found themselves disenfranchised, landless, homeless and without the means to support themselves. The missionaries, who played a great role in the liberation movement, had built up their expectations of a better life in a free Jamaica, but this proved to be nothing more than empty talk. The great Revival is thus better understood as a rejection of Christianity and a revival of the African force-vitale…. What really took place was a forcible amalgamation of Christianity with the African ethos.[21]

Among many Jamaicans, Revivalism is associated with Alexander Bedward, the best known and most popular of the Revivalists. Bedward was arrested for teaching that Afro-Jamaicans should overthrow white rule in Jamaica. Born in 1859, Bedward models for us some of the traits of the Revivalist spirit. In a visit to Colon, Panama, he received a vision to return to Jamaica and save the souls of his people. The spirit instructed him to fast three times per week, during which time the gift of healing was bestowed on him. With the gift of the Revivalist spirit on him, Bedward began his ministry in 1895 in Kingston, Jamaica.

One of the marks of his ministry was the use of the water of the Mona River in Kingston for healing purposes. People came from as far away as Panama and throughout Jamaica for the water, which is purported to have had medicinal properties. He attracted the most oppressed among the poor, the group at the bottom of the social ladder, from which Rastafari would emerge in the 1930s. In a context in which health care was not provided by the government for its citizens and in which thousands among the Jamaican peasants were landless, the Revivalists, through baths, and in this case baptisms, provided healing for weary, forlorn, and sick bodies. This was also one way in which Revivalist churches counteracted the tendency of mainline churches to focus on healing the

---

[21] Barrett, *Soul-Force*, 115.

souls of the people but neglecting their bodily needs. Indeed, during slavery the master and quite often the missionary taught that while the soul belonged to God, the body belonged to the master. The Revivalists, steeped in African cosmology, made the connection between body and soul, teaching that to heal the body is at the same time to care for the soul, contending that many illnesses have spiritual causes. The material and the spiritual were connected.

I should like here to draw on my own experience and recollections of Revivalism and church in Jamaica. The Revivalist spirit had spilled over into the Baptist Church in which I was brought up as a boy in St. Thomas, Jamaica. Although this church was what is referred to by the local people as Regular Baptist (in distinction from Native Baptists), its celebration of the sacraments of baptism and Holy Communion exemplified the influence of Revivalism. I recall how my baptismal experience at the age of twelve drew upon African cosmology.

It was early Good Friday morning about 5:00 A.M. All the candidates for baptism met at the church with the "mothers" and the deacons, and being moved by the spirit, we testified and sang. After much praying in the spirit, we all set out with the church mothers and deacons leading—all of us dressed in white—to the place where our sins would be washed away. It was about three miles that we walked in the early morning, many of us children not quite understanding the ways of the spirit. My father was the minister, and being filled with the Revivalist spirit, he asked each of us if we believed in Jesus Christ. Being assured that we did, he then immersed us in the river. Standing close to him with towels in hand to cover us, and ready to calm us if we were overpowered by the spirit, was the "water mother," who took charge of each of us and safely guided us out of the water.

I suspect that the Regular Baptist Church in which I was baptized was closer to the church model represented by George Liele than that which emerged among the Native Baptists and later the Revival Church. For example, Alexander Bedward would not have asked those who came to him at the Mona River to receive water for healing and baptism if they believed in Jesus Christ as a prerequisite for salvation and healing. This emphasis on Jesus Christ as divine and as equal with God came to Baptists through the tradition and teaching of George Liele and the Baptist missionaries who followed him. Earlier it was noted that many Native Baptists saw John the Baptist as essential for faith, as he baptized Jesus and, so to speak, received him into his church. Revivalists believed Jesus was one of the prophets and was not equal with God. Therefore, it should not surprise us that Alexander Bedward, following in the tradition of the Native Baptists, could change his title from "Shepherd" to the "Incarnation of Christ" with the promise that on 31 December 1920 he would ascend to heaven, thereby destroying the rule of white people and establishing the kingdom of Bedwardism on earth. In the same vein, Bedward could claim that he was Jesus

Christ who was crucified. Some Christians may find this sacrilegious, because it sounds as if Bedward were equating himself with God. But the Revivalists did not see Jesus as God but rather as a prophet who had the power to heal, prophesy, and change the oppressive order that was killing black people.[22]

George Liele introduced Afro-Jamaicans to a radical version of Christianity that they interpreted through Afro-centric lenses. Perhaps because it was within the context of slavery and radical oppression that two forms of spirituality emerged: Native Baptists and the Revival Church. Both departed from Liele's teaching at critical points, choosing a hermeneutic of freedom and liberation over Baptist orthodoxy, which seemed to be very important to Liele. But without Liele's contribution neither expression of freedom would have emerged.

Resources

Barrett, Leonard E. *Soul-Force.* Garden City NY: Anchor Press/Doubleday, 1974.

Beckwith, Martha Warren. *Black Roadways.* New York: Negro University Press, 1929.

Bennett, Hazel and Philip Sherlock. *The Story of the Jamaican People.* Kingston Jamaica: Ian Randle Publishers, 1998.

Curtin, Philip D. *Two Jamaicas.* New York: Atheneum, 1970.

Gates, J. P. "George Liele: A Pioneer Negro Preacher." *The Chronicle* 6/3 (July 1943).

Gardner, W. J. *A History of Jamaica.* London: T. Fisher, 1873.

Hinton, John Howard. *Memoir of William Knibb.* London: Houlston and Stoneman, 1847.

Lawson, Winston. *Religion and Race.* New York: Peter Lang, 1996.

Munroe, Trevor and Don Robotham. *Struggles of the Jamaican People.* Kingston Jamaica: E. P. Printery, 1977.

Stewart, Robert J. *Religion and Society in Post Emancipation Society.* Knoxville: University of Tennessee Press, 1992.

---

[22] Martha Warren Beckwith, *Black Roadways* (New York: Negro University Press, 1929) 168.

David George:
George Liele's Legacy in Sierra Leone

JENEEN BLEASE ROSCOE

David George was a protégé of George Liele. David George was first known only as "David." He took the name "David George" in honor of George Liele, the man who preached the sermon that liberated him to spiritual freedom.[1] David George's act of adopting Liele's first name as his last name was a profound attestation to David George's outstanding respect for George Liele. Through David George, we can see the legacy of George Liele take shape and grow globally. Liele's story of an enslaved man being converted to Christianity and freed from slavery, his ordination, gifted preaching, and evangelizing, and his missionary endeavors have been told in the preceding chapters of this anthology. Liele made disciples of many who became preachers, missionaries, and world leaders. One of those disciples was David George. David George emulated Liele and went on to live a life of service in three countries on two continents. On the continent of North America, David George started Baptist churches in the United States and Canada. He later started a Baptist church in Sierra Leone in West Africa. Indeed, David George is the personification of Liele's legacy, but the David George story must be told because of its significance in the spreading of the gospel in spite of the dangers both men faced.

In the early 1740s David George was born in Essex County, Virginia, to enslaved parents, John and Judith, who had been born in Africa. Also born in Virginia to enslaved parents, Liele and Nancy, George Liele (1750–1820) was about ten years younger than David George.

In the first-hand account of his life, David George told of the cruel system of slavery from which he wanted to be free. David wrote:

> My older sister was called Patty; I have seen her several times so whipped that her back has been all corruption, as though it would rot. My brother Dick ran away but they caught him, and brought him home, and as they were going to tie him up, he broke away again, and they hunted him with horses and dogs, till they took him, and they hung him up to a cherry tree in the yard, by his two hands, quite naked, except his breeches, with his feet about half a yard from the

---

[1] Simon Schama, *Rough Crossings: Britain, the Slaves, and the American Revolution* (New York: Harper Collins, 2006) 96.

ground. They tied his legs close together, and put a pole between them, at one end of which one of the owners sons sat to keep him down, and another son at the other. After he had received five hundred (500) lashes or more, they washed his back with salt water, and, whipped it in, as well as rubbed it in with a rag and then directly set him to work in pulling off the suckers of tobacco. I also have been whipped many a time on my naked skin, and sometimes till the blood has run down over my waistband, but the greatest grief I then had was to see them whip my mother, and to hear her on her knees, begging for mercy. She was masters cook, and if they only thought she might do anything better than she did, instead of speaking to her as to a servant, they would strip her directly and cut away. I believe she was on her deathbed when I got off, but I have never heard since. Master's rough and cruel usage was the reason for my running away.[2]

David George was about nineteen years when he ran away from that cruel slaveholder. He lived among the Natchez Indians[3] who traded deerskins with George Galphin.[4] David sewed the deerskins together and tended the horses. Every year David "took the skins downstream, piled high in a leather canoe, to Mr. Galphin at Silver Bluffs."[5] David asked George Galphin if he could live with him. Mr. Galphin said yes to David's request and David stayed there for four years.[6] Another writer said that a white man named George Galphin (Gaulfin, Gaulphin) bought him from the Indians and put him to work on his plantation at Silver Bluff.[7] Regardless of how he came to live and work on the Galphin estate, this is where George Liele and David George met and became friends. Although younger than David George, Liele was older in conversion to Christ. Liele's preaching was, in part, the reason David George came to know Christ and was

---

[2] "Black Loyalist. An Account of Life of Mr. David George from S. L. A. given by himself. In a conversation with Brother Rippon of London and Brother Pearce in Birmingham," 2000, http://www.blackloyalist.com/canadiandigitalcollection/documents/diaries/george_a_life.htm (accessed 15 September 2009).

[3] Schama, *Rough Crossings*, 96.

[4] Alfred Lane Pugh, *Pioneer Preachers in Paradise: The Legacies of George Liele, Prince Williams, and Thomas Paul in Jamaica, the Bahamas and Haiti* (East Peoria IL: Versa Press, 2003) 12.

[5] Schama, *Rough Crossings*, 96.

[6] Ibid.

[7] "David George," in *Dictionary of Canadian Biography Online*, http://www.biographi.ca/009004-119.01-e.php?&id_nbr=2417&&PHPSESSID= ychzfqkvzape (accessed 22 December 2010).

baptized. David George said that soon after he heard Liele preach, he gave his life to Christ.[8] In his own words, David George gives this account:

> Soon after I heard Brother George Liele preach, who, as you both know, is at Kingston in Jamaica. I know him ever since he was a boy— [Liele preached] 'Come unto me all ye that labour, are heavy laden, and I will give you rest.' When it was ended I went to him and told him I was so, that I was weary and heavy laden and that the Grace of God had given me rest. Afterward Brother Palmer, who was pastor at some distance from Silver Bluff, came and preached to a large congregation at a mill of Mr. Gaulfin's. He was a very powerful preacher, and as he was returning home Lords day evening, I went with him two or three miles, and told him how it was with me. About this time more of my fellow creatures began to seek the Lord. Afterwards Brother Palmer came again and wished us to beg Master to let him preach to us, and he had leave, and came frequently. There were eight of us now who had found the great blessing and mercy from the Lord, and my wife was one of them, and my brother Jessie Gaulfin that you mention in the History of us poor slaves, was another. Brother Palmer appointed Saturday evening to hear what the Lord had done for us, and the next day he baptized us in the Mill stream.[9]

The two men became friends at Silver Bluff and enjoyed a joint ministry in preaching the word.[10] After the Revolution, the two men left America. Liele established the Baptist denomination in Jamaica. David George left with hundreds of people and sailed to Nova Scotia. For ten years, David George endured persecution in the form of lynch threats and arson. He was threatened harm if he did not stop preaching. Even in the face of such danger, David George founded the first Baptist Church in Shelburne.[11] After that decade of threats and constant consternation, David George migrated with a group called Black Pioneers in 1792 from Nova Scotia to Freetown in West Africa. He became one of the founders of Sierra Leone. There, he planted the first Baptist church in West Africa.[12]

---

[8] Schama, *Rough Crossings*, 96.

[9] David George, "Black Loyalist: An Account of the Life of Mr. David George from S. L. A. Given by Himself, in Conversation with Brother Rippon of London and Brother Pearce in Birmingham," 2000.

[10] W. H. Brooks, "The Evolution of the Negro Baptist Church," *Journal of Negro History* 7/1 (January 1922).

[11] Sidney Kaplan and Emma Nogrady Kaplan, *The Black Presence in the Era of the American Revolution* (Amherst: University of Massachuetts Press, 1989).

[12] Ibid.

David George was a family man. At Silver Bluff he married Phillis, another slave who was part Creek Indian. David and Phillis George had children. Soon, upon being introduced to the Christian religion by a fellow black man named Cyrus, from Charleston, David George started attending religious services held on the Galphin estate.[13] Those services were conducted by George Liele.[14]

David George took a trip to London, England to visit Dr. John Rippon shortly after establishing himself on the continent of Africa in Sierra Leone in West Africa. The purpose of that trip was to secure the support and financial aid of the English Baptists.

David George told his own life story to John Rippon of London.[15] In that story, David George indicated that on each departure from a place, he preached a farewell sermon. This held true when David George left his beloved Sierra Leone to visit John Rippon in London. In that farewell sermon, David George reminded the people of the importance of showing godly and brotherly love. He stated, "When I came away from Sierra Leone, I preached a farewell sermon to the church, and encouraged them to look to the Lord, and submit to one another."[16] In that statement, David George showed himself to be a dedicated shepherd of the Christian flock.

The Legacy of Similarities

Protégés, preachers, and pastors, David George and George Liele's lives were similar in many ways. Each was born in Virginia on the same plantations as their respective parents. Each was separated from their parents by slaveholders. Each left the shores of the United States to escape slavery. Each left the United States in 1782 when the British evacuated after the war. Each planted churches where they went. George Liele brought the Baptist Church to Jamaica and David George brought the Baptist Church to Sierra Leone. Each was treated harshly in their new-found homelands. George Liele was jailed in Jamaica. David George endured economic and societal mistreatment in Nova Scotia. Each traveled around within the lands where they dwelled.

Both David George and George Liele were literate. They kept in close contact with John Rippon of London and with each other by letter. With this close friendship and commitment to spreading the gospel, it is no wonder that we see the legacy of George Liele through the life of David George.

---

[13] Schama, *Rough Crossings*, 96.

[14] "David George," Dictionary of Canadian Biography Online.

[15] Pugh, *Pioneer Preachers*, 22–23.

[16] George, "Black Loyalist."

Resources

Alie, Joe A. D. *A New History of Sierra Leone*. Oxford: Macmillan Publishers, 1990.

Barbington-Johnson, Tanie, senior pastor of the Regent Road Baptist Church, to missionary Jeneen Roscoe. Personal interview. 20 November 2007.

Barbington-Johnson, Tanie and Edward Dumbuya. "Brief History of the Regent Road Baptist Church (Church of God)." Unpublished archival records. Freetown, Sierra Leone. n.d.

Bichner, Carrie. "Slave & Religion in America: A Time Line 1440–1866." The Regents of the University of Michigan online Public Library. 1995. Accessed 15 April 1998. http://www.mamiwata.com/bchurch.html

Burton, Orville Vernon. *In My Father's House Are Many Mansions: Family and Community in Edgefield, South Carolina*. Chapel Hill: University of North Carolina Press, 1985.

George, David. "Black Loyalist. An Account of Life of Mr. David George from S.L.A. given by himself. In a conversation with Brother Rippon of London and Brother Pearce in Birmingham." http://www.blackloyalist.com/canadiandigitalcollection/documents/diaries/george_a_life.htm

Jeffries Jr., Leonard. "The African-Americans Search for Truth and Knowledge, Part 20: African-American Church in the Revolutionary Era." The National Black United Front. The Leonard Jeffries Virtual Museum. 5 June 1999. http://www.nbufront.org/mastersmuseums/lenjeffries/africanamericans/aapart20.html.

Kaplan, Sidney and Emma Nogrady Kaplan. *The Black Presence in the Era of the American Revolution*. Amherst: University of Massachusetts Press, 1989.

Lewis, Marilyn. "Overcoming Obstacles. The Broad Sweep of the African American and Missions." *Mission Frontiers*. The U.S. Center for World Mission. April 2000.

Miltenberger, Scott A. *Encyclopedia of African-American History, 1619 to 1895: From the Colonial Period to the Age of Frederick Douglas*. Oxford: Oxford University Press, 2008.

Pugh, Alfred. *Pioneer Preachers in Paradise: The Legacies of George Liele, Prince Williams, and Thomas Paul in Jamaica, the Bahamas, and Haiti*. East Peoria IL: Versa Press, 2003.

Rippon, John. "An Account of several Baptist Churches, consisting chiefly of Negro Slaves...." *The Baptist Annual Register* (London, 1793).

Russell, Horace O. *The Missionary Outreach of the West Indian Church: Jamaican Baptist Missions to West Africa in the Nineteenth Century*. New York: Peter Lang, 2000.

Sernett, Milton C. *African-American Religious History: A Documentary Witness* Durham NC: Duke University Press, 1999.

Sundkler, Bengt and Christopher Steed. *A History of the Church in Africa.* Cambridge: University Press, 2000.

Wardin, Albert. "Who are the Baptists [Africa]?" Baptist World Alliance Heritage & Identity Commission. 1990. http://www.bwa-baptist-heritage.org/hst-afr.htm (accessed 20 December 2007).

The Last Will and Testament of George Liele
...Without a trace

VERNITIA A. SHANNON, ESQ.

The lifetime experiences of George Liele were forever etched in the chambers of his mind.[1] Out of abundance of his love for persons who were struggling in the fight for justice and utilizing his intellect, Liele committed himself to preach about the good news of Jesus Christ. His impervious hope that flowed forth was a symbol of his courage, dedication, and kindness. He had been in the fight for justice so long at the time of his death that he embraced a Christlike love for humanity.

The significance of George Liele's will to church history and scholarship cannot be underestimated. It is essential because it is a legal record of an early African-American evangelist's possessions and his desired means of disposing them. The will is also important because it reveals aspects of Liele's life that we might not have known otherwise. Most of what scholars know about Liele is obtained from his letters (1791–1793) to John Rippon, minister and editor of the *Baptist Annual Register*, published in London. The will allows us to get an informed glimpse of Liele's life in the early eighteenth century. As an evangelist, Liele proved himself to be a Christian—a man of God who believed in the saving power of Jesus Christ. The will indicates that before making any disposition of his estate, Liele "gives thanks" to God for his "worldly goods" and goes so far as to "commend his soul to Jesus Christ" and his "body to the earth." Nonetheless, George Liele was a responsible person as well as a spiritual one. He was a free black man who was thinking of departing Jamaica for the United Kingdom. As the head of his household and family, he felt duty bound to make the legal arrangements necessary to provide for his dependents. Moreover, Liele was thinking of his mortality in 1822, at the time he wrote the will, and realized that he might not return from such a long journey.

George Liele's will contains information that shows him to have been a responsible Christian businessman who was interested in ensuring the economic, physical, and religious well being of those persons in his care. George Liele was a well-known Baptist evangelist in Jamaica. His will was registered 12 June 1830.

---

[1] Last Will and Testament of George Liele. June 1830. George Liele referred to himself as George Liele, the elder. Island Record Office at Spanish Town, Jamaica, Record No. 744. In Appendix B, see a transcription of the will.

At the time of the registration of the will, Liele was deceased and the courts needed a living witness to Liele's signature. The witnesses were James Fendlater of "the city of Kingston, a gentleman" and two other men. Under oath, they attested to the authenticity of George Liele's will according to the Jamaican courts. The official who administered the oath writes:

> I have administered an oath to James Fendlater, who, being duly sworn on the Holy Evangelists, deposeth and said that he was present and did see George Liele, the Testator in the annexed Instrument of writing named, being at that time of sound and disposing mind, memory and understanding, sign, seal, publish, and declare the same as and for his last will and testament—and at the same time Robert Whair, Zachariah Galfon were also present and together with him subscribed their names as witnesses to the Same in the presence of the said Testator and further that he knows nothing of any will or codicil that can lend to the disadvantage of the will hereunto annexed. Given under my hand and Seal this 19 day of April, in the year of our Lord 1830.—R. Chamberlaine

The authentication of the will indicates that Liele understood the necessity and the process of legally solidifying his wishes. Liele sought three witnesses (no doubt the number required by the court) who were responsible citizens of Jamaica. We learn that one was a gentleman, that they were summoned by Liele, and they were all three together to witness the signing. Here is their written testimony referring to their meeting with Liele: "...of us whom his presence at his request and in the presence of each other have hereunto set and subscribed our hands as Witnesses thereto." It was signed by Robert Whair, Z. Galfon, and James Fendlater.

The fact that Liele goes to the trouble to draft the last will and testament, following the laws and protocol required for making his last will and testament a valid process, suggests his business acumen. Another indication of his business sense is his penchant for details, which are spelled out in the specific items to his wife and children. Land, money, and enslaved persons are specified.

George Liele's Last Will and Testament shows that he was concerned about the physical comfort of his family as well as their continued and future economic freedom. Liele seems to have been financially comfortable in Jamaica. His letter of 1791 to John Rippon indicates that he was a farmer who owned a team of horses and wagons. He reports that he and his sons supplemented the family's income by using his wagons to do work for businesses and the government. Presumably by the time of his death in 1825 or 1828, he had gained more wealth, including real estate, as his will suggests. Naming his wife, Hannah Hunt Liele, as his first heir, Liele states:

> I give, devise, and bequeath unto my dear and beloved wife, Hannah Hunt Liele, all my lands and tenements with all and singular the buildings thereon standing, erected and built, to hold the same to her, her heirs and assigns forever. Items, I give, devise, and bequeath unto the said Hannah Hunt Liele my Negro slaves named Neptune, Anney, and her son James, Betsy and her children Indjoe and Nancy, Peggy and Margaret, for and during the run of her natural life and no longer and from and immediately after the decease of the said Hannah Hunt Liele. Then I do by this my will absolutely manumize, enfranchise and set free from all manner of bondage and slavery whatsoever all and singular the said slaves with their then and future issue, offspring, and increase in as full and ample manner as if they had been born of free parents and never had been slaves.[2]

Not only did Liele own land and buildings, he owned eight slaves whom he wished to be freed after his wife's death. It is not absolutely clear why Liele owned slaves, but it is likely that they were free laborers for the family's farming and household chores. This conjecture seems to have additional support by the publication of Hannah's will, filed in 1828. She clearly wished to hold on to some of the slaves, as is evidenced by this statement:

> A Negro woman slave named Betsy, and her children are (from mistake or inadvertence) directed to be manumitted at my decease but as the said Negro woman slave named Betsy and her children, Nancy and Cudjoe, are my sole and separate property, my said late husband George Liele had no legal power to make such bequest. It is therefore my will and desire that the said Negro woman slave named Betsy, and her children Nancy and Cudjoe, and their future issue, offspring and increase shall form part of my estate and pass under this my will and go to my said Daughter Lucy [Liele] Price to hold to her the said Lucy Price and to her heirs and assigns forever.[3]

Creature comfort and financial security equaled a well-to-do economic status, guaranteed by slave labor for the Liele family. They had become accustomed to such a livelihood. George Liele wished his family to continue enjoying this level of comfort, but not at the expense of withholding freedom from any of the slaves. According to her will, Hannah differed. Unlike Liele, who wanted all of the slaves in the family to be free, Hannah placed comfort and economic status above freedom. The enslaved servants were important to the survival of healthy crops and other enterprises that demanded hard labor that was crucial to the

---

[2] Ibid.

[3] The Last Will and Testament of Hannah Hunt Liele. Island Record Office at Spanish Town, Jamaica, Record No. 744.

family's economic security. Hannah was thinking particularly of daughter Lucy, who had evidently married between 1822, the date of Liele's will, and Hannah's in 1828.

The content of Liele's will regarding his children is both admirable and disturbing. Liele is concerned that his children and future generations hold on to the economic resources that he has accumulated, which is indeed admirable.

> All the Rent, Resources and Remainder of my Estate either real, personal or mixed and not herein before disposed of and wheresoever situated, I give, devise, and bequeath the same and every part and parcel thereof unto my dear and beloved son George Liele and my dear and beloved daughter Lucy Liele of the city and parish of Kingston, free black persons, to hold the same to them and their heirs and assigns for ever equally to be divided, Share and Share alike, and on this express condition, and it is my will and meaning that unless the said George Liele and Lucy Liele do continue to embrace the true church of Christ and become Anabaptists, that they shall in such event absolutely forfeit all right, interest and benefit which I have given them by this my will and be divested and barred absolutely therefrom to all manner of intents and purposes whatsoever.

Here, Liele specifies that "rent" and other "resources...personal and mixed" are to be bequeathed to George and Lucy Liele, his children. We learn from this portion of the will that Liele owned rental property and perhaps investments that were providing some returns. It seems that Liele was not sure of a harmonious relationship between the two or their religious pro-activities. Liele specifically announces that his children are "free black persons," and he admonishes them to "Share and Share alike." Liele's resources are to be equally divided between the two of them and their heirs "forever." The religious uncertainty is suggested when Liele adds his disturbing requirement for his children. His will states that if George or Lucy change their Anabaptist affiliation that they will forfeit all their inheritance from him. Further, he makes plain that if they are disinherited, their resources from his will go to the Anabaptist Church.

The provision of Liele's will insisting that his children adhere to the Anabaptist Church certainly indicates his concern for the religious and spiritual well-being of his children and the future of the Anabaptist Church. He refers to the Anabaptist Church in the will as the "true church of Christ." Common beliefs among the Anabaptist are that a person must experience conversion and rebaptism by immersion. Anabaptists believe that baptism at birth is not sufficient for salvation. In his letter to Rippon in 1791, Liele stated that his wife and children were all "members of the church."[4]

In the same letter, Liele gives some idea of his Anabaptist Church in Jamaica. His members were poor people, both free and enslaved. He makes the point that these people wished to worship God freely: "Thanks be to God we have the liberty to worship Him as we please in the Kingdom."[5] Liele goes on to state that about "four hundred and fifty had been converted to Christ "and that he had "baptized four hundred" in Kingston and Spanish Town combined.[6] No doubt his children were among them. Liele's concern about his children's allegiance to the Anabaptist Church most surely underscores his desire to know that his children would remain committed to the religious denomination of his passion and faith. Undoubtedly, his children's continued commitment to the church of their youth and its ideals would assure Liele of the future of the Anabaptist faith within the family. Therefore, if George and Lucy choose to desert the Anabaptists, Liele promised to ensure the legacy of the Anabaptist Church in Jamaica.

> I do give, devise, and bequeath all and singular of such estate as the said George Liele and Lucy Liele would have been entitled to have and receive under this my will for the benefit and use of the Anabaptist Church in the said city and parish of Kingston and to and for no other use, intent or purpose of Kingston and to and for no other intent or purpose whatsoever.

Liele's promise reflects his love for Jesus Christ and his effort to perpetuate the gospel for generations to come.

George Liele's will, registered in Kingston, Jamaica, county of Surrey, in 1830, is a testament to history. His business-like sense of responsibility combined with his evangelism make him one of the most outstanding black leaders of late seventeenth and early eighteenth-century Jamaica. Despite the fact that part of his will was contested and refuted by his wife Hannah, the record shows that he was a strong family man who left his wife and children sufficient resources for a comfortable living.

Although the will itself does not overtly dwell on the subject of freedom, Liele makes the point that he and his family are free and that he wished the same status for the enslaved persons in his care. As the executrix of her husband's will, we learn that when Hannah's will was probated, she refused freedom to one of

---

[4] George Liele to John Rippon, 1791, *The Baptist Annual Register 1790, 1791, 1792, and Part of 1793* (London)

[5] Ibid.

[6] Ibid.

the families. Liele would have been disappointed with her decision. It was George Liele's desire that everyone under his domain would embrace freedom without a trace of their enslaved heritage.

Epilogue

George Liele

A Religious Figure in America and Abroad

LINDA REED

George Liele's life became an intersection of American and British endeavors in North America and eventually Jamaica as Great Britain militarily engaged herself to maintain sovereignty over her original thirteen colonies, and the colonies did the same to break away and declare independence from British rule. Outside of the many economic issues that burdened the colonial and Mother Country relationship, religion also grew to be very important to the everyday life of colonists in North America. The narrative is a familiar one: those who supported and held loyalty to Great Britain called themselves Loyalists; the colonial backers and so-called instigators were identified as Patriots. Between 1775 and 1782 Loyalists and Patriots fought in a war for America's independence historically known as the American Revolution. Thomas Jefferson's Declaration of Independence, signed by the colonies on 4 July 1776, marked one of the greatest moments in the midst of the conflict. Once the military fighting drew to a close in 1782, Americans set out to establish a way of life for themselves that resulted in the U.S. Constitution which was ratified by the states by 1788, and which also included the Bill of Rights. Americans set firmly a foundation for religious freedom within the Bill of Rights. However, evidence of America's religious fervor showed up as early as the 1740s and 1750s in what historians call the Great Awakening. The Great Awakening proved to be a significant watershed and historical moment because of the huge interest of so many colonists in the religious conversion of their fellowman. Within this religious context we find the lives of George Liele, his owner, Henry Sharp, George Galphin, Liele's converts, and eventually the religious missionary work of Liele, physically aided (there may have also been spiritual aid) by a British soldier who assisted Liele's travel to Jamaica in 1782, the closing year of the American Revolution. This is the story told by all of the scholars within the chapters of this book, whose timeline reaches from the 1750s, the decade of Liele's biological birth, to his religious work in Jamaica and the establishment of Baptists churches there and his death in the 1830s, the decade in which the British universally freed enslaved persons there and others of its Caribbean possessions. This is most ironic since the British entered Europe's competition for overseas colonies after Portugal, Spain, the Netherlands, and the French, even declaring that Britain only followed the pattern set by her European neighbors in their use of the institution of slavery to make their New World empires or possessions produce a profit for respective empire builders.

George Liele's place in history is also intriguing because his life of enslavement gave way to a freed person's life full of zeal for consistent efforts to have other peoples (African Americans, the British, Jamaicans) learn about Jesus Christ and to accept him as their Lord and Savior. He took to heart the Great Commission as found in Matthew 28 and verses 19–20, "Go ye therefore and baptize all nations, baptizing them in the name of the father, son, and holy ghost; teaching them to observe everything that I have commanded. And lo, I am with you, always, even to the end of the world."

Like the evangelists or preachers of the Great Awakening, such as George Whitefield, George Liele proved himself to be a fascinating religious leader. His zeal probably followed the example of Whitefield, who became widely known for his fiery preaching, summarized in today's terms as sermons filled with significant emotional moments where the deliverer raises and lowers his voice to catch and hold the attention of the listener or congregation. David Shannon's piece puts this all together when he illustrates how Liele caught the attention of his owner, who freed him spiritually as well as physically. Milledge Galphin Murray furthers our thinking along these lines in his work on Liele on the Galphin plantation, where he preached so powerfully that the white plantation owner allowed him to deliver sermons to the enslaved, freed persons, and to whites on the plantation and neighboring farms. Liele's preaching is a historical marker for Silver Bluff, South Carolina. As the first ordained African-American preacher with such a wide group of listeners, Liele deserves his rightful place in history because he was able to move and work in the physical locations of Silver Bluff, Augusta, and Savannah to win souls to Christ when most African Americans were yet enslaved, and if free, were confined to segregated seating within the confines of white church service or worship. Many persons of African descent felt so confined by the limitation of the separate seating and watered-down messages of "slaves obey your master" that they took to brush-arbor gathering so that they could worship in their own way, again, as illustrated in the work of David Shannon in this book. Their culture tied them to a particular religious expectation and experience.

Liele identified with the British Loyalists like George Galphin, and so American Patriots would not have cared for him. As he made his way to Savannah, he accepted his fate with the British, which had proven to be beneficial as soon as the American Revolution started militarily, for the British under Lord Dunmore promised freedom to all enslaved persons who engaged in the war on the side of the British. American Patriots lagged in such a strategic military decision, only coming to the same conclusion under George Washington late in the war. Hence, it becomes clear why Liele and many persons of African descent had a greater hope in the Loyalist position. Historians have long established that in many areas landowners or plantation owners had to move their slaves to a different location whenever the British engaged the Patriots in those places. Imagine, if you will, even the logistical difficulty this must have posed as the Patriots and the British fought a war!

In the midst of the war George Liele continuously preached the gospel, winning converts in David George, Jesse Peter, and Andrew Bryan. Bryan met Liele when Liele reached Savannah with the British. We are reminded of just how much the Patriots disliked those who affiliated with the Loyalists because the historical narrative from Savannah is that Bryan's owners whipped him for his choice of listening to Liele and then his religious conversion under the preaching of Liele. Liele's message might not have been the reason behind Bryan's public whipping as much as the Loyalist persuasion of the person delivering the message.

George Liele proved to be very resourceful because of his intellect. Julia Frazier White captures Liele as an intellect of his time only to be compared with the likes of Phillis Wheatley, Benjamin Banneker, Richard Allen, and Absalom Jones. Liele cleverly managed to earn and keep the trust of white plantation owners, British soldiers, and the enslaved persons whom he came to know, as well as other freed persons. In brief, he learned how to walk a tightrope, so to speak. Moreover, he managed to live a balanced life by choosing a wife and having a family that he managed to also arrange for the British to bring into Jamaica when they departed from the shores of Savannah in 1782.

Liele continued his work in Jamaica, just as he had managed to do while he was still in America. He preached the gospel, but went a step further when he set up churches so that a greater number of people could choose Jesus Christ as their personal savior. Noel Leo Erskine's "George Liele, Native Baptists and the Revival Church" tells the story of Liele's religious work in Jamaica.

Beyond Jamaica, Liele's influence reached as far away as Nova Scotia and Sierra Leone through his converts David George and Andrew Bryan. The American Revolution narrative also has an impact here, because as British soldiers departed America and the fighting of the Revolutionary War, Great Britain kept its wartime promise of freedom for the enslaved who assisted the British in the war. Departing from the port cities of New York, Charleston, and Savannah, the British took thousands of former slaves, carrying them into Nova Scotia, Sierra Leone, and other destinations, including Great Britain. Of course, the authors of this book tell of the influence of Liele through David George and Andrew Bryan. In this way Liele's religious work or missionary work reached

Americans and people abroad. It has passed on to future generations who still tie his work to the religious fervor forever present from colonial time to the present.

By numbers alone, Christians are the top-ranked religious group of the world, with well over two billion believers. Christians, then, account for a third of the world's religious believers because the world population in 2010 is roughly six and one-half billion people.[1] Baptists are represented in the largest numbers in the United States of America, Africa, and other parts of the world, including Jamaica. Interestingly, George Liele became enslaved in the North American colonies and also was set free in the same environment. However, he considered himself spiritually free before he was set physically free. In Liele's spiritual freedom he found that he wanted many others to share the same experience, to be spiritually free in his Lord and to have salvation. He started his missionary work, then, just as the Bible advised in Acts 1: 8, which reads, "But ye shall receive power, after that the Holy Ghost is come upon you: and ye shall be witnesses unto me both in Jerusalem, and in all Judaea, and in Samaria, and unto the uttermost part of the earth." Liele evangelized in America to those close to him, and once he left with the British in 1782, he continued to evangelize in Jamaica. He was forever concerned about the salvation of another person.

Liele's historical significance is bound to his religious fervency. He established safe havens for African-American Baptists, whether they were enslaved or free. Just as significantly, he established places of worship for his fellowman, African American or European American, in the church where black people and white people could hear his sermons at once. Through the conversions of David George, Jesse Peter, and Andrew Bryan, other sanctuaries sprang up in Savannah, Nova Scotia, and Sierra Leone. When we include the missionary work of this masterful preacher, teacher, worker, and intellectual in North America and Jamaica, we really cannot overlook the global impact of this one great missionary. Some twelve to fourteen years before Richard Allen and Absolom Jones set up the African Methodist Episcopal Church in Philadelphia, Liele had begun the work that God purposed for his life. The record needs to be clear that Liele sought to witness to any person, regardless of background. Liele focused on winning souls, and because his work had that dimension, as others experienced spiritual conversion, their missionary work and ministry followed a similar pattern. Liele's divine purpose and work leaves little doubt how the zeal of a few has made Christians the largest number of religious believers the world over.

---

[1] http://www.adherents.com/Religions_By_Adherents.html (accessed 12 July 2010).

Contributors

David T. Shannon, Sr.

Dr. David T. Shannon was an educator, scholar and pastor. He shared his expansive knowledge with the church, the academy, and the global community. He served as president of three institutions: Andover Newton Theological School (Newton Centre, Massachusetts); Virginia Union University, (Richmond, Virginia.); and Allen University (Columbia, South Carolina). Shannon served as Dean of Faculty at Pittsburgh Theological Seminary (Pittsburgh, Pennsylvania) and at the Interdenominational Theological Center (Atlanta, Georgia). Known for his ecumenical and interfaith endeavors, he was a leader in the National Council of Churches and World Council of Churches. His published works include: *Studies in the Life and Works of Paul* (Nashville, TN: Townsend, 1961), *The Old Testament Experience of Faith* (Valley Forge, PA: Judson Press, 1977), coeditor of *Black Witness to the Apostolic Faith* (Grand Rapids, MI: Eerdmans, 1985), and articles in *Stony the Road We Trod* (Minneapolis, MN: Augsburg Fortress, 1991), and *The Africana Bible: Reading Israel's Scriptures from Africa and the African Diaspora* (Minneapolis, MN: Fortress Press, 2010).

B. Carlisle Driggers

Dr. B. Carlisle Driggers is the Executive Director Emeritus of the South Carolina Baptist Convention. He served as a pastor and also as the Associate Director of the Black Church Relations Department of the Home Mission Board, Southern Baptist Convention. He is the author of three books and has written numerous articles. Dr. Driggers holds degrees from Mars Hill College and Carson-Newman College along with two degrees from the Southern Baptist Theological Seminary in Louisville, Kentucky. He earned his doctor of ministry degree at the Pittsburgh Theological Seminary, where he first met Dr. David T. Shannon, Sr., who was the dean of faculty. He has been awarded three honorary degrees. His wife, Jeanette, has been helpful in the writing project. They reside in Shady Dale, Georgia.

Noel Leo Erskine

Dr. Noel Leo Erskine is professor of theology and ethics at Candler School of Theology and the Graduate School of Arts and Sciences at Emory University. A native of Jamaica, Dr. Erskine holds a diploma in Theology from the University of London, a Master of Theology from Duke University, and from Union Theological Seminary a Master of Sacred Theology, a Master of Philosophy and a PhD in Systematic Theology. His books include: *Black Theology and Pedagogy* (New York: Palgrave Macmillan, 2008), *From Garvey to Marley:*

Rastafari Theology (Gainesville: University Press of Florida, 2005), *King Among the Theologians* (Pilgrim Press, 1994), *Decolonizing Theology: A Caribbean Perspective* (African World Press, 1981, 1998), and *Black People and the Reformed Church in America* (Reformed Church Press, 1978). Forthcoming is *The Black Church: Caribbean and African American* (New York: Oxford University Press). He resides in Atlanta with his wife Glenda. They have three children: Donna, June, and Leo.

Ernestine Pickens Glass

Dr. Ernestine Pickens Glass is former professor and chair of the Department of English at Clark Atlanta University in Atlanta. A graduate of Tennessee State University, she earned an MA in English from Atlanta University and PhD from Emory University. A Phi Beta Kappa, Dr. Glass is the author of *Charles W. Chesnutt and the Progressive Movement* (New York: Pace University Press, 1994), the editor of *Frederick Douglass by Charles W. Chesnutt: a Centenary Edition* (Atlanta: Clark Atlanta University Press, 2001), and the co-editor of *Passing in the Works of Charles Waddell Chesnutt* (Jackson: University of Mississippi Press, 2010). Dr. Glass is the recipient of an award for outstanding teaching at Clark College, the Sylvia Lyons Render Award from the Charles W. Chesnutt Association, and the Aldridge-McMillan Award for excellence in research and scholarship. Professor Emerita at Clark Atlanta University, Dr. Glass is an active member of Friendship Baptist Church in Atlanta, along with her husband, William Glass.

Winston A. Lawson

Rev. Dr. Winston A. Lawson is senior pastor of Hillside Presbyterian Church in Decatur, Georgia. Prior he was professor of religion and philosophy at Stillman College in Tuscaloosa, Alabama, where he also served as pastor of the Brown Memorial Presbyterian Church. Dr. Lawson was college chaplain at the University of the West Indies in Kingston, Jamaica, of which country he is a native. He has been a parish minister in Kingston, Jamaica; New York City; Pittsburgh, Pennsylvania; Atlanta, Georgia; Columbia, South Carolina; Jackson, Kentucky; Gadsden, Alabama; and Tuscaloosa, Alabama. He also served four years as denominational executive for the General Assembly of the Presbyterian Church, during which time he was adjunct professor of theology at Columbia Theological Seminary in Decatur, Georgia. Dr. Lawson is the author of the book *Religion and Race: African and European Roots in a Jamaican Testament* (New York: Peter Lang, 1996) and several scholarly articles. Dr. Lawson is married to Verona, a psychiatrist, and is the father of two adult children, Kwame, an Arabic literature and language scholar, and Indira, a high school principal.

Milledge Galphin Murray

Mr. Milledge Galphin Murray is a seventh-generation direct descendant of George Galphin, who owned Silver Bluff Plantation in Beech Island, South

Carolina, where George Liele preached to enslaved persons prior to the American Revolution. Murray was born in Augusta, Georgia. He received a Bachelor of Science degree in Industrial Education from Clemson University, and a Master of Science degree from the Graduate School of Banking of the South at Louisiana State University. An active member of St. James United Methodist Church in Augusta, Mr. Murray teaches the adult men's Bible class. Mr. Murray is also a member of the Beech Island Agriculture Club, Beech Island Historical Society, Historic Augusta, the Augusta Museum of History, and serves on the board of directors for the North Augusta Arts and Heritage Center. Retired as first vice president at SunTrust Bank after thirty-nine years, Mr. Murray remains active in community affairs.

Linda Reed

Dr. Linda Reed is associate professor in the Department of History at the University of Houston. She is a scholar in African-American history with a particular interest in women and the South. She has served as the director of the University of Houston's African-American Studies Program and the national director for the Association of Black Women Historians. She received fellowships from the University of North Carolina, the University of Michigan, the Ford Foundation, and Princeton University. Dr. Reed received her PhD from Indiana University, Bloomington. Dr. Reed's book, *Simple Decency and Common Sense: The Southern Conference Movement, 1938-1963*, concentrates on the forgotten years of the civil rights movement. Professor Reed is also coeditor, along with Darlene Clark Hine and Wilma King, of *We Specialize in the Wholly Impossible: A Reader in Black Women's History*. Dr. Reed is currently completing two books, *Black Women in America, 1619-2001* (Malden, MA: Blackwell Publishers) and *I'm Sick and Tired of Being Sick and Tired: The Life and Times of Fannie Lou Hamer*, a biography of the influential Mississippi civil rights activist. She also contributed sections to volume 1 of *America's Past in Global Perspective*.

Jeneen Blease Roscoe

Missionary Jeneen Roscoe holds a Bachelor of Science degree in Psychology from Howard University in Washington, DC, and has pursued theological seminary training toward a Master of Divinity degree in missiology at the Interdenominational Theological Center in Atlanta. She has served as a licensed missionary with Campus Crusade for Christ International, with assignments worldwide, including in Bolivia, Nigeria, Kenya, Ghana, and South Africa. Ms. Roscoe has served as a licensed missionary in Sierra Leone, West Africa, with the missionary organization Christians in Action. She currently serves at the Regent Road Baptist Church in Sierra Leone, West Africa, where she was inducted as a missionary in 2008, becoming their first African-American female missionary since the nineteenth century.

Horace O. Russell

Educated at London University, Calabar Theological College in Jamaica, and Regent's Park College, Oxford University, in England, the Rev. Dr. Horace O. Russell has devoted his life to the Church and education. Russell was instrumental in the formation in 1965 of the United Theological College of the West Indies and served as its President. He created the *Caribbean Journal of Theology*, a publication for learned theological discourse. In 1976, Dr. Russell was called to the historic East Queen Street Baptist Church in Kingston (started by George Liele), where he served for thirteen years. In 1990 Dr. Russell became professor of historical theology and dean of the chapel of Eastern Baptist Theological Seminary, Philadelphia (now Palmer Theological Seminary), and while there he was pastor of Saints Memorial Baptist Church, Bryn Mawr, from 1992 to 2010. Dr. Russell is author of numerous articles and several books, including *The Missionary Outreach of the West Indian Church: Jamaican Baptist Missions to West Africa in the Nineteenth Century* (New York: P. Lang, 2000). He was recently honored for his work by the Jamaican government.

Averett Powell Shannon

Mrs. Averett Powell Shannon is a retired educator and college administrator. She received her undergraduate Bachelor of Science degree from Virginia State University in Petersburg, Virginia and the Master of Education Degree from University of Pittsburgh in Pittsburgh, PA. She studied painting at the Boston Museum of Fine Arts in Boston, MA; the Atlanta School of Arts in Atlanta, GA and continues to enjoy helpful painting instructions at the Darnell Senior Multipurpose Facility in Atlanta. Mrs. Shannon's paintings have been exhibited in Boston; Columbia, South Carolina; and in Atlanta where several were juried by the Atlanta and Fulton County Arts and Community Affairs Departments. Two of her paintings received second and third place awards respectively. She was commissioned to paint the portrait of George Liele by her husband Dr. David T. Shannon, Sr. Averett Shannon is a key researcher and counselor for the George Liele Research Project.

Vernitia A. Shannon

Ms. Vernitia A. Shannon, Esq. graduated from Bucknell University in Lewisburg, PA, and from Howard University School of Law in Washington, DC. She has practiced law for more than twenty years in Atlanta and served on the White House Task Force on the Environment during the Clinton Administration and serves on the Fulton County Commission on Disability Affairs. She has been a missionary to Zambia, Africa and Fiji and participated as co-moderator for the International Conference on Medical Volunteerism in Atlanta, and as a panelist at the Global Summit on Medical Volunteerism. She is a volunteer for the Friends of Disabled Adults and Children and serves on the Board of Deacons of Friendship Baptist Church in Atlanta, Georgia.

Deborah Bingham Van Broekhoven

Dr. Deborah Van Broekhoven has been executive director of the American Baptist Historical Society since 1998, where she is also managing editor for *The American Baptist Quarterly*. Prior to the Historical Society position, Dr. Van Broekhoven taught history and American studies for twenty years, at Grand Rapids Baptist College, Barrington College, and Ohio Wesleyan University. She has written numerous articles and a book, *The Devotion of These Women: Rhode Island in the Antislavery Network* (Boston: Boston University Press, 2002). A member of the International Collegium of Scholars at Morehouse College, she also is a member of the Society for Historians of the Early Republic.

Julia Frazier White

Dr. Julia Frazier White, project manager for the George Liele Research Project, is the author of *Forgiveness: Learning How to Forgive* (Indianapolis: Xlibris Publishers, Inc., 2005) and *Poems, Prose, and Prayers* (Indianapolis: Xlbris Publishers, Inc, 2012). Dr. White graduated from Murray State University (BS), Colorado Technical University (MA); and Newburgh Theological Seminary (Phd). Dr. White worked at IBM as a senior systems engineer, senior instructor of computer systems, and project manager. After retiring from IBM, Dr. White founded Cintech Computer Center, Inc., and later worked for Georgia-Pacific Corporation as an Information Systems Manager of Development. Dr. White has three adult children: Richard Frazier White, Anthony Brewer White, and Cheryl A. White.

Rev. Victor G. Williams, I

Rev. Victor G. Williams, pastor of Greenspoint Baptist Church in Houston, Texas, is technical consultant and Internet and Web page advisor for the George Liele Research Project. He attended University of North Texas where he graduated with a Bachelor of Science in History and a Master of Science in Education, after which he worked for Southwestern Bell Communications for 26 years. Rev. Williams was founder and president of Saturday Academy USA: Computer and Business Education. He started and equipped computer education learning centers in seven states in the United States and three sites in Jamaica and has been an instructor of computer education for the National Baptist Convention USA, Incorporated and for the National Missionary Fellowship of Churches. Rev. Williams is presently Christian Educational Director of the Independent Missionary Baptist General Association of Texas. He has two sons, Victor G. Williams II, and Curtis Brandon Williams, an attorney.

Appendixes

Appendix A

Chronologically Significant Dates

1607:	British ship lands at Jamestown in the New World.
1608–1609:	John Smyth and Thomas Helwys went to Holland from England.
1611–1612:	Thomas Helwys returned to London to start a Baptist church and give rise to General Baptist views as Arminians.
1619:	Indentured servants from Africa brought to Virginia followed by thousands of slaves.
1620:	Pilgrims (or Separatist Puritans) began arriving at Plymouth, Massachusetts.
1638:	Particular Baptists and Calvinism emerged in England.
1639:	Roger Williams started First Baptist Church at Providence, Rhode Island.
1696:	William Screven moved to Charleston, South Carolina, with his Particular (or Regular) Baptist congregation.
1704:	London Baptist Association was formed.
1740–1775:	First Great Awakening in America.
1740s:	George Galphin came from Ireland and began the Silver Bluff settlement in South Carolina.
1755:	Shubal Stearns came to Sandy Creek in North Carolina to start a Separatist Baptist church.
1764:	Henry Sharp and his family plus nine slaves, including George, moved from Virginia to Georgia. George was separated from his parents, Nancy and Liele.
1772:	Daniel Marshall began the First Baptist Church in Georgia called Kiokee, a Separatist church.
1773:	Edmund Botsford began the second Baptist church in Georgia, a Regular church, called Botsford's Old Meetinghouse
1773:	Wait Palmer started the Silver Bluff Baptist Church, which would become the first black Baptist church in America.
1773 or 1774:	Matthew Moore began a Baptist church near Buckhead Creek in what became Burke County Georgia.
1774:	George Sharp [Liele] was converted to Christ by Matthew Moore and was soon ordained as the first ordained black Baptist preacher in America.

1774:	George Sharp [Liele] preached to slaves at surrounding plantations including Silver Bluff and led David George to Christ.
1775:	American Revolutionary War began.
1775:	Wait Palmer ordained David George and Jesse Peters as Baptist preachers, and David George became the pastor at Silver Bluff, the first black Baptist pastor of a congregation in America.
1776–1777:	Matthew Moore's church disbanded and George Sharp [Liele] and family went to Savannah.
1776–1777:	Silver Bluff church disbanded and David George and Jesse Peter went to Savannah.
1778:	George Sharp [Liele], assisted by David George, began the First Colored Baptist Church near Savannah with Sharp [Liele] as pastor.
1778–1779:	George Sharp [Liele] was made a freed man by Henry Sharp. George Liele changed his last name to Liele in recognition of his father.
1781:	David George went to Canada and later to Sierra Leone in West Africa.
1782:	George Liele ordained Andrew Bryan and established him as pastor of the Savannah church.
1782–1783:	George Liele and family left America for Kingston, Jamaica, in December 1782, arriving in January 1783. Established the first Baptist church in Jamaica. Liele's work is now recognized as the first missionary endeavor by an African-American Baptist.
1783:	The Revolutionary War ended.
1788:	Jesse Peter returned to Silver Bluff, reorganized the church, and became its pastor.
1790–1803:	John Rippon, London, edited the *Baptist Annual Register*.
1791:	George Liele wrote from Kingston, Jamaica, to John Rippon in London. Dr. Rippon's compilations in *The Baptist Annual Register* are the oldest known documents that authenticate the written words of George Liele.
1792:	David George started the first Baptist church on the continent of Africa in Sierra Leone, West Africa. The church today is named Regent Road Baptist Church (Church of God).
1793:	Jesse Peter started the First African Baptist Church of Augusta and became its pastor.
1828:	George Liele passed to Glory.

Appendix B

Last Will and Testament of George Liele

Transcription Earle D. Clowney

The last Will and Testament/Jamaica Island.

George the 4th by the Grace of God of the United Kingdom of Great Britain and Ireland King

George Liele/and of Jamaica Lord Defender of the Faith, Lc Ent. 12 June 1830

To our trusty and well-beloved, Richard Chamberlains and William Henry Hall of the city of Kingston Esquires.

Know ye that we have constituted, authorized, and appointed and by these presents do constitute, authorize and appoint Ye or either of ye to administer an oath unto James Findlater of the City of Kingston, Gentleman or any other that are witnesses and can make oath, of the signing, sealing, publishing and declaring of the last will and testament of George Liele, late of the City and Parish of Kingston, a free Black man deceased, and thereof you or either of you are to make a due return under your or either of your Hands and Seals unto our Governor or Commander in Chief of our said island or to the Governor in Chief of the same for the time being with this power annexed so that such proceedings may be ordered therein as may be according to law.

Witness his Excellency the Right honorable Somerset Lowry, Earl of Belmore, Captain General and Governor in chief of our Said Island at San Jago de la Vega, the 15th day of April in the year of our Lord 1830 and in the 11th Year of our Reign.

Belmore Passed the Secretary's office

W. Bullock

Secretary

In obedience to the dedimus potestatem and agreeable to the purport thereof, I have administered an oath unto James Findlater, one of the Subscribing Witnesses to the Execution of the last will and Testament of George Liele, late of the city of Kingston, a free Black man deceased, as I am within directed as witness my hand and seal this 19th day of April 1830.

R. Chamberlains

Jamaica Island. In the name of God, Amen, I, George Liele the Elder, of the City and Parish of Kingston, in the county of Surry and Island aforesaid, a free Black man but shortly intending to depart the said Island for the United Kingdom of Great Britain and Ireland—having taken into mature consideration the certainty of Death and the uncertainty of this transitory and the duty incumbent on me of disposing of my worldly concerns so as to prevent all disputes hereafter respecting my estate, do for that purpose, while in a State of Sound and disposing Mind, memory and understanding (thanks be to God for the Same), do make, publish and declare this my last will and Testament in manner and form following; that is to say, first and principally, I commend my soul unto the Hands of Almighty God, hoping for remission of all my sins through the merits of Jesus Christ, my blessed Saviour and Redeemer, and my body to the earth when it shall please God to call me, as my Executrix or Executor or either of them hereinafter named shall direct. Secondly, that all my just and lawful debts, which I may owe at the time of my decease and the expenses of my funeral and the charges approving and recording this my will, may be fully proved and satisfied by my Executrix and Executor or such of them as shall qualify and act under this my will as soon as conveniently may be after my decease for the payment of which I hereby subject and make liable all my real and personal Estate of what nature and kind so ever and as to what worldly Estate God has been pleased to bless me with, I give and dispose of the same as followeth: Item. I give, devise, and bequeath unto my dear and beloved wife, Hannah Hunt Liele, all my lands and tenements with all and singular the buildings thereon standing, erected and built, to hold the same to her, her heirs and assigns forever. Item. I give, devise, and bequeath unto the said Hannah Hunt Liele my Negro slaves named Neptune, Anney, and her son James, Betsy and her children Indjoe and Nancy, Peggy and Margaret, for- and during the run of her natural life and no longer and from arid immediately after the decease of the said Hannah Hunt Liele, then I do by this my will absolutely manumize, enfranchise and set free from all manner of bondage and slavery whatsoever all and singular the said slaves with their then and future issue, offspring, and increase in as full and ample as if they had been born of free parents and never had been slaves. All the Rent, manner Resource and Remainder of my Estate either real—personal or mixed and not herein before disposed of and wheresoever situate, I give, devise, and bequeath the same and every part and parcel thereof unto my dear and beloved son George Liele and my dear and beloved daughter Lucy Liele of the city and parish of Kingston, free black persons, to hold the same to them and their heirs and assigns for ever equally to be divided, Share and Share alike, this express condition, and it is my will and meaning that unless the said George Liele and Lucy Liele do continue to embrace the truth of Christ and become Anabaptists, that they shall in such event absolutely forfeit all right, interest and benefit which I have given them by this my will and be divested and barred absolutely therefrom to all manner of intents and purposes whatsoever, and in case of such event, then I do give, devise, and bequeath all and singular of such estate as the said George Liele and Lucy Liele would have been entitled to have and receive under this my will for the benefit and use of the Anabaptist Church in the said city and parish of Kingston and to and for no other use, intent or purpose whatsoever, and I do hereby nominate, constitute and appoint my dear and beloved wife, the said Hannah Hunt Liele, Executrix and the said George Liele Executor of this my last will and Testament, and I do recommend to them to hold my memory dear to them to see the same executed fairly and honestly and that they will act in a friendly manner and see to the Execution of what I have left in charge to them, so as to prevent any dispute or disagreeable litigation. And do hereby revoke and make void all former and other will or wills by me at any time heretofore made and do declare this only to be and contain my last will and Testament. In witness whereof I have hereunto set my hand and Seal this twenty-fifth day of February in the year of our Lord one thousand Eight Hundred and Twenty-two.

George Liele The Elder

Signed, sealed, published and / declared by George Liele the / Elder as and for his last will / and Testament in the presence / of us whom his presence / at his request and in the presence of each other have hereunto set and sub- / scribed our hands as Witnesses thereto.

Robert Whair

Z. Galfon

James Fendlater

Jamaica Island. In obedience to the dedimus potestatem hereunto annexed, I have administered an oath to James Fendlater, who, being duly sworn on the Holy Evangelists, deposeth and saith that he was present and did see George Lisle, the Testator in the annexed Instrument of writing named, being at that time of sound and disposing mind, memory and understanding, sign, seal, publish, and declare the same as and for his last will and Testament—and at the same time Robert Whair, Zachariah Galfon were also present and together with him subscribed their names as witnesses to the Same in the presence of the said Testator and further that he knows nothing of any will or codicil that can lend to the disadvantage of the will hereunto annexed.

Given under my hand and Seal this 19 day of April, in the year of our Lord 1830.

R. Chamberlains

Jamaica Island

Foster Henry March of the Parish of Saint Catherine, Gentleman, being duly sworn, deposeth and saith that the paper writing or will and Papers hereunto annexed contain, according to the best of this deponent's reckoning and belief thereof, Eight Legal Sheet (of one Hundred and Sixty words to a Sheet) and ninety-five words over.

F. Henry March

Sworn before me this 12th day of June 1830

R. Williams

Appendix C

The George Liele painting was commissioned by the founder of the George Liele Research Group, Dr. David T. Shannon, Sr. The inspiration was drawn from Dr. Shannon's contagious commitment to the research of George Liele's life and accomplishments during a very difficult period in history. In the painting, George Liele has been depicted as a strong, determined man of faith wearing the typical attire of a preacher during that time. Liele was able to garner the courage in spite of the challenges Africans and African Americans were forced to endure. Liele was apt enough to recognize the true source of life—the Creator.

The painting is depicted at night, which represents this dark, unbelievable, and unknown period of human history. The stars represent the hope that mankind can wonder about, study, learn from, and use as a guide for escaping to freedom and a better life. The two churches represent Liele as founder of a church in Savannah, Georgia, and Kingston, Jamaica, where he preached the gospel of Jesus Christ as Lord and Master. Those two structures also represent the church-related schools that George Liele founded. He influenced colleagues to educate their people at their mission sites. The trees in the background represent the enormous strength, endurance, protection, and growth of the thousands of enslaved people. Trees are usually thought to have deep roots and most of them are able to weather storms for many years. Similarly, the enslaved people have been steadily anchored in the Creator and have been able to survive that very painful period thrust upon them. Thanks to George Liele's faith in his "Lord and Master" as to what could be done, others dared to follow him and future generations can dare to hope.

About the Artist: Mrs. Averett Shannon earned a Bachelor of Science at Virginia State College and a Master of Education at University of Pittsburgh. Ms. Shannon's paintings have been exhibited in Boston, Massachusetts, Allen University, Columbia, South Carolina, and in Atlanta. Two of her paintings received second- and third-place awards in juried art shows sponsored by the City of Atlanta and the Fulton County Arts and Community Affairs Department.

Appendix D

Last Will and Testament of George Galphin

The will and codicils of George Galphin, entered at the court of Ninety-Six District (Box 40, Pack 898, dated April 6, 1776), read as follows:

In the name of God Amen. I George Galphin of the Province aforesaid, Gentleman, do make this my last will and Testament in manner and Form following, First it is my will that all and every the Legatees herein after named or mentioned who are not free shall from and immediately after my Death be and remain forever free and discharged from all and all mannr of Slavery and Bondage, particularly I will that my mulatto Girl named Barbara be free and I do hereby give her her freedom. Also I give to my mulatto girls Rachel and Betsey, (Daughters of a mulatto woman named Sapho) their Fredom, Also I give to my half breed Indian Girl Rose (Daughter of Nitehuckey), her freedom and also five Cows and Calves and two mares and Colts, and my will is that they severally shall be forever free and discharged from all Bondage and Slavery. Also I give and devise to Thomas Galphin Son of Rachel Dupre all my household furniture and plate and Ten mares and Colts and all the riding horses belonging to him and his sisters Cowpen in Ogeechee with the half of Stock of Cattle at Ogeechee aforesaid with his and his sisters mark and brand. Also I give and devise to the said Thomas son of the said Rachel Dupre (without impeachment of waste) for the Term of his natural life the use occupation and enjoyment of my Grist Mill and Saw Mill, situate lying and being on the North side of Town Creek together with all the lands on the same side of said creek containing about one thousand acres, also the use of my new Brick House with four hundred acres of land belonging to it and all the improvements thereon situate in the province of South Carolina. Also the use of all the land from Mr. Shaw's lower line upon Savannah River at the Spanish Cutoff down said River to Mr. McGillvery's lower line containing about one thousand three hundred acres in the province of Georgia. Also one tract of land on the out side of the Swamp in said province of Georgia which I bought from James McHenry, also two thousand acres of the ceded land in any part he may choose that belongs to me or may belong to me, also three hundred and fifty acres of land upon Ogeechee which I bought off Patrick Denneson. Also a tract of land on the Back Swamp in the said province of South Carolina containing four hundred acres, all without Impeachment of waste, also the use work and labour of the following Slaves (that is to say) Petersisom and his wife Nanncy, their Children and future issue, Cato his wife Bess their children and future Issue, Syefa Negro Man, Joe and Cornelia his wife their Children and future Issue, Kelley, Tom, his wife Lucey, their Children and future Issue, Michal his wife Sarah their Children and future Issue, Coffee his wife Betty, their Children and future Issue, Goodfellow (a Negroe man), Sarah I had off James Deveaux, her Children and future Issue, Little Frank (a mustee Boy), Davey (a Negroe Man), Pompey and his wife Sarah and issue, Rachel (Fridays wife), her children and future issue, and upon the Death of the Said Thomas I give my said Mills, Brick House and all the said Lands and Slaves with their future Issue unto the Child or Children of the Said Thomas that shall be then living in such parts and proportions, and for such Estate and Estates, and at and under Such Limitations, Restrictions and Contingencies as he the said Thomas shall by his last will and Testament in writing or by any deed by him to be duly Executed in his lifetime direct limit or appoint, and for want of Such direction limitation and appointment I give and bequeath the said Mills, houses, lands and Slaves and their Issue to and amongst all and every of the children of said Thomas that shall live to come of age or have issue to be equally divided amongst them and their respective heirs and assigns forever as tenants in Common and not as joint tenants and if but one child of the said Thomas shall live to come of age or have issue then to that child alone and his or her heirs and assigns forever.

Also I give and bequeath to Martha Galphin (Daughter of the said Rachel Dupre) for and during the term of her natural life without impeachment of waste the use of two tracts of land containing five hundred acres each, situate lying and being above Mr. Raes above Augusta in the Province of Georgia. Also the use of two lots of land in Augusta, also fifty acres of land in Augusta which I bought of John Joachim Zubly where Gray lived with all the improvements thereon, also one tract of land on the outside of the Swamp I bought off Wade joining McHenry's Land in the said Province of Georgia, also two thousand acres of the ceded land in any part she may that belongs or may belong to me all without Impeachment of waste. Also I give and devise unto the said Martha, ten horses and seven mares with the half of all the stock of cattle at Ogeechee aforesaid here and her brother's mark and brand likewise all cattle and horses with her own mark and brand. Also the use, work, and labour of the following Slaves (that is to say) Dick his wife Cler and their Children and future issue, Billey his wife Dina their children and future Issue, Dutch-Jemmy, Beckey her children and future issue, Jemima her children and future issue, Deborah and her future issue, Swind Tom his wife Juba, their children, and future issue, Trump his wife Tina their children and future issue, French Peter his wife Silvia their children and future issue, and little Jacob and upon the death of the said Martha, I give all the said several tracts and lots of land last above mentioned unto the child or children of the said Martha (together with the last mentioned slaves and their issue) that shall upon such contingency be living in such way and manner parts and proportions and for such estate and estates and at and under such contingencies limitations and restrictions as the said Martha shall by her last will and testament in writing or other writing by her duly executed directed limited and appoint, and for want of such direction limitations or appointment I give and bequeath the said several slaves and their issue and increase to and among all and every the children of the said Martha (that shall live to come of age or have) issue to be equally divided amongst and their respective Heirs and Assigns forever as Tenants in Common and not as joint Tenants and if but one child of the said Martha shall live to come of age or have issue then to that Child alone and his or her heirs and assigns forever.

Also I give to George the son of Metawney (an Indian woman) ten horses and seven mares with the one third of all the stock of cattle, with his own and sisters Judith's and brother John's mark and branch wheresoever they be found, likewise all cattle and horses with his own mark and brand, also I give and bequeath unto the said George for and during the term of his Natural life without Impeachment of waste the old Brick House with one hundred acres of land whereon it stands, also two hundred acres joining, one hundred acres more joining all below said Brick House in said province of South Carolina, Also all that tract of Land containing five hundred acres above the Spanish Cutoff on Savannah River in the province of Georgia. Also I give and bequeath unto the said George, and John his brother, the saw mill on the south side of Town Creek with the tract of land whereon it stands containing about one hundred acres together with all the land I run upon the South side of and joining the said Creek above the said Saw Mill containing about one thousand acres to hold to them jointly, also I give to the said George two thousand acres of the Ceded Land in any part he may choose, that belongs or may belong to me, to be disposed of as he the said George shall think proper, also I give the said George the use work and labour of the following slaves (that is to say) Coboy, his wife Sarah their children and future Issue, August a Mulatto man and his children except Rose, whose freedom I have herein given, Moll her Children and future issue, Ingston, his wife Darkey, their children and future issue, Grays March his wife Claranda and any issue she may have of him, Sue her children and future issue, Joe his wife Hannah their children and future issue, Long John his wife Sarah, their children and future issue, Leander, Frank and Harry, and upon the Death of the said George, I give the said Brick House with the said one hundred acres of land whereon it stands, and the said two hundred acres joining one hundred acres more joining, all below the said brick house with the said track of five hundred acres; likewise his joint part of the said Saw Mill with the said one hundred acres of land; with the joint part also of the said one thousand acres of land, and also the slaves and their future issue unto the child or children of the said George that then shall be living in such parts and proportions, and for such estates and estates and at and under such limitations restrictions and contingencies as the said George shall by his last will and testament in writing or by any deed by him to be duly executed in his life time direct limit or appoint and for want of directions limitation and appointment I give and bequeath (the said brick house and land, with his join part of) the said saw mill and joint part of the said lands there after mentioned and the slaves and their issue to and amongst all and every of the children of the said George that shall live to come of age or have issue to be equally divided amongst them and their respective heirs and assigns for ever as tenants in common and not as join tenants and if but one child of said George shall live to come of age or have issue then to that child alone and to his or her heirs and assigns for ever

Also I give to John (son of said Metawney) ten horses and seven mares with the one third of all the stock of cattle with his own and sisters Judith's and brother George's mark and branch wheresoever they be found, likewise all cattle and horses with his own brand and mark. Also I give and bequeath unto the said John for and during the term of his natural life without Impeachment of waste the tract (or tracts) of land upon Ogeechee in the province of Georgia called the Old Town which I run out containing about one thousand five hundred acres, also that tract of land below it that was John Sallers's, also that tract of land in the swamp called Dunifin's Place which I bought off him, also two hundred acres of land which I run out joining it with the tract of land I bought off Joel Walker behind it; Dunifin's place fronting the River, also I give and bequeath unto the said John and the Said George his brother the saw mill on the saouth side of Town Creek with the tract of land whereon it stand containing about one hundred acres together wilh all the land I run up the south side of and joining the said Creek above the said saw mill containing about one thousand acres, to hold to them jointly also I give to the said John two thousand acres of the Ceded land in any part he may choose that belongs or may belong to me, to be disposed of as he the said John shall think proper, also I give to the said John the use work and labour of the following slaves (that is to say) Stepney his wife Margret their children and future issue, phin her children and future Issue, Mingo his wife Maria her children and future issue, Ockera his wife Cakte their children and future Issue, Limerick, King, Nero, Negro Men, Colo Peter a Negro man, Olipher his wife Cresha, their children and future Issue, New Negro Dick, Peter (I bought of Joseph Butler) his wife their Children and future issue, Sapho (a Mulatto women) her children and future Issue (except her daughters Rachel and Betsey whom I have herein before made free), New Negro Jack, Bulley, and Chevers, Negro Men, also Delia a half breed Indian woman, she to serve him seven years, then to be free, and the said John on the day of her freedom to give her five cows and calves, and upon the death of the said John I give the said several tracts of land, together with his joint part of the said Saw Mill and tracts of land thereafter mentioned, and also the Slaves and their future issue unto the child or children of the said John that shall be then living in such parts and proportions and for estate and estates and at and under such limitations restrictions and contingencies as he the said John shall by his last will and testament in writing or by any deed by him to be duly executed in his life time direct limit or appoint, and for want of such [rest of line missing]…[ap]pointment I give and bequeath the said several tracts of land together with his joint part of the said saw mill and tracts herein before mentioned, with the slaves and their future issue to and amongst all and have issue to be equally divided amongst them and their respective heirs and assigns for ever as tenants in common and not as join tenants, and if but one child of said John shall live to come of age or have issue then to that child alone and to his or her heirs and assigns for ever. Also I give unto Judith (Daughter of the said Metawney) for and during her natural life, without impeachment of waste, the use of the upper half three tracts of land, which said tracts run from Mr. Newman's line down to the point, containing in the whole about thirteen or fourteen hundred acres with the dwelling house and all other improvements thereon where she now lives called Silver bluff in the province of south Carolina. Also I give to the said Judith two thousand acres of the ceded land in any part she may choose that belongs or may belong to me to be disposed of as she shall think proper, also I give and devise unto the said Judith ten horses and seven mares with the third of all the stock of cattle wheresoever they may be found, with her own, her brother George's and her brother John's mark and brand, likewise all cattle (and horses) with her own mark and brand, also the use work and labour of the following slaves (that is to say) Warick his wife Marcha their children and future issue, Billey, Peter and Cela, (Mustees) her children and future issue, Sally an Indian wench her children and future issue, Kelly's Abraham his wife Elcey their children and future Issue, Cyrus his wife Sue their children and future issue, Joe his wife Emma their children and future issue, old Cyrus his wife Maria their children and future issue, Gabriel his wife Minerva their children and future issue, Jacob his wife Cloe their children and future issue, Charlotte her children and future issue, and upon the death of the said Judith, I give the use of the said upper half of the said three tracts of land with the dwelling house and improvements and slaves and their future issue; unto the child or children of the said Judith that then shall be living in such parts and proportions, and for such estates and estates and at and under such contingencies and limitations and restrictions as the said Judith shall by her last will and testament in writing or other writing by her duly executed direct limit or appoint and for want of directions limitation and appointment I give and bequeath the said upper half of the said three tracts of land with the dwelling house and improvements and the said slaves last mentioned with their future issue to and among all and every of the children of the said Judith that shall live to come of age or have issue to be equally divided amongst them and their respective heirs and assigns for ever, as tenants in common and not as joint tenants and if but one child of said Judith shall live to come of age or have issue then to that child alone and to his or her heirs and assigns [part of the line missing]....

Barbara, the daughter of [part of line missing]...during her natural life...[missing line] waste, the use of the lower half of three tracts of land which said tracts run from Mr. Newman's line down to the point containing in the whole about thirteen or fourteen hundred acres with all the improvements thereon called the Silver bluff in the Province of South Carolina, also I give unto said said Barbara ten horses and seven mares likewise all cattle and horses with her own brand and mark, also the use, work, and labour of the following slaves (that is to say) Little March, Katte that was his wife, their children and future issue, Ponpon, Jemmey, his wife Betty, their children and future issue, Ned and his sister Dido, (son and daughter to Dido deceased), her children and future issue, Bidgo, Sib his wife, Young Sib, her children and future issue, Indian Peter, his wife Capuchey, their children and future issue, and Georgia Dublin. And upon the death of the said Barbara, I give the use of said lower half of the said three tracts with the improvements and slaves with their future issue; unto the child or children of the said Barbara that shall then be living in such parts and proportions and for such estates and estates and at and under such contingencies limitations and restrictions as the said Barbara shall by her last will and testament in writing or other writing by her duly executed [last will and testament in writing or other writing by her duly executed directed limit and appoint] and for want of such directions limitation and appointment I give and bequeath the said lower half of the said three tracts of land with the improvements and the said last mentioned slaves and their future issue to and amongst all and every of the children of the said Barbara that shall live to come of age or have issue to be equally divided amongst them and their respective heirs and assigns for ever as tenants in common and not as join tenants and if but one child of said Barbara shall live to come of age or have issue then to that child alone and to his or her heirs and assigns.

Also I give to the said Thomas a negro man named Abraham which I had off Mr. Barnard, also Indian Prince, under the same restrictions with the rest of the salves hereinbefore mentioned. Also I give unto the said Thomas all my great guns, with my silver mounted gun and pistols, the rest of my guns I give to the said George and John equally between them, Also it is my will that in case any of the six devisees and legatees herein before mentioned, namely George, Thomas, John, Judith, Martha, Barbara, shall happen to die without leaving issue or their issue die, that then and whenever a contingency of that kind happens to any of the said devisees or any of their issue that the estates, slaves, and issue of slaves hereby intended for such devisee or devisees and issues shall be shared equally by my Executors or the Survivors of them amongst the survivors of the said six devisees and legatees, and the lands to be shared between (the said George) [remainder of line missing] and their issue to be [remainder of line missing]

Devisees and legatees and their heirs. Likewise it is my will that the six devisees and legatees shall during their respective minorities be respectively maintained clothed schooled and educated out of the profits of the estate hereby intended for them respectively, and that upon any of their deaths leaving issue living, such issue shall during their respective minorities be maintained clothed schooled and educated out of the issues and profits to arise out of the estate and labour and services of the slaves hereby intended for such issue.

Also I give unto the said six devisees and legatees all my sheep to be equally divided between them and after my debts and the other legacies to other persons herein after mentioned shall be paid and delivered, I give and devise all the rest residue and remainder of my real and personal estate of what nature or kind soever and wheresoever to and between the said Thomas and Martha and their children share and share alike and in case the said six devisees and legatees should all die intestate and without issue I leave all the estate hereby given to them among my sisters and their heirs share and share alike. Also I give to David Holms five hundred pounds sterling also two tracts of land on the long reaches where Galfin lived and one tract on the long reaches in the Georgia side I bought off Benjamin Stedham and two thousand acres of the ceded lands, to him and his heirs in lieu of any part of my estate he may lay claim to, I leave to Judith Galphin my sister one hundred and fifty pounds sterling, in lieu of any part of my estate she may lay any claim to, I leave Catherine Galphin living in Ireland one hundred fifty pounds sterling, in lieu of any part of my estate she may lay any claim to, I leave to my sister Margaret Holms fifty pounds sterling, to each of her children now in Ireland, fifty pounds sterling and to her son Robert now living here fifty pounds sterling and one thousand acres of the ceded lands, in lieu of any part of my estate they or any of them may lay claim to. I leave to Mrs. Taylor fifty pounds sterling, to each of her children now in Ireland fifty pounds sterling and to each of her children also five cows and calves to each of them in lieu of any part of my estate she or they may lay claim to.

I leave my sister Crossly fifty pound sterling, a paceing horse and a new side saddle in lieu of any part of my estate she may lay any claim to and each of her children fifty pounds sterling and five hundred acres of the ceded lands, with a horse and mare to each of them in lieu of any part of my estate they may lay claim to, I leave to my cousin George Rankin in Ireland seventy pounds sterling to him or his children in lieu of any part of my estate he may lay claim to, I leave to my Aunt Sennard's daughter in Ireland to her and her children fifty pounds sterling in lieu of any part of my estate she or they may lay claim to. I leave to my Cousin John Foster, fifty pounds sterling to him and his children in lieu of any part of my estate he or they may lay claim to.

I leave to Rachel (daughter of Sapho) herein before mentioned two negro men and two negro women to be bought out of the first ship that comes in with negroes, ten cows and calves, three mares and colts, one horse, and twenty pounds sterling, also that tract of land where John Raton lived called Clouds Place between Macbean and Briar Creek to her and her children but if she dies without children then to her sister Betsey (daughter to the said Sapho) I leave to the said Betsey one new negro man and women to be bought her, ten cows and calves, two mares and colts, one Horse, and that tract of land below the Cowpen on Macbean to her and her children but if she dies without children then the whole to fall to the said Thomas (son of the said Rachel Dupre) and his children to be maintained and schooled on the plantation until they are married or of age and then to receive what is left them.

I leave to Betsey Callwell (daughter of Mary Callwell) one new negro wench, ten cows and calves, two mares and colts, one riding horse, and saddle, and that tract of land at the Three Runs at the old Stomp above Tim's Branch and fifty pounds Carolina Currency to be laid out in cloathing, for her the whole to be put in her own possession after my death to her and her children.

I leave to all the poor widows and fatherless children within thirty miles of where I live in the province of South Carolina (and Georgia) fifty pound sterling, I leave fifty pounds sterling to be shared among the poor of Eneskilling and fifty pounds sterling to be shared among the poor of Armagh in Ireland; I leave to Timothy Barnard two hundred pounds sterling, I leave to all the orphan children I brought up ten pounds sterling each and Billey Brown to be bound out to a trade; I leave John McQueen and Alelxander his brother each a good riding horse and each of them and their wives a ring. I leave to Mr. Netherclift and his wife each a ring, I leave all of my executors a suit of mourning and a ring each, I leave to Mr. and Mrs. Wylly each a ring. I leave to their daughter Suckey Wylly Fifty pounds sterling and a suit of mourning, I leave to each of my sisters their husbands and children a ring, I leave to Mrs. Campbell a ring, I leave to Mr. Cartin Campbell a ring, I leave to Mrs. Frasier a ring and ten pounds sterling, I give to Mr. Newman a ring and twenty pounds sterling. I give to the widow Atkins twenty pounds sterling and a ring. I give to her two sons William and Alexander each a good riding horse, and to her daughter I give a good pacing horse of the value of ten or twelve pounds sterling. I give to Mr. and Mrs. Greirson each a ring, I give to person Seymore and his wife each a ring. I give to George Parsons a likely negro boy to be bought him out of the first ship that comes in, and one of my best riding horses. I leave to Quinton Pooler of the ceded lands, and to all the rest of my Cousins Pooler (man and woman) each a ring (in lieu of any part of my estate they may lay claim to).

I leave to the said Rachel Dupre the use of one Negro man called Foot, one negro wench called Charlott and her children during her natural life and then to her son Thomas, and that her son Thomas and her daughter Martha are to pay her twenty pounds sterling yearly as long as she is virtuous or lives single, and then to leave her ten cows and calves and Martha's negro boy called Jacob as long as they think proper, and they may let her live upon any of their land. I leave her also a paceing horse and side saddle, and also one bed, one pair of sheets, three blankets, two counterpains, one set of china cups and saucers, tea pot and tea kettle, the rest of the cups, saucers, kettles and so forth together with the plate that is in the house, and all my other plate and so forth I leave to the said Thomas and Martha. Also I leave to each of the said six legatees a bed and furniture.

I leave my sister Young in Ireland, fifty pounds sterling, to each of her children fifty pounds sterling and to each of them five hundred acres of the ceded lands and five cows and calves and a horse and mare to each of them in lieu of any part of my estate they may lay claim to. I give to Clotworthy Robson five hundred acres of the Ceded lands to him and his heirs. I give to each of the six legatees first mentioned a stallion to run with their mares (three of the likeliest to the boys and three Jack Asses) and as soon as they or any of the said six legatees shall arrive at the age of twenty one years or be married whichever shall first happen I will that he she or they shall immediately have possession of all the estate hereby given to him her or them.

I give to all my Hunters and House wenches a suit of mourning to all the Cowpen wenches, and a new shirt and shift to each of the rest of my men and women slaves. I will that the said Metawney do live at her said children's Cowpen and be maintained and clothed by them, and I give to her and the said Rachel Dupre each a suit of mourning, and that the said Thomas, Martha, and John be sent to Charlestown or Savannah to school. And in case there is not sufficient to pay of the said legatees I will that all the remainder of my horses and mares not herein willed and lands be sold, and the profits of the saw mills and work of all my slaves be applyed for that purpose, after the maintainance schooling and clothing of the said six legatees.

Also I will that the said Thomas and Martha may dispose of their tracts of the ceded lands as they shall think proper. And lastly I do herby nominate constitute and appoint James Parsons, John Graham, Lauchlin McGillvery Esqurs., John Parkinson, Mect., the said George, Thomas and John Galphin's and the survivors and survivor of them Executors and Executor of this my last will and testament and guardians of the real and personal estates hereby given to the said legatees and in case the said George, Thomas and John Galphin or any of them shall be under age or incapable of acting at the time of my death, that then they shall with the consent of the other executors nominate and appoint other persons to act in their stead until such time as they come of age or are capable of acting.

In Witness Whereof I have to this my last will and testament contained in nine sides of papers set my hand and seal the sixth day of April in the year of our lord one thousand seven hundred and seventy six.

George Galphin

Seal

Signed and sealed published and declared by the

said Testator George Galphin as and for his last will
and testament in the presence of us who in his
presence and at his request have subscribed our
names and witnesses hereto
> David Zubly
> Michael Meyer
> John Stuzenggar

Isabele Vandervelde, *Aiken County, The Only South Carolina County Founded during Reconstruction* (Spartanburg, SC: Art Studio Press, for the Reprint Co. Publishers, 1999) 218-231. Reprinted with permission.

Index

East Queen Street Baptist Church, 3, 6,
    11, 127, 160
Edwards, Morgan, 27, 28
emancipation, 25, 30, 128, 137
English Baptists, 77, 125, 143
Erskine, Noel, 3, 4
Erskine, Noel Leo, 129, 154, 157
Ethiopia, 9
Ethiopians, 9
evangelical movement, 7

First African Baptist Church, 52, 62, 65,
    90, 94, 95, 164
Franklin, John Hope, 72

Galphin, 2, 3, 4, 13, 15, 16, 17, 18, 19, 20,
    21, 42, 49, 52, 87, 100, 107, 141, 143,
    153, 159, 170, 171, 176, 178
Galphin Plantation, 2, 3, 18, 48, 52, 87,
    100, 107, 108
Galphin, George, 13, 15, 16, 17, 18, 20,
    21, 42, 43, 48, 49, 50, 52, 54, 87, 101,
    141, 152, 153, 159, 163, 170, 178, 179
Galphin, Jesse Peters, 19
Galphinton, 17
Garner, W. J., 124
Garvey, 9, 137, 158
Gaulfin, Jessie, 142
Gaulfin's, 142
Gayle, Clement, 6, 89, 127
General Baptists, 33, 34, 35
George Liele Research group, 3
George Liele Research Project, The, 2, 4,
    160, 161
George, David, 3, 7, 9, 18, 19, 42, 49, 50,
    51, 52, 76, 87, 88, 92, 93, 95, 106, 107,
    108, 113, 140, 141, 142, 143, 144, 154,
    155, 164
Gibbs, George, 113, 125
Gill, John, 28, 29
Glass, Ernestine Pickens, 4, 158
Grant, Sir John Peter, 11
Great Awakening, 1, 23, 24, 27, 38, 39,
    100, 103, 104, 105, 106, 112, 114, 152,
    153, 163

Great Revival, 137

Habersham, Major Joseph, 18
Hanover Street Baptist Church, 6
Helwys, Thomas, 33, 34, 35, 163
hermeneutical, 5, 75

Indian traders, 14, 15, 16, 19
itinerant, 22, 24, 26, 27, 40, 49, 108

Jamaica Assembly, 76, 77
Jamaica House of Assembly, 119
Jamaican Assembly, 124
Jamaican Baptists, 9, 11, 28
Judson, Adoniram, 1

Kirkland, Colonel Moses, 8, 51, 61, 70,
    76, 109, 116
Knibb, William, 126, 127, 135, 139

Last Will and Testament of George
    Liele, 146
Lawson, Winston, 3, 4, 124, 130, 131
Lawson, Winston A., 115, 158
Lewis, George, 131
liberation theological posture, 125
liberation theology, 71, 73, 76, 82, 128
Liele, Hannah, 61, 66
Liele, Hannah Hunt, 61, 147, 148, 166,
    167
Liele's Wife and Children, 61
literacy, 84
London Baptist Association, 35, 163
Lord and Master, 47, 68, 75, 78, 82, 92,
    112, 115, 122, 168
Love, E. K. Love, 61, 90
Loyalists, 97, 108, 129, 152, 153, 154

Marshall, Daniel, 23, 39, 40, 106, 163
Master and Lord, 4, 71
Mercer University, 3, 12, 45, 66
Methodists, 23, 29, 39, 110, 119, 120
Moore, Matthew, 42, 43, 44, 45, 46, 47,
    48, 50, 53, 54, 72, 73, 81, 91, 92, 100,
    101, 103, 106, 115, 163, 164